OXFORD MEDICAL PUBLICATIONS

AN INTRODUCTION TO THE
PSYCHOTHERAPIES

SECOND EDITION

An Introduction to the Psychotherapies

EDITED BY

SIDNEY BLOCH

Department of Psychiatry
St Vincents Hospital
Fitzroy
Victoria 3065
Australia

Second Edition

Oxford   New York   Tokyo
OXFORD UNIVERSITY PRESS

Oxford University Press, Walton Street, Oxford OX2 6DP

Oxford New York Toronto
Delhi Bombay Calcutta Madras Karachi
Kuala Lumpur Singapore Hong Kong Tokyo
Nairobi Dar es Salaam Cape Town
Melbourne Auckland Madrid
and associated companies in
Berlin Ibadan

Oxford is a trade mark of Oxford University Press

Published in the United States by
Oxford University Press Inc., New York

First edition 1979
Second Edition 1986
Reprinted 1986 (with corrections), 1988, 1989, 1990, 1992, 1993

A catalogue record is available from the British Library

Library of Congress Cataloging in Publication Data
Main entry under title:
An Introduction to the psychotherapies.
(Oxford medical publications)
Includes bibliographies and index.
1. Psychotherapy.   I. Bloch, Sidney.   II. Series.
[DNLM: 1. Psychotherapy. WM 420 1611]
RC480.159   1985   616.89'14   85–13706
ISBN 0–19–261469–X

Printed in Great Britain by
Bookcraft Ltd, Midsomer Norton, Avon

Preface to first edition

The most striking memory I have of my first few months in psychotherapy training was how bewildering it all seemed. No one could define it, controversy raged over the question of its effectiveness, different schools engaged in constant warfare with one another, and the training programme itself lacked goals and a coherent structure. I realized later when I continued my training in the United States and Britain that this sense of bewilderment was not indigenous to my native Antipodes. The 'acute confusional state' was universal! In recent years I have noted, as a teacher of psychotherapy, that contemporary trainees still undergo a similar type of experience to the one I had.

This situation is not at all surprising. Psychotherapy after all *is* a nebulous term with widely differing connotations; the controversy over its value is still with us; dozens of psychotherapy schools, each with its own theories on psychopathology (often contradictory) and particular set of techniques, compete for the trainee's attention; and there is no apparent link between research and clinical practice—psychotherapists are influenced only occasionally by the results of research.* Overwhelmingly, theory determines practice and works vigorously to protect itself from forces that might lead to change.

I hope that this book, mainly an introduction for students in the mental-health professions, will help to remove at least some of the hurdles that commonly obstruct them in approaching the complex and demanding subject of psychotherapy. The general objectives of the book are: (1) To make the concept of psychotherapy more understandable. To this end I have used the term *psychotherapies* in the sense that there are several forms of psychotherapeutic treatment which can be distinguished from one another according to their goals, techniques, and target of intervention. We can therefore differentiate, for example, between crisis intervention, supportive psychotherapy for chronically disabled psychiatric patients, family

---

*Malan, D. H. (1973) The outcome problem in psychotherapy research. A historical review, *Archs gen. Psychiat*. **29**. 719–29.

therapy, sex therapy, long-term intensive individual psychotherapy, and so forth. The clinician's task is to match the needs of the patient, couple, or family with the appropriate psychotherapy rather than the converse of fitting the patient to the treatment. By using this approach psychotherapy as a generic term may fade into oblivion. (2) To minimize the differences between schools of psychotherapy and to emphasize the features they have in common. Alongside this aim, the book attempts to eschew the dogmatism and doctrinaire attitudes that have tended to permeate the field. Jerome Frank, who has made such a valuable contribution in bringing the issue of 'shared factors' to our attention, considers it in his introductory chapter and the other contributors have been guided by it. A central focus in this book is on what Yalom refers to as 'core' factors (in contrast to 'front' factors).* The significance of theory is not denied; trainees must ultimately familiarize themselves with various models for each of the psychotherapies but they should not be swamped by them before they have grasped basic common principles. Each contributor therefore comments on theoretical aspects and provides a guide to further reading. (3) To draw a relationship betweem research and clinical practice. Although psychotherapy research is still in its infancy, the therapist needs to keep abreast of it in order to maximize his effectiveness. For example, the value of preparing the patient for psychotherapy has been replicated in several studies and the procedure should logically be incorporated into clinical work. When appropriate, reference is made to the contribution of such investigations on clinical practice. By taking cognisance of research findings, I hope that the heat will also be removed from the lingering debate over whether psychotherapy works or not. This debate is futile because we have no way as yet of even attempting to answer the basic questions. In any event, a more suitable question is whether each of the psychotherapies is of value, for whom and in what circumstance. Limitations of space do not allow more than a superficial examination of pertinent research but references are recommended for the interested reader at the end of each chapter. (4) To guide the trainee in his reading. A common problem in psychotherapy education is the bombardment of the novice with references. Inevitably he wonders how to get into the material, and once having entered, often how to extricate himself.

---

*Yalom, I. D. (1975) *The theory and practice of group psychotherapy*. Basic Books, New York.

Since the literature is voluminous, reading must of necessity be done rationally. The contributors hope that the recommended reading lists following each chapter will help the trainee to reconnoitre without injury.

I hope that the book comes some way in meeting these objectives.

The presentation of eight different psychotherapies does not mean that the reader should be able to master them all. Presumably he will select therapies which are intrinsic to his particular work and those which he finds interesting. However, he should also be in a better position to refer appropriately patients who require one of the treatments in which he has not trained.

The masculine pronoun is used, where appropriate, to represent both sexes so as to avoid clumsiness and unnecessary repetition.

Oxford   S.B.
April 1978

Preface to second edition

For the second edition, coverage of the psychotherapies has been broadened by the inclusion of new chapters on brief, focal psychotherapy and child psychotherapy. In addition, the existing chapters have been updated by their authors to take into account recent developments in each particular field.

I hope the book will continue to prove helpful to students seeking an introduction to what remains a most complex subject.

Oxford   S.B.
April 1985

Acknowledgements

First edition

I have been helped by many colleagues in editing this book. To the contributors, with whom collaboration proved smooth and pleasant, my thanks. I am grateful to several colleagues who reviewed sections of the manuscript and offered valuable suggestions—Derek Bergel, Pepe Catalan, Michael Gelder, Dave Kennard, Michael Orr, William Parry-Jones, Bob Potter, and Nick Rose. Professor Gelder was helpful in many ways and I thank him for his support.

I would like to pay special tribute to the late Dr. Phyllis Shaw. She not only provided the encouragement I needed to initiate the project but also agreed to contribute the chapter on supportive psychotherapy. Many ideas contained in this chapter come from her preparatory notes.

I am grateful to several secretaries in the Oxford University Department of Psychiatry who helped to prepare the manuscript. Finally, I thank my wife, Felicity, for her constant support and editorial suggestions.

Second edition

Again it is a pleasure to thank the contributors for their helpful collaboration. Gillian Forrest, Ian Goodyer, Keith Hawton, and David Mushin reviewed sections of the manuscript—to them my gratitude. My secretary Ann Robinson was most obliging in helping to prepare the final typescript.

Contents

List of contributors

JOHN BANCROFT, M.D., M.R.C.P., F.R.C.Psych.,
Clinical Scientific Officer, MRC Reproductive Biology Unit, Edinburgh.

ARNON BENTOVIM, M.B., B.S., F.R.C.Psych.,
Consultant Psychiatrist, The Hospital for Sick Children, London.

SIDNEY BLOCH, M.B., Ch.B., Ph.D., F.R.C.Psych.,
Clinical Lecturer in Psychiatry, University of Oxford, and Consultant Psychotherapist, Warneford Hospital, Oxford.

SIDNEY CROWN, Ph.D., F.R.C.P., F.R.C.Psych.,
Consultant Psychotherapist, The London Hospital, London.

JACK DOMINIAN, D.Sc., M.R.C.P.E., M.R.C.Psych.,
Consultant Psychiatrist, West Middlesex Hospital, London.

JEROME FRANK, M.D., Ph.D.,
Emeritus Professor of Psychiatry, Johns Hopkins University, Baltimore.

MICHAEL GELDER, M.D., F.R.C.P., F.R.C.Psych.,
Professor of Psychiatry, University of Oxford.

BERNARD ROSEN, M.B., Ch.B., M.R.C.Psych.,
Senior Lecturer in Psychiatry, Guy's Hospital Medical School, and Honorary Consultant, Guy's Hospital, London.

SULA WOLFF, B.M., Ch.B., F.R.C.P., F.R.C.Psych.,
Honorary Fellow, Department of Psychiatry, University of Edinburgh (late Consultant Psychiatrist, Royal Hospital for Sick Children, Edinburgh).

1

What is psychotherapy?

Jerome D. Frank

In this introductory chapter Frank attempts to answer the complex question 'what is psychotherapy?' by approaching the subject in historical and cultural contexts. After describing psychotherapy's practitioners, the kinds of treatment they offer, and the patients who receive it, he pays particular attention to the common therapeutic functions of the rationales and procedures of all psychotherapies. The chapter ends with general principles and guidelines for the trainee setting out to practise psychotherapy. Recommended reading covers historical background, different theoretical approaches and techniques, and research aspects.

As social beings, humans are totally dependent on each other for maintenance of their biological and psychological well-being. When this is threatened in any way, they typically turn to each other for help, whether this be protection against a physical danger such as an enemy group, protection of a food supply endangered by drought, or for assuagement of distress created by the vicissitudes of life.

This book is concerned with the attempt of one person to relieve another's psychological distress and disability by psychological means. These are typically words, but include other communicative or symbolic behaviours, ranging from laying a reassuring hand on someone's shoulder to elaborate exercises aimed at combatting noxious emotions and promoting inner tranquillity.

Informal psychological help in the form of solace, guidance, advice, and the like is frequently sought and received from family members and other intimates. Other sources may sometimes be casual acquaintances and even strangers, especially if they occupy roles like that of the bartender, for example, that create the expectation that they will be good listeners.

Psychotherapy, the form of help-giving with which we are here concerned, differs from such informal help in two significant ways. First, the practitioners are specially trained to conduct this activity and they are sanctioned by their society or by a subgroup to which they and the patients belong. Second, their activity is systematically guided by an articulated theory that explains the sources of the patients' distress and disability and prescribes methods for alleviating them. Psychotherapy differs from medical and surgical procedures in its major reliance on symbolic communications as contrasted with bodily interventions. This implies that it is concerned with the content of the symptoms and their meaning for the patient's life—what the hallucinated voices are saying, or what the patient is depressed about, or what he fears when anxious. Drugs, when used, are regarded as facilitative adjuncts, and their choice is determined by the form and severity of the patient's symptomatology, such as auditory hallucinations, depressed mood, and the like.

An important consequence of the primacy of communication as the medium of healing is that the success of all forms of psychotherapy depends more on the personal influence of the therapist than do medical and surgical procedures. Even when the success of psychotherapeutic procedures is believed to depend solely on their objective properties, as some behaviour therapists maintain, the personal influence of the therapist determines whether the patient carries out the prescribed treatment in the first place, as well as having healing effects in itself. While important in all medical treatment, the personal impact of the therapist is crucial to psychotherapy (Sloane, Staples, Cristol, Yorkston, and Whipple 1975; Greben 1983).

A historical-cultural perspective

Although there are a bewildering number of schools of psychotherapy, each proclaiming its own special virtues, viewed from a historical-cultural standpoint, all can be subsumed under two categories: the religio-magical and the empirical-scientific (Frank 1977*b*; Zilboorg and Henry 1941). The former is as old as human culture and continues to predominate in most non-industrialized societies. Although viewed askance by many persons in industrialized societies, healing cults continue to have large followings in them as well.

Religio-magical therapies are grounded in what has been termed the perennial philosophy (Huxley 1941). This underlies all major religions and avers that humans are manifestations of the 'Divine Ground' which links us into a kind of seamless web. Each individual, as it were, contains the universe. The conventional or sensory reality in which we live is only one of reality. Health is a harmonious integration of forces within the person coupled with a corresponding harmony in his relations with other persons and the spirit world. Illness is a sign that he has transgressed the rules of nature or society, thereby disrupting his internal harmony and creating vulnerability to harmful influences from other persons and spirits.

Such a conceptualization takes for granted that mental states can powerfully affect bodily functions and that the state of bodily health, conversely, can affect mental functions. The therapist's goal is to restore the patient's harmony within himself, with his group, and with the spirit world through special rituals requiring the participation of the patient and, usually, those important to him, the purpose of which is to intercede with the spirit world on the patient's behalf. The religio-magical healer is as well trained in special techniques as his scientific colleague but attributes his healing powers to supernatural sources which are linked to a religious system that he and the patient share. Healing involves a special state of consciousness of both healer and patient, in which both temporarily enter another reality characterized by such phenomena as clairvoyance, communion with the spirit world, and out-of-the-body experiences.

Empirical-scientific psychotherapy was foreshadowed by Hippocrates. It has been practised continuously in the West since the mid-eighteenth century, beginning with the charismatic physician Anton Mesmer, who viewed his treatment as the scientific application of animal magnetism. Although his theories and he himself were discredited, empirical-scientific psychotherapy continued as hypnosis and then experienced a sharp rise in popularity and influence thanks to the genius of Freud (see Chapter 2). More recently empirical-scientific psychotherapy has been expanded by therapies based on the theories of Pavlov and Skinner (see Chapter 6), and therapies that seek to help the patient correct pathogenic cognitions (Beck 1976; Mahoney 1974).

The empirical-scientific approach is conducted with the patient in an unaltered state of consciousness but may involve hypnotic states, fantasies, dreams, and the state of reverie which may accompany free association in psychoanalysis. The therapies which appear most scientific however, notably behaviour therapy, depend on full utilization of the patient's waking intellect. Healers in the scientific tradition, instead of basing their powers on supernatural sources, invoke science as the sanction for their methods.

Despite striking differences in their underlying world-views, religio-magical and empirical-scientific therapies have much in common. They share the aim of restoring the patient's harmony with himself and with his group. Both approaches, furthermore, depend on a belief system shared by the patient and the therapist that the treatment has been empirically validated. This is as true for the religio-magical systems of pre-scientific cultures as for the supposedly scientifically based systems in our own. The therapeutic procedures express the belief system in tangible form, thereby reinforcing it. In both, a trained healer derives his power from the belief system—whether it be as scientifically-grounded Western practitioner or a supernaturally-inspired shaman—and in both he serves as an intermediary between the patient and his group. Finally, empirical-scientific healers, no less than shamans, expend considerable effort to mobilize the patient's faith in their procedures (Klein, Dittman, Parloff, and Gill 1969).

Practitioners of psychotherapy

Starting with Mesmer and until the middle of the twentieth century, empirical-scientific psychotherapy was conducted by physicians, initially neurologists, later psychiatrists. In recent decades they have been joined by psychiatric social workers and later by clinical psychologists and psychiatric nurses. In Britain these mental health professionals usually work under medical supervision but in the United States many, especially in large cities, have achieved virtually complete autonomy. To these must be added clergymen, for whom psychotherapy is a natural extension of pastoral counselling.

In addition, in the United States the excess of demand for help over the supply of trained practitioners has led to a proliferation of self-appointed healers and cult leaders, with or without training, who work not only in conventional settings but in ones specially designated as 'growth centres' as well as in hotel rooms, meeting halls, and private homes. Most utilize group approaches, some of which are similar to those of healing religious cults such as 'scientology'. Although many do not set themselves up as therapists, the great majority of their clientele have had previous psychotherapy or are currently in treatment (Lieberman and Gardner 1976). Also important on the American scene are groups composed of fellow sufferers. These 'peer self-help psychotherapy groups' (Hurvitz 1970; Dumont 1974) function autonomously and maintain various degrees of rapport with the medical profession. Some, such as Recovery Incorporated (Wechsler 1960), welcome all comers, but most, such as Alcoholics Anonymous, are proffered only for those suffering from a specific common problem.

Kinds of psychotherapy

The goal of all forms of pyschotherapy is to enable a person to satisfy his legitimate needs for affection, recognition, sense of mastery and the like through helping him to correct the maladaptive attitudes, emotions, and behaviour which impede the attainment of such satisfactions. In so doing, psychotherapy seeks to improve his social interactions and reduce his distress, while at the same time helping him to accept the suffering that is an inevitable aspect of life and, when possible to utilize it in the service of personal growth.

Although all psychotherapies take into account all aspects of personal life, different schools vary considerably in emphasis. They can be roughly ordered in accord with their primary target, their temporal orientation, and whether they seek primarily to modify thoughts and attitudes, emotional states, or behaviour.

To oversimplify vastly, insight-therapies focus on the individual patient and see distress as arising primarily from unresolved internal conflicts. Some, such as psychoanalysis, focus on the past. They see the internal conflicts as caused by traumatic experiences of early life and seek to unearth their sources and thereby resolve them (Menninger 1958). Behaviour therapies based on desensitization (Wolpe and Lazarus 1966) or implosion (Stampfl and Lewis 1967) also are primarily concerned with counteracting the effects of previous damaging experiences.

Other behaviour therapists who emphasize modelling (Bandura 1968) or operant conditioning (Krasner 1971) view the primary difficulties as located at the interface between the patient and his immediate social environment and are orientated to the present; that is, they try to help the patient identify and modify the proximate causes and consequences of behaviour that create distress. Existentially oriented therapists are apt to emphasize helping the patient to open up the future—that is, to discover new potentialities for personal satisfaction and growth (Frankl 1965).

Therapists who regard the primary focus of treatment as the patient in his family (see Chapters 7 and 9) or in an artificially composed group (see Chapter 4) pay particular attention to the patient's reactions to other family or group members as casting light on the sources of their symptoms and seek to mobilize therapeutic group or family forces. Family and group therapists differ in the extent to which they search in the patient's past for source of current problems, and in whether they focus on the individual patient or on the pathogenic or healing potentials of the family or group as a system.

For psychoanalytically derived therapies, the kind of treatment the patient receives depends primarily on the therapeutic school of the therapist to whom he is referred. That is, these therapists tend to apply their particular method to all their patients, and justify this on the grounds that their goal is to enhance the patient's general integration or to foster personality growth. Relief of specific symptoms is assumed to follow automatically. Cognitive and behaviour therapists reverse this. They believe that the patient's success in correcting faulty cognitions or overcoming specific symptoms will promote more general improvement by enhancing social competence and self-confidence. Hence they attempt to tailor their methods to combat the patient's specific complaints. As is reported in Chapter 6, behaviour therapists have succeeded to some extent with complaints that are fairly circumscribed. Unfortunately, patients whose chief complaints are of this kind represent a very small proportion of those seeking help (Marks 1976). Most feel a pervasive distress or sense of incompetence or alienation, and evidence is still lacking that they respond better to one approach than another, a point to be considered more fully below.

Receivers of psychotherapy

Since psychotherapy is a cultural institution, those who are considered suitable candidates for it vary among different societies. In the West, psychotherapy is believed to be appropriate for all persons in whom psychological factors are perceived as causing or contributing significantly to distress and disability. Although this criterion is more generously applied in the United States than elsewhere, by and large persons are selected from the following categories in Western societies:

(1) *Psychotics*, such as schizophrenics, whose symptoms in all likelihood stem predominantly from an organic source. The aim of psychotherapy for these patients is to help them to recognize and try to deal more effectively with life stresses to which they are particularly vulnerable (see Chapter 11).

(2) *Neurotics*, who suffer from persistent faulty strategies for dealing with the vicissitudes of life, based presumably on important early experiences that were either damaging or lacking, thereby distorting the processes of maturation and learning. These patients and those in the next category constitute the vast majority of individuals in psychotherapy.

(3) The *psychologically shaken*, who are temporarily overwhelmed by current life stresses such as bereavement (see Chapter 5). Relatively brief and superficial help usually suffices to restore their emotional equilibrium. Since such persons can manifest the entire gamut of neurotic and psychotic symptoms and respond gratifyingly to any form of help, they fan the competitiveness between different schools of psychotherapy.

(4) The *unruly*, whose behaviour upsets other people but is attributed to illness rather then wickedness. This category includes 'acting-out' children and adolescents, spouses whose heedless or self-indulgent behaviour distresses their partners, as well as antisocial personalities and addicts. Some could be classified under the preceding categories. The distinguishing feature is, perhaps, the degree of motivation for help. The neurotics and the psychologically shaken seek psychotherapy; the unruly are brought to it by others, which makes them, by and large, poor candidates.

Two additional categories of persons receiving psychotherapy exist in affluent or intellectual circles: the discontented, struggling with boredom or existential problems, and professionals who undergo training in psychotherapy as a prerequisite to offering it to others.

How effective is psychotherapy?

This is an easy question to ask but a surprisingly hard one to answer

(Frank 1968*b*, 1979, 1981; Malan 1973). Evaluation of therapies bristles with methodological problems of which two important ones are how to measure improvement and how to disentangle the effects of psychotherapy from those of other concurrent life experiences. Criteria of improvement, to the extent that they depend on the conceptualizations of therapeutic schools, are not readily comparable. Thus psychoanalysts define improvement in part as being able to consciously experience previously unconscious feelings and thoughts, while behaviour therapists look for overcoming of symptoms elicited by particular situations. They are interested in whether the agoraphobic patient can leave the house or the socially inhibited one can enjoy a party, not in the relationship of unconscious to conscious experiences.

Moreover, improvement is not unitary, and so can change in different directions on different criteria. If a husband's chronic abdominal pain disappears after he takes to mistreating his wife instead of submitting to her, is he better or worse?

Another problem of evaluation arises from the fact that psychotherapeutic sessions constitute only a small proportion of a person's waking life and he may well be seeking informal help at the same time. Hence improvement during therapy my primarily reflect this outside help or beneficial changes in his life situation (Voth and Orth 1973). To complicate matters further, these changes may be the result of shifts in the patient's attitudes and behaviour resulting from psychotherapy.

These and other problems present more difficulties for the evaluation of long-term psychotherapies with loosely defined, open-ended goals such as increased personality integration than of short-term therapies focused on the relief of particular target complaints.

Nevertheless, findings from many studies have consistently found that all the types of psychotherapy that have been studied produce greater beneficial change than 'spontaneous improvement'; that is improvement occurring over the same time interval in the absence of psychotherapy (Luborsky, Singer, and Luborsky 1976; Shapiro and Shapiro 1982; Sloane *et al.* 1975; Smith, Glass, and Miller 1980). 'Psychotherapy is beneficial, consistently so and in many different ways. Its benefits are on a par with other expensive and ambitious interventions, such as schooling and medicine.' (Smith *et al.* 1980, p. 183). Findings are less clear with regard to the relative effectiveness of various types of therapy for different conditions. Some studies have found no significant differences in effectiveness

(Luborsky *et al.* 1976; Sloane *et al.* 1975; Smith *et al.* 1980). One found behavioural or cognitive approaches to produce slightly more improvement than psychodynamic approaches, but only for relatively circumscribed and minimally disabling symptoms (Shapiro and Shapiro 1982).

It must be emphasized that failure to demonstrate significant differences between various therapies by no means excludes the possibility that such differences exist; failure may be due to the lack of criteria for classifying patients with respect to their relative response to various therapeutic approaches. As a result, if a cohort of patients, selected by any criterion, are divided into two groups, one receiving therapy A and one receiving therapy B, each may contain some patients who respond to neither and some who do well with both, and those who respond differentially may get lost in the statistical shuffle.

Improvement in methods of diagnosis and evaluation of change may yet reveal some differences in effectiveness of different therapies that present methods fail to detect. In the meanwhile, a reasonable conclusion is that, whatever their specific symptoms, most patients share a source of distress that responds to the common features of all forms of psychotherapy (Frank 1973).

The demoralization hypothesis

This common source of distress my be termed demoralization, a state of mind that ensues when a person feels subjectively incompetent—that is, unable to cope with a problem that he and those about him expect him to be able to handle (DeFigueiredo and Frank 1982; Frank 1974). Demoralization can vary widely in duration and severity, but the full-blown form includes the following manifestations, not all of which need be present in any one person. The individual suffers a loss of confidence in himself and in his ability to master not only external circumstances but his own feelings and thoughts. The resulting sense of failure typically engenders feelings of guilt and shame. The demoralized person frequently feels alienated or isolated, as well as resentful because others whom he expects to help him seem unable or unwilling to do so. Their behaviour in turn may reflect their own irritation with him, creating a vicious circle. With the weakening of his ties often goes a loss of faith in the group's values and beliefs, which have formerly helped to give him a sense of security and significance. The psychological world of the demoralized person is constricted in space and time. He becomes self-absorbed, loses sight of his long-term goals and is preoccupied with avoiding further failure. His dominant moods are usually anxiety, ranging from mild apprehension to panic, and depression, ranging in severity from being mildly dispirited to feeling utterly hopeless.

Most episodes of demoralization are self-limiting. These responses to crisis can enhance a person's mental health by stimulating him to seek better solutions to his problems, strenghtening his emotional ties with others, and demonstrating to himself that he can overcome obstacles. Prolonged states of demoralization, however, are self-perpetuating and self-aggravating, since they lead to increasing discouragement which impedes recovery. Those who seek psychotherapeutic help are usually in the middle range of demoralization. Mild forms are relieved by advice or reassurance from family or friends, or changes in life situation such as a change of job, as a result of which the person regains his sense of mastery and links with his group. At the other extreme, if demoralization is sufficiently severe, the person, believes he is beyond help and simply withdraws into a shell. Such persons do not seek help and some, such as derelicts, seem unable to use it.

In order to come to psychotherapy, the patient must experience certain symptoms, which are viewed as especially amenable to this form of treatment. Many of these, such as anxiety, depression, and feelings of guilt, seem to be direct expressions of demoralization. Others, such as obsessions, dissociative phenomena, and hallucinations have a variety of causes, many of which are still not understood (Dohrenwend, Shrout, Egri, and Mendelsohn 1980). Sometimes they seem to be symbolic ways through which the patient expresses or attempts to resolve the problems which demoralize him.

Whatever their ultimate aetiology, symptoms interact in two ways with the degree of demoralization. First, the more demoralized the person is, the more severe these symptoms tend to be; thus patients troubled with obsessions find them becoming worse when they are depressed. Secondly, by crippling the person to some degree, symptoms reduce his coping capacity, thereby aggravating his demoralization. The demoralization hypothesis asserts that the shared features of psychotherapies, which account for much of their effectiveness, combat demoralization, as a result of which symptoms diminish or disappear.

Features of all psychotherapies which combat demoralization are:

(1) An intense, emotionally changed, confiding *relationship* with a helping person, often with the participation of a group. In this relationship the patient allows himself to become dependent on the therapist for help, because of his confidence in the latter's competence and good-will. The patient's dependence is reinforced by his knowledge of the therapist's training, the setting of treatment (see below), and by the congruence of his approach with the patient's expectations. While these factors determine the therapist's ascendancy initially, after they are face to face the main source of the therapist's power increasingly becomes his personal qualities, especially his ability to convince the patient that he can understand and help him; that is, his ability to establish what has been termed a therapeutic alliance.

(2) A *healing setting* which reinforces the relationship by heightening the therapist's prestige through the presence of symbols of healing: a clinic in a prestigious hospital, or an office complete with bookshelves, impressive desk, couch, and easy chair. The setting often contains evidence of the therapist's training such as diplomas and pictures of his teachers.

Furthermore, the setting is a place of safety; that is, the patient is secure in the knowledge that his self-revelation will have no consequences beyond the walls of the office. As a result, he can dare to let into awareness of and come to terms with thoughts and feelings that had been avoided or repressed.

(3) A *rationale* or conceptual scheme that explains the cause of the patient's symptoms and prescribes a ritual or procedure for resolving them. The rationale must be convincing to the patient and the therapist; hence it is validated by being linked to the dominant world-view of their culture and cannot be shaken by therapeutic failures. In the Middle Ages the belief system underlying what we today call psychotherapy was demonology. In many primitive societies it is witchcraft. In the Western world today it is science.

(4) Linked to the rationale is a *procedure* which requires active participation of both patient and therapist and which is believed by both to be the means for restoring the patient's health.

Proponents of all schools of psychotherapy agree that they offer essentially the same kind of therapeutic relationship, but each claims special virtues for their particular rationales and procedures.

Shared therapeutic functions of the rationales and procedures of psychotherapy

Despite marked differences in content, all rationales and procedures in psychotherapy, reinforced by the setting, share six therapeutic *functions*:

(1) *They strengthen the therapeutic relationship.* Since the therapist represents society, his mere acceptance of the patient as worthy of help reduces the latter's sense of isolation and re-establishes his sense of contact with his group. This is further reinforced by the fact that therapist and patient adhere to the same belief system (Frank 1977*a*), a powerful unifying force in all groups. Explanations of the patient's symptoms or problems in terms of a theory of therapy, moreover, implicitly convey to him that he is not unique, since the rationale obviously must have developed out of experiences with many patients. The treatment procedure also serves as a vehicle for maintaining the therapist–patient relationship over stretches when little seems to be happening, by giving both participants work to do.

(2) The rationales and procedures of all therapies inspire and maintain the patient's *hope for help*, which not only keeps him coming but is a powerful healing force in itself (Frank 1968*a*). Hope is sustained by being translated into concrete expectations. Thus experienced therapists spend considerable time early in treatment teaching the patient their particular therapeutic 'game' and shaping his expectations to coincide with what he will actually experience.

(3) The rationales and procedures provide the patient with opportunities for both *cognitive and experiential learning* by offering him new information about his problems and possible ways of dealing with them, or new ways of conceptualizing what he already knows. All schools of psychotherapy agree that intellectual insight is not sufficient to produce change. The patient must also have a new experience, whether this be related to reliving the past, discovering symptom-reinforcing contingencies in the environment, or becoming aware of distortions in interpersonal communications. Experiential learning occurs through, for example, emotionally charged self-discovery, transference reactions, and the feelings aroused by attempts to change the contingencies governing behaviour. It is facilitated by the therapist and, in therapy groups, by the group members, both of whom the patient uses as models and as sources of knowledge.

(4) Experiential learning implies *emotional arousal*; this supplies the motive power for change in attitudes and behaviour (Frank, Hoehn-Saric, Imber, Liberman, and Stone 1978, Chapter 3). The revelations emerging in psychotherapy may be pleasant surprises, but more often they are unsettling shocks, as the patient discovers features of himself he had previously not let himself face. Some therapists deliberately cultivate emotional arousal, since they see it as central to treatment.

(5) Perhaps the chief therapeutic effect of the rationales and procedures is enhancement of the patient's sense of *mastery*, self-control, competence, or effectiveness (Frank *et al*. 1978, Chapter 2). Ability to control one's environment starts with the ability to accept and master one's own impulses and feelings, an achievement which in itself overcomes anxiety and strengthens self-confidence. Nothing is more frightening than feeling oneself to be at the mercy of inchoate and mysterious forces. A powerful source of a sense of mastery is being able to name and conceptualize one's experiences, an activity facilitated by each of the therapeutic rationales. That naming a phenomenon is a means for gaining dominance over it is a frequent theme in folklore and religion as in the fairy tale of Rumpelstiltskin, and the book of Genesis in which the first task God assigns Adam is to name the animals, thereby asserting his dominion over them.

The sense of mastery is reinforced by *success experiences*, which all therapeutic procedures provide in one form or another. These successes maintain the patient's hopes, increase his sense of mastery over his feelings and behaviour, and reduce his fear of failure. The role of success experiences is most obvious in behaviour therapy, which is structured to provide continual evidence of progress and aims to have every session end with a sense of attainment. For example, flooding, by showing the patient that he can survive the full impact of feelings he feared would destroy him, powerfully enhances his sense of self-mastery. Psychoanalytically and existentially-oriented therapies, being less clearly structured, yield more subtle but equally potent successes. Patients who respond well to these approaches master problems through verbalization and conceptualization, so that the achievement of a new insight or ability to formulate clearly previously muddled thoughts can powerfully raise their self-confidence.

(6) Finally, all therapies tacitly or openly encourage the patient to

digest or *'work through'* and practise what he has learned in his daily living, thereby fostering generalization of the therapeutic gains beyond the psychotherapy situation itself. Some therapies assign homework and require the patient to report back how well he has carried out his assignment. For others, this remains an implicit, but nevertheless strong, expectation.

Differences in the length of therapy used by different schools depend in part on the expectations implicit in their rationales. Behaviour therapies are expected to be brief, psychoanalytically-oriented ones long. Within each school, differences in duration may depend primarily on how long it takes to establish a genuine therapeutic alliance—i.e. win the patient's trust—and how much practice he needs to unlearn old attitudes and habits and develop new, healthier ones.

In short, evidence available to date strongly suggests that in treating most conditions for which persons come or are brought into psychotherapy, the shared *functions* of different rationales and procedures, not their differing *content*, contribute most of their therapeutic power. These functions, which are interwoven, all help to re-establish the patient's morale by combating his sense of isolation, re-awakening his hopes, supplying him with new information as a basis for both cognitive and experiential learning, stirring him emotionally, providing experiences of mastery and success, and encouraging him to apply what he has learned.

Implications for psychotherapy practice

The probability that the rationales and procedures of all psychotherapies differ little in their effectiveness for most patients by no means implies that familiarity with a particular psychotherapeutic rationale and procedure is unnecessary. Most psychotherapists need a conceptual framework to guide their activities, maintain self-confidence, and provide adherents of similar orientation to whom they can turn for support.

The demoralization hypothesis does imply, however, that a therapist will probably do best with the method most congenial to his personality. Some therapists are effective hypnotists, others are not; some welcome emotional outbursts, others avoid them; some work best with groups, others with an individual patient; some enjoy exploring the psyche, others prefer to try to change behaviour. In so far as possible, therefore, the trainee therapist would do well to look into a variety of approaches with the aim of mastering one or more that best accord with his own personal predilection and, if he can handle several, selecting the one most appropriate for a given patient (Lazarus 1976). Criteria that could help guide his choice, as well as the procedures themselves, are described in the remainder of this volume.

This chapter concludes with some general principles and guidelines on which almost all schools of psychotherapy agree, and which therefore can be put to immediate use while the student is learning to master a particular approach. The suggestions concern primarily the first encounter with the patient but apply in varying degree throughout treatment.

Most patients enter therapy with more or less covert conflicts and doubts that distort or impede free communication with the therapist. Your success in overcoming these obstacles in the initial interview may determine whether the patient returns for a second visit as well as the course of therapy thereafter. Hence, from the very beginning, cultivate sensitivity to patients' attitudes that may be blocking the interview. They can be grouped into three classes: those arising from the patient's internal state, those reflecting his attitude toward the interview situation, and those springing from his feelings towards you.

With respect to patients' internal states, most are more or less demoralized; their self-esteem damaged. They may also experience a conflict between wanting to change and unwillingness to surrender their habitual ways of dealing with life, especially since change usually entails the distress felt in confronting their own repressed feelings and the anxiety of venturing into new, uncharted territory. Like Hamlet, many prefer to bear the ills they have than fly to others they know not of.

As to the interview situation, patients have a wide range of sophistication concerning psychotherapy. Some are fully informed; others are bewildered, even frightened, and do not know what to expect. They may suspect that referral to a psychotherapist means that others regard them as crazy, and they may fear what you may discover about their less admirable qualities. The route by which they have arrived at your office influences their initial attitude. A self-referred patient usually feels differently than one who has been referred by his physician in such a way that he experiences it as a brush-off, or one who faces criminal charges or has been referred by his probation officer.

Finally, many patients have doubts about your competence and trustworthiness, especially if you are young and inexperienced. It is prudent to assume that the patient is covertly forming an impression of you at the same time that you are evaluating him.

Hence your initial aim is to help the patient to overcome these blocks to open communication. Central to this is your ability to convince the patient that you desire to help him and are competent to do so (Greben 1983). To this end, try to act in such a way as to show that you are trustworthy, concerned about his welfare, and seeking to understand him. Try to elicit hidden doubts and misgivings and respond appropriately. The sense that one's message is being received and understood by someone who cares is a powerful reliever of anxiety.

This implies suggestions as to some general attitudes and specific procedures that facilitate patient–therapist communication, thereby supplying the necessary basis for the success of all forms of psychotherapy:

(1) *Be yourself* within the boundaries of the professional role. A stiff, artificial therapist discourages communication. Accordingly, you should not fear being spontaneous within wide limits, expressing pleasure, concern, sorrow, or even anger, admitting when you are sleepy or uncertain as to what is going on, and the like. If humour is within your repertoire, it can be a great help in enabling the patient to achieve some detachment from his troubles, as long as he feels that you are laughing with him and not at him.

By being open with the patient you make it easier for him to be open with you and also to use you as a model. While relying on spontaneity increases the likelihood of making errors, if the patient is convinced that you genuinely care about his welfare, he will forgive and forget almost any blunder you may commit.

(2) *Maintain an attitude of respectful, serious attention.* For many patients, especially lower-class ones, the psychotherapist may be the first person with status who is willing to hear them out. You should keep in mind that, especially in early interviews, the patient is covertly testing you to see how understanding and trustworthy you are. The best way to pass the test is to maintain an attitude of respectful attention no matter how shocking, trivial or ridiculous the patient's productions are. This does not mean that the patient should be allowed to ramble. It is possible tactfully to guide the patient while preserving a respectful attitude.

(3) Throughout the interview *emphasize the positive*. It is necessary, of course, to explore what is going wrong in the patient's life. After all, it is because of this that he has come for help. Exclusive pursuit of this goal, however, can increase the patient's demoralization by turning the interview into what has been aptly described as a degradation ceremonial. Remember that patients would not have survived to be in your office today unless they had some assets and coping skills. So be sure to listen for these and remind the patient of them, especially after particularly damaging self-disclosures. This must be done with care. Nothing is more harmful to the progress of an interview than unwarranted or empty reassurance, because the patient hears it as evidence that you don't take his troubles seriously or have not understood their gravity. It is always reassuring, however, after listening to a patient's worst misgivings without implying that you share them, to utilize every appropriate opportunity to remind him of what is going well, or of latent abilities that he is not fully utilizing.

In prolonged therapy, a patient's. goals often seem to become more ambitious as he improves. Because the goals keep receding in this way, he may feel he is making no progress. If you sense this, a reminder of the patient's state when he first entered therapy and the gain he has made since can be powerfully reassuring.

(4) *Make sure the patient understands the interview situation.* Depending on the patient's sophistication, take sufficient time to find out his understanding of the nature and purpose of the interview and, to the degree necessary, explain them to him. Let him know how much, if any, of what he reveals will be reported back to the referring agent. Usually the patient can be reassured that information he reveals will be given to others only with his explicit permission. In the rare cases where complete confidentiality in this sense cannot be guaranteed, as in some court referrals, the patient should be so informed at the start.

(5) *Pay attention to physical arrangements.* The chairs should not be separated by a desk, and be so placed that you and the patient can comfortably maintain or avoid eye contact. It may be facilitative sometimes, for example, for you to avert your gaze when the patient embarks on an acutely embarrassing topic. The lighting should be arranged so that illumination is equal for both parties, or more on you than the patient, to avoid the impression that the patient is being interrogated.

(6) *Be alert to the patient's non-verbal behaviour*. These include tone of voice, hesitancies of speech, facial expression, as well as gestures and bodily postures. Is the patient's manner ingratiating, challenging, tense? Does he maintain eye contact? Are his responses forthright or defensive and evasive? Such clues as to covert attitudes may help you to evaluate what the patient is saying.

Evidence of autonomic activity like sweating or flushing may signal that the topic under discussion is emotionally significant. If a patient indicates that he has non-visible autonomic responses such as heart-pounding, abdominal pain, or headache during the interview, he should be asked to report when they occur.

Since commenting on non-verbal communication may increase the patient's uneasiness, you should reserve comment until you are sure that his trust in you is sufficiently strong to enable him to hear and use the information. Then you may offer immediate feedback of your own reactions, so as to clarify for the patient responses of others that have disturbed him in the past. This is most apt to happen when the patient is unaware of aspects of his communicative behaviour that upsets others. In this connection, a useful manoeuvre is to call the patient's attention to discrepancies between his verbal and non-verbal communications—for example, that he states he is angry in a sweet tone of voice while smiling. Videotape playback, by sharply confronting a patient with the way he presents himself to others, can enhance this aspect of therapy.

(7) *Focus on the present*. The patient comes to therapy for help in resolving current problems, however long-standing they may be. He wants to talk about the here and now, and encouraging this helps to establish rapport. It is also the most direct route towards understanding the patient's characteristic ways of coping. Another reason for focusing primarily on the present is that, although maladaptive patterns of perceiving, feeling, and behaving are rooted in the past, they are sustained by present forces and, therefore, it is these that must be changed.

(8) *Take a history*. Emphasis on the present must not preclude taking a history, especially in the first interview, and returning to aspects of it periodically when relevant. Irrespective of its contents, and therapists of different persuasions emphasize different aspects, taking a full history is the best way to get acquainted with someone. Moreover, it is essential to a full understanding of the patient's current reactions, for we perceive events and react to them not as

they exist objectively but in terms of what they mean to us. The same objective event, such as the death of a close relative, may be experienced as a tragedy or a relief. Since the meaning of present events is largely determined by past experiences, considerable review of the latter may be needed to understand the patient's predicament today. Sometimes a review of the past serves to enhance rapport: a patient may be able to reveal embarrassing or anxiety-provoking features of his history before he can discuss his current difficulties, and may need to test the therapist's reactions to remote material before he can bring up present feelings. As the patient progresses in therapy, moreover, changes in his interperetations of past events may be important clues as to his progress.

(9) *Reflect what you have heard.* Repeating back what the patient has said, either precisely or with modifications to emphasize a point, is evidence that you are listening attentively and are not angered, frightened, or otherwise disturbed by what you have heard. This implicity encourages the patient to continue.

(10) *Interpret, but sparingly.* Calling attention to points a patient has overlooked, bringing together statements he had not realized were linked, or offering explanations for his feeling and actions, if skilfully done, shows that you not only heard him but can make sense of what you have heard in ways he had not considered, thereby demonstrating your competence. Premature or implausible interpretations, however, may have the opposite effect, so it is well to be sure of one's ground before offering them.

(11) *Ending the interview.* At the close of the first interview offer the patient an opportunity to make comments and ask questions. He may need encouragement to bring up matters of concern that were not adequately dealt with, seek additional information, ask for further clarification of some of your comments, and the like. Review the mundane aspects of therapy with the patient including the fee (if appropriate), frequency of interviews, and tentative duration. If possible, try to establish with the patient preliminary goals of therapy, recognizing that they might require subsequent revision. At the close of every interview, it is well to sum up the major topics and call attention to significant points. Sometimes it is also possible to offer a formulation in terms of a theme which links the topics together. Finally, when appropriate, suggest homework. This may be to think more about a certain issue, to record dreams, to keep a diary noting when certain symptoms occur, or to try to put into

action what has been learned. At the next interview ask the patient to report on the assignment. This helps to preserve the continuity of psychotherapy during the intervals between sessions.

Summary

This chapter has attempted to answer the question: 'What is psychotherapy? by considering it in a historical-cultural perspective and by discussing its practitioners, the kinds of therapies they offer, and to whom. Particular emphasis has been placed on the shared therapeutic functions of the rationales and procedures of all psychotherapy. Finally some general principles and guide-lines common to all the psychotherapies covered in this book are briefly dealt with.

References

Bandura, A. (1968). Modelling approaches to the modification of phobic disorders. In *The role of learning in psychotherapy* (ed. R. Porter). Churchill, London.

Beck A. (1976). *Cognitive therapy and the emotional disorders*. International Universities Press, New York.

Defigueiredo, J. M. and Frank, J. D. (1982). Subjective incompetence, the clinical hallmark of demoralization, *Comprehen. Psychiat.* **23**, 353-63.

Dohrenwend, B. P., Shrout, P. F., Egri, G., and Mendelsohn, F. S. (1980). Nonspecific psychological distress and other dimensions of psychopathology, measures for use in the general population, *Archs Gen. Psychiat.* **37**, 1229-36.

Dumont, M. P. (1974). Self-help treatment programs, *Am. J. Psychiat.* **131**, 631-5.

Frank, J. D. (1968*a*). The influence of patients' and therapists' expectations on the outcome of psychotherapy, *Br. J. med. Psychol.* **41**, 349-56.

—— (1968*b*) Methods of assessing the results of psychotherapy. In *The role of learning in psychotherapy* (ed. R. Porter). Churchill, London.

—— (1973) *Persuasion and healing: a comparative study of psychotherapy*, 2nd edn. Johns Hopkins University Press, London.

—— (1974) The restoration of morale, *Am. J. Psychiat.* **131**, 271-4.

—— (1977*a*) Nature and functions of belief systems: humanism and transcendental religion, *Am. Psychol.* **32**, 555-9.

—— (1977*b*) The two faces of psychotherapy, *J. nerv. ment. Dis.* **164**, 3-7.

—— (1979). The present status of outcome studies, *J. consult. clin. Psychol.* **47**, 310-16.

—— (1981). Reply to Telch, *J. consult. clin. Psychol.* **49**, 476-7.

—— Hoehn-Saric, R., Imber, S. D., Liberman, B. L., and Stone, A. R.

(1978). *Effective ingredients of successful psychotherapy.* Brunner/ Mazel, New York.

Frankl, V. (1965). *The doctor and the soul: from psychotherapy to logotherapy.* Knopf, New York.

Greben, S. E. (1983). *Love's labor: twenty-five years in the practice of psychotherapy.* Schocken, New York.

Hurvitz, N. (1970). Peer self-help psychotherapy groups and their implications for psychotherapy, *Psychother.: Theory Res. Pract.* 7, 41–9.

Huxley, A. (1941). *Introduction to Bhagavad-Gita* (translation by Swami Prabhavananda and C. Isherwood). New American Library, New York.

Klein, M. H., Dittman, A. T., Parloff, M. R., and Gill, M. W. (1969). Behavior therapy: observations and reflections, *J. consult. clin. Psychol.* 33, 259–66.

Krasner, L. (1971). The operant approach in behavior change. In *Handbook of psychotherapy and behavior change* (eds A. E. Bergin and S. L. Garfield). Wiley, New York.

Lazarus, A. A. (1976). *Multimodal behavior therapy.* Springer, New York.

Lieberman, M. A. and Gardner, J. R. (1976). Institutional alternatives to psychotherapy, *Archs gen. Psychiat.* 33, 157–64.

Luborsky, L., Singer, B., and Luborsky, L. (1976). Comparative studies of psychotherapies: is it true that 'Everyone has won and all must have prizes'? In *Evaluation of psychological therapies* (eds R. L. Spitzer and D. L. Klein). Johns Hopkins University Press, London.

Mahoney, M. J. (1964). *Cognition and behavior modification.* Ballinger, Cambridge, Maryland.

Malan, D. H. (1973). The outcome problem in psychotherapy research, *Archs gen. Psychiat.* 29, 719–29.

Marks, I. M. (1976) The current status of behavioral psychotherapy: theory and practice, *Am. J. Psychiat.* 133, 253–61.

Menninger, K. (1958) *Theory of psychoanalytic technique.* Basic Books, New York.

Shapiro, D. A. and Shapiro, D. (1982). Meta-analysis of comparative therapy outcome studies: a replication and refinement, *Psychol. Bull.* 92, 581–604.

Sloane, R. B., Staples, F. R., Cristol, A. H., Yorkston, N. J., and Whipple, K. (1975) Short-term analytically oriented psychotherapy vs. behavior therapy, *Am. J. Psychiat.* 132, 373–7.

Smith, M. L., Glass, G. V., and Miller, T. I. (1980). *The benefits of psychotherapy.* Johns Hopkins University Press, Baltimore.

Stamfl, T. G. and Lewis, D. J. (1967). Essentials of implosive therapy: a learning-theory-based psychodynamic behavioral therapy, *J. abnorm. Psychol.* 72, 496–503.

Voth, H. and Orth, M. (1973). *Psychotherapy and the role of the environment.* Behavioral Publications, New York.

Wechsler, H. (1960). The self-help organization in the mental health field: Recovery Inc., a case study, *J. nerv. ment. Dis.* **130**, 297–314.
Wolpe, J. and Lazarus, A. A. (1966). *Behavior therapy technique: a guide to the treatment of neuroses.* Pergamon Press, New York.
Zilboorg, G. and Henry, G. W. (1941) *History of medical psychology.* Norton, New York.

Recommended reading

(The list below should be referred to in conjunction with the recommended readings that follow each of the subsequent chapters.)

General

Bloch, S. (1982). *What is psychotherapy?* Oxford University Press, Oxford.
Brown, D. and Pedder, J. (1979). *Introduction to psychotherapy.* Tavistock, London.
Brown, J. A. C. (1961). *Freud and the post-Freudians.* Penguin, Harmondsworth.
Ellenberger, H. (1970). *The discovery of the unconscious.* Basic Books, New York; Allen Lane, London.
Frank J. D. (1973). *Persuasion and healing.* Johns Hopkins University Press, London.

Approaches and techniques

Beck, A. T. (1976). *Cognitive therapy and the emotional disorders.* International Universities Press, New York.
Berne, E. (1961). *Transactional analysis in psychotherapy.* Grove Press, New York.
Fagan, J. and Sheperd, I. L. (eds) (1972). *Gestalt therapy now.* Penguin, Harmondsworth.
Fromm-Reichman, F. (1950). *Principles of intensive psychotherapy.* University of Chicago Pres, Ill.
Haley, J. (1963). *Strategies of psychotherapy.* Grune and Stratton, New York.
Malan, D. H. (1979). *Individual psychotherapy and the science of psychodynamics.* Butterworth, London.
Rogers, C. (1961). *On becoming a person.* Houghton-Mifflin, Boston, Mass.
Sifneos, P. E. (1972). *Short-term psychotherapy and emotional crisis.* Harvard University Press, Cambridge, Mass.
Storr, A. (1979). *The art of psychotherapy.* Heinemann, London.
Wolberg, L. R. (1977). *The technique of psychotherapy*, 3rd edn. Grune and Stratton, New York.

Research aspects

Garfield, S. L. and Bergin, A. E. (eds) (1978). *Handbook of psychotherapy and behavior change: an empirical analysis*, 2nd edn. Wiley, New York.

Sloane, R. B., Staples, F. R., Cristol, A. H., Yorkston, N. J., and Whipple, K. (1975). *Psychotherapy versus behaviour therapy*. Harvard University Press, Cambridge, Mass.

2

Individual long-term psychotherapy

Sidney Crown

In this chapter Crown describes that form of individual long-term psychotherapy whose aims are symptom relief and personality change. Following an outline of its psychoanalytic basis, he describes the practical aspects of treatment: patient selection, assessment, preparation of therapy, the negotiation and re-negotiation of contracts, and termination. Detailed attention is paid to the stratagems that the therapist uses and to the problems he may face in the course of therapy. The chapter ends with a section on the type of training necessary for long-term psychotherapy.

Psychoanalysis (Freud 1976) was the first systematic attempt to use a psychological method to alleviate psychological symptoms and to modify aspects of personality. Psychoanalytic theory also attempted to link a general psychology of mental functioning and behaviour (e.g. dreaming, lapses of memory, slips of the tongue or pen) with the varied and often obscure clinical manifestations of what we now call neurosis, particularly hysteria.

Psychoanalysis as a psychotherapeutic procedure has prescribed rules: four or five sessions per week, each 50 minutes long, using the method of free association to gather data and the method of interpretation, particularly of the patient's relationship with the therapist (transference) to induce inner understanding (insight). Infantile problems are delineated and how these problems are reflected in current inhibitions and difficulties, in symptoms, in the psychopathology of everyday life, and in dreams are looked at (worked through) from many angles to complete the process of therapeutic change. The therapist tends to remain silent apart from his interpretations and the patient is not helped over a difficult phase of therapy (resistance) other than by identifying its source and inter- preting the reason for its presence. The therapeutic results of psy- choanalysis tend to be judged in terms of personality change and freedom from the residue of infantile conflicts rather than in terms of loss of symptoms or significant progress in the patient's extra- therapeutic world (Luborsky and Spence 1971). Psychoanalysis is an individual therapy and the term 'significant others' has little meaning: spouse and relatives, children or parents are not included in the therapy even initially for information gathering.

Psychoanalysis today cannot be considered a therapeutic tech- nique relevant for patients other than private ones, because of the demands it makes on therapist and patient's time. It is more a method of training for psychoanalysts and psychotherapists interested in those psychotherapies directly related to psychoanalysis of which individual long-term psychotherapy is one. Psychoanalysis is also a research tool especially for those interested in exploring the extremes of personality functioning and complexity in the treatment of schizophrenics (Rubenstein and Alanen 1972) or in those severe personality disorders called 'borderline' or 'narcissistic' (Hartocollis 1977).

There has been, in recent years, an explosive development of psy- chotherapeutic methods other than psychoanalysis. These newer psychotherapies are based on two major theoretical traditions: learning theory, particularly social learning theory (Bandura 1969) and humanist-existentialism (Bugental 1967). It occurred to me, while preparing this chapter, that the current and developing psy- chotherapies reflect the personality, interests, and psycho- therapeutic practice of two of the early three 'giants': Adler and Jung. Psychoanalysis rapidly became authoritarian and controlling of its practitioners in its struggle for identity. A number of the early pioneers could apparently express themselves within the major psy- choanalytic tradition. Adler and Jung, however, relating both to the developing incompatibility of their ideas with those of Freud and also, probably, as is the way of things, to individual clashes of per- sonality, broke away from the mainstream; but their approaches to psychotherapy are expressed in the two continuing and developing traditions, the humanist-existential and social learning.

Jung perhaps expresses some men's need for a spiritual dimen- sion, for self-expression and individation, for self-fulfilment as a positive goal. This overlaps with, but is different from, the goal of freeing oneself from early psychic fixations and conflicts so that the 'energy' from basic drives (sexuality and aggression) can be more appropriately sublimated. Jung's divergence is reflected in the newer therapies (Marteau 1976) with their anti-theoretical and anti-authority bias, with their emphasis on self-actualization and personal fulfilment. Adler introduced a social dimension into therapy, a development that was later extended to include a cultural dimension by the neo-Freudians especially Karen Horney. Adler, with his basic ideas such as striving to overcome 'organ inferiorities' by over-compensation within a social milieu, directly anticipated techniques such as social skills training (Argyle, Bryant, and Trower 1974). Adler's emphasis on the importance of social relationships anticipates group (Yalom 1975), marital (Crown 1976*b*; Gurman and Kniskern 1978), family (Skynner 1976), and other techniques of therapy which incorporate a social dimension.

Individual long-term psychotherapy in the 1980s uses basic psychoanalytic concepts and also draws on concepts from both learning and humanist-existential theory, the whole being adapted for once-weekly psychotherapy. Emphasis is given both to intra-psychic and extra-psychic (social) components of man, and the aims, perhaps grandiose, are both to relieve symptoms and to modify basic personality. It is with the features of this technique that the remainder of this chapter is concerned.

Background of psychotherapy: concepts from psychoanalysis

The majority of the basic concepts by psychotherapists today had been established by Freud by the early 1920s. These include psychosexual development, anxiety, defences, the structure of the ego and superego (conscience), free association as a basic method of recall, and the therapeutic technique of interpretation, including that of transference, defences, and dreams.

A number of the early psychoanalysts suggested modifications of treatment technique to try to expedite therapy or suggested the application of psychoanalysis to clinical entities outside the classical neuroses. The interested reader is referred to Brown's (1961) *Freud and the post-Freudians* for details of suggested modifications to the number of sessions, the state of deprivation (e.g. sexual) under which therapy should be conducted, early examples of touch technique, etc. Alexander (1957) is a more recent influential psychoanalyst who extended the development of psychotherapy as distinct from psychoanalysis. Groddeck (1977) proposed to Freud's receptive ear the relevance of psychological components to all physical illness thus anticipating our present multifactorial approach to disease (Lipowski 1975). Aichorn (1935) extended psychoanalytic concepts into the field of delinquency.

If psychosexual development and the psychology of the ego and its defences against anxiety represent the theoretical developments of classical psychoanalysis relevant to psychotherapy, the third area of interest is in the field of object-relations theory. An 'object' is a person or part of a person (e.g. breast) of psychological significance to the patient. The theory focuses on the relationships of the developing infant with other people. An object might exist in the real world as sibling, father, mother, etc. or it might be an internalized representation of that person or part of the person, in which case it may or may not conform to the reality seen by other people. The ambiguity of the concept—internal or external object—is one of the difficulties with this theory because, like so many things in psychoanalysis, it can mean different things relatively arbitrarily (Rycroft 1972). This area is more relevant to classical psychoanalysis than to other psychotherapies and particularly to theoretical developments starting with Melanie Klein. The reader who wishes a straightforward account should refer to Segal (1964) for the theory, and to Hughes (1974) for the practice of Kleinian psychoanalysis.

To the more eclectic psychotherapist, the obverse of the object relations approach is more important. If, during assessment of the patient, there is evidence in the symptomatology, personality traits, or relationships with significant other people, that the patient has not successfully negotiated early stages of development, he is likely to be unsuitable for psychotherapy. Thus there may be evidence of: lack of 'basic trust' (Erikson 1965); permanent or semi-permanent depression and pessimistic life-style; poorly developed reality sense ('reality testing'); a tendency to develop clinging, dependent, interpersonal relationships; the expression of emotion restricted to anger and hostility; crude and massive defences against anxiety such as denial and depersonalization; the use of 'splitting' mechanisms such as dissociation and the division of 'objects', whether internal or external, into good and bad. Object-relations psychoanalysts tend to concentrate their clinical practice upon the treatment of severe personality disorders especially the borderline state (Hartocollis 1977) and also on the psychoses (Rubenstein and Alanen 1972). I suggest however that there is little justification for the relatively inexperienced psychotherapist to take on patients with such severe disorders.

Development of psychotherapy

The development of contemporary, individual, long-term psychotherapy has advanced, or been pushed along, by several forces. One of these was the challenge by Eysenck (1952) that psychotherapy is no more efficacious than the factors leading to spontaneous recovery. Another has consisted in a number of able reviewers and synthesizers who advocate how psychotherapy should be researched. Representative textbooks are those of Meltzoff and Kornreich (1970), Gottschalk and Auerbach (1966), and Bergin and Strupp (1972). A third, more important, force has been a relatively small number of active psychotherapy researchers of whom Frank (1973, 1974), Malan (1963, 1975, 1976), Luborsky and his colleagues (Luborsky and Spence 1971; Luborsky, Chandler, Auerbach, Cohen, and Bachrach 1971), Strupp (1975), and Sifneos (1968, 1969) are outstanding in the quality of their writing. Frank's general writing endures, perhaps permanently, in his classical book *Persuasion and healing* (1973) (see Chapter 1). This raised for the first time systematically curative factors common to all therapies. Frank surveyed methods of healing that resembled Western psychotherapy. Part of the success of all forms of psychotherapy, he suggested, may be the therapist's ability to mobilize the patient's expectation of help. Psychotherapies differ in their emphasis on influencing emotions, cognition, or behaviour. Illustrative is the emphasis in the encounter or new therapies on eliciting intense emotional reactions as a step to insight and changed behaviour. It is even more interesting, in view of a controlled study by Yalom, Bond, Bloch, and Zimmerman (1977) that it is now clear that intense emotion alone is not enough to achieve significant change; cognitive understanding ('working through') is also important. Frank suggested that all forms of psychotherapy, when successful, provide new opportunities for learning, both cognitive and experiential; enhance the patient's hopes of relief; increase his sense of mastery over himself and his environment, and lead to a better approach to previously avoided problems and to experiments with new ways of tackling them. These ideas were developed and confirmed over a 25-year period of clinical practice and research which Frank has usefully summarized (Frank 1974).

In Britain Malan and his collaborators have worked assiduously to develop and study an effective mode of brief, psychodynamic psychotherapy in an atmosphere far less favourable to psychotherapeutic research than that pertaining in the United States (see Chapter 3). His work is summarized in two books (Malan 1963, 1976) both of which review the field comprehensively and provide replicated clinical and experimental data particularly on the selection of patients likely to have a favourable outcome. Malan's contributions are also notable for their unusual candour about methodological problems and because he writes with a refreshing humour. He has ploughed a lonely furrow, developing methods to research psychotherapy which, while remaining true to psycho-dynamic principles, also operate within the accepted canons of orthodox methodological and statistical practice—by assessing the validity and reliability of observations and by making systematic predictions about patients and confirming or refuting these in studies of outcome. Psychodynamic criteria have been developed to compare the effectiveness of psychotherapy with spontaneous remission (Malan, Bacal, Heath, and Balfour 1968; Malan, Heath, Bacal, and Balfour 1975). The Malan group has also demonstrated the relevance of the therapist's intuition that he can help a client and wishes to do so, and that interpretation of the transference relation-ship, particularly the parent transference, is related to good outcome.

Definition

Once-weekly psychotherapy with 50-minute sessions has become the accepted form. What is less clear is the question of length of treat-ment. In Malan's (1963) 'brief' psychotherapy the number of sessions seems to vary between 10 and 40. For Frank (1974) therapy is short-term, i.e. 3–6 months. It is impossible to be precise about what is meant by 'long-term' but 6–18 months would perhaps cover at last two-thirds of patients. I do not think length can be decided definitively at the start of treatment—this decision may depend on the results of a trial of therapy; also, because of the importance of flexibility, length should be a negotiable part of the therapeutic contract (both these matters are dealt with later in this chapter).

Aims

Long-term individual psychotherapy has two broad aims: symptom relief and personality change. Neurotic symptoms which can be dealt with include anxiety in its free-floating (anxiety state) or focal (phobic) forms, obsessions and compulsions, depression, and hysterical conversion symptoms. Psychosomatic symptoms (e.g. asthma, diarrhoea, headache, and palpitations) are also frequently tackled in treatment. Sexuality may be involved in psychotherapy either as the central consideration or in conjunction with other symptoms and personality problems. Psychosexual problems (Crown 1976*a*) thus bridge the gap between symptoms as such, and enduring personality traits and overall mode of adjustment.

Emphasis on symptomatic relief has come to psychotherapy through the recent influence of learning theory; the second aim, personality change, from psychoanalysis. Personality change is a poor term and needs further consideration. Sometimes it relates to the modification of traits such as aggressiveness or timidity which are reasonably easy to delineate both for patient and therapist. The term also includes higher order concepts like personal 'effectiveness' (Parloff, Kelman, and Frank 1954) which in turn may be operationally defined in the context of work, interpersonal relationships, and sexuality. Commonly, however, clients enter psychotherapy with more vague, but none the less pressing, aims most conveniently reflected in concepts like self-realization or self-fulfilment. A patient wishes to finish therapy much closer to realizing his true potential intellectually and emotionally; relating effectively to others of both sexes; having developed his own identity to the full (Erikson 1959); having become separated (autonomous) from early figures, especially parents, yet retaining a good relationship with them; achieving mature dependence within a marriage or other continuing relationship; and feeling concern for others in general as distinct from being dependent on them.

Although these aims are, by their very nature, personal and difficult to define, they are the ones which psychotherapists, especially those working with young adults, must accept as a common reason for self-referral.

Some practitioners of long-term individual therapy aim for evidence of 'psychodynamic change'. This may include progress towards psychosexual maturity ('genitality'); evidence that ego strength has increased so that it is more capable of controlling stresses from the drives, the external would, and the conscience; and evidence that the superego exerts a guiding function rather than a harsh, punitive one leading to excessive guilt.

Selection of patients

The selection of patients for long-term individual psychotherapy needs to take into account currently accepted clinical criteria and how, through research, these criteria are constantly being refined. The therapist should remain abreast of new research findings so that his therapeutic effectiveness is maximized. It is an intriguing fact that some highly experienced psychotherapists have failed to modify their clinical work despite unequivocal results of their own research (Malan 1973).

Clinical criteria of selection

It is widely agreed that traditional diagnostic categories provide only the crudest filter in selecting patients for psychotherapy and relate more to those who should be rejected rather than giving a guide to those who should be accepted. Thus, on the whole, patients with psychotic illness whether depressive or schizophrenic, borderline syndrome (Hartocollis 1977), psychopathic personality, drug and alcohol dependence, long-standing severe personality disorder, and an organic state like a post-head-injury personality deficit are not suitable candidates. However since some individuals within these broad categories can be successfully helped—some alcoholics and schizophrenics for example—clinicians and researchers have looked for other more general indications and contra-indications for psychotherapy. At this general level are a number of vague but identifiable factors such as psychological-mindedness, flexibility, motivation, and desire to change. Psychological-mindedness is the opposite to what Nemiah, Freyberger, and Sifneos (1976) have called 'alexythymia'. Alexythymia refers to the tendency to conceive psychological problems in physical terms—to feel, for example, more comfortable with headache than with anxiety. As these people also tend to dream less, there may be a constitutional basis in the structure of their central nervous system. Clearly the psychologically minded patient who can feel anxious, sad, happy, frustrated, fulfilled, loving—and say so—is likely to benefit from a verbally based psychological therapy. Flexibility in the present context refers to the ability of a patient to see problems and conflicts in a variety of ways and may relate to psychological concepts from education and learning such as creativity, divergent thinking (Hudson 1967), and 'syllabus-freeness' (Parlett 1969).

Motivation has always been rated highly by psychotherapists as a selection criterion. It is, however, a dynamic and changing quality within a relationship rather than a static, measurable personality trait; this is particularly relevant to psychotherapy. It is undoubtedly increased by an element of personal suffering, particularly anxiety or depression. In some patients motivation is present initially and expresses itself best in a loose concept such as 'desire to change'; in others this attitude seems to be absent. Some therapists attempt to influence motivation. One strategem during the preliminary assessment is to impress on the patient—or certain patients—how arduous therapy will be. This technique is carried to an extreme in dealing with the multifaceted resistance of patients with chronic hysteria by Taylor's (1969) 'prokaletic therapy' in which he virtually dismisses a patient as beyond help in order mobilize his remaining reserves of motivation. There is however an important paradox noted by Entwistle and Wilson (1977) in their research on the relationship between students' personality and background variables and their examination results. The authors suggest that motivation may be the result of certain events happening to a person rather than the cause of them. Thus a student who unexpectedly succeeds in an examination may suddenly become motivated to have an interest in the subject concerned. Interest and ability are, after all, correlated. Behaviour therapists have always stressed that the treatment of symptoms directly is justified because if a symptom such as premature ejaculation can be overcome, improvement in sexual functioning leads secondarily to other gratifying changes in the patient.

In applying the dynamic concept of motivation to individual psychotherapy, the relevant question is what goes on between patient and therapist *and* between patient and his general environment, to the systems of personal and family reward and punishment contingencies. The idea that motivation can be assessed in relation to psychotherapy alone is too simplistic.

Contra-indications

The contra-indications to psychotherapy can be conveniently categorized as intra-psychic or situational in type.

Paranoid traits and attitudes are the first intra-psychic contra-indication; they are exceptionally resistant to change and patients with them as a prominent personality feature are difficult to work with. Possibly this is because of their development in early life, perhaps in the first year: Erikson's (1965) basic mistrust concept, Klein's paranoid-schizoid position (Segal 1964). In therapy the practical difficulty lies in modifying these patients' constant use for primitive disowning defences like splitting people into good and bad, and projection of their unfavourable personal qualities onto others. The second intra-psychic contra-indication is poor impulse control. Combined, as so frequently, with low frustration tolerance, these patients have great difficulty in 'staying with', i.e. understanding and working through the inevitable conflicts that arise in long-term psychotherapy. They tend to drop out suddenly and without thought or to engage in such impulsive, self-damaging behaviour as attempted suicide. Inevitably episodes of crisis and in-patient admission disrupt the progress of therapy and also, unless the therapist is a saint, undermine the therapist–patient relationship. Persons with drug dependency problems, including alchohol, are particularly likely to show impulsiveness as an obvious part of their personality pattern.

A third intra-psychic contra-indication is a life-long attitude of pessimism—that is a basic view of the world; this is different to the low mood that might occur as part of a depressive illness. It may also overlap with the idea in transactional analysis of the person with a 'losing script' whose life tends to be punctuated by repeated episodes of failure (James 1977).

The extra-psychic contra-indication is the patient's impossible social situation (Goffman 1972). This relates to people who are caught in a totally unresolvable marital or family problem, or who are severely disadvantaged financially or educationally, or who may be physically handicapped, or who have demonstrable, even if largely unconcious, 'gain' from a difficult social situation (e.g. the alcoholic's wife who 'needs' to be married to a weak or crippled man). People in these sorts of situations which are unmodifiable, are extremely difficult, if not impossible, to help by psychotherapy.

Research criteria of selection

Selection for psychotherapy is closely relate to what has become called 'outcome research' (to differentiate it from 'process research which attempts to study factors in psychotherapy which lead to patient change). The pertinent question is stated by Bergin and Strupp (1972): 'which patient characteristics and problems are most amenable to which techniques conducted by which type of therapist in what type of setting?' We can complicate the question by adding: in what weighted combination of these four factors—patient, therapy, therapist, and social situation? Malan (1973) suggests outcome is the crucial issue in psychotherapy research and refers somewhat contemptuously to investigators who have made the 'flight from outcome into process', i.e. from *how well* psychotherapy works to how it works.

These are deep waters and in a chapter of limited remit I will restrict myself mainly to commenting on factors that relate to the patient since both researchers and reviewers of psychotherapy agree that the characteristics of the patient are the most crucial. To Freud is attributed the reply 'not too old, not too ill' to the question of suitability for psychotherapy and as a simple guide this is still acceptable. Young, attractive, verbal, intelligent, and successful—the so-called YAVIS patient—is a more detailed variant of this theme.

Luborsky *et al.* (1971) have made an extensive review of the quantitative research on factors influencing outcome in psychotherapy. Predictive factors include a global estimate of the adequacy of personality functioning; absence of schizoid trends; motivation and/or positive expectation; intelligence; initial anxiety and other strong affects like depression; educational and social assets; and 'experiencing'—rated from early psychotherapy sessions, i.e. the patient is capable of deep and immediate feelings and of being reflectively aware of these feelings. Several American reviewers have noted that low socio-economic status is negatively related to improvement with conventional, dynamic, long-term psychotherapy (Garfield 1971). Barron (1953) designed an 'ego-strength' scale to predict response to psychotherapy and found a relationship between good outcome and the following: good physical health in the previous few years; spontaneity and the ability to share emotional experiences with others as compared with seclusiveness; good reality sense; a permissive morality rather than a repressive, punitive one; undogmatic religious convictions; personal adequacy and ability to cope and plan; general capacity for personality integration despite vivid psychopathology; intelligence; and lack of racial prejudice.

Malan (1973) reviewing outcome in his own research noted that, of the original selection criteria, motivation for insight appeared to be the most important. Sifneos (1969) confirmed this in finding in his studies that there should be motivation for change, not just for symptom relief. He systematically evaluated motivation by using a number of criteria in the patient: his recognition of the psychological nature of his symptoms; an introspective tendency; a preparedness to give an honest account of difficulties and to take an active part in the treatment process; a curiosity and willingness to understand oneself; a desire to change, explore, and experiment; realistic expectations of the results of psychotherapy; and preparedness to make sacrifices in time and money. Other patient features used by Sifneos in selection are: above average intelligence; a history of at least one meaningful relationship; expression of affect during the interview; and a specific chief complaint.

In conclusion, therefore, the currently accepted clinical criteria of selection for psychotherapy overlap with, and do not in any significant way contradict, the findings of research. Cognitive and demographic variables are probably not as important as factors suggesting total involvement in therapy of which motivation to change and psychological awareness are probably the most relevant.

Assessing the patient

A general assessment of the patient, including history-taking and mental state examination, should be followed by a psychodynamic evaluation. In addition a final decision as to suitability for long-term treatment may be delayed until the completion of a trial of psychotherapy. Attention should be paid both to extra- and intra-psychic factors. Extra-psychic factors have been discussed earlier in the chapter and will not be considered further. Intra-psychic ones can be classified under four broad headings: psychosexual development, defences, conscience (superego), and relationships.

Psychosexual development

For long-term psychotherapy an age-appropriate heterosexual adjustment is regarded as highly advantageous. Sexual dysfunction, deviance, or infantilism (e.g. masturbation or pornography as a main sexual outlet) are still treatable, but with some difficulty. Inquiries should be directed to sexuality in the past and present, both performance and relationship aspects; in particular, has the patient managed to sustain a sexual relationship for a significant period at any stage of his life. If not, what is the orientation and quality of his sexual fantasies (e.g. homo–heterosexual, narcissistic, sadistic).

Defence mechanisms

Defence mechanisms are used by the ego to help in a person's adaptation to stress, whether this stress arises internally (from the drives or superego) or externally (from the outside world). Does the patient deal effectively with anxiety? Has he a balanced defence repertoire or does he rely on the sole use of particular defences (e.g. denial, projection, or intellectualization)? Does he show an inadequate defence structure as illustrated by symptoms like anxiety, depression, and obsessive–compulsive phenomena; or a defence structure leading, for example, to a work block (Lucas, Crown, Stringer, and Supramanium 1976) or to a sexual inhibition; or a distorted defence structure as seen in hysterical, paranoid, depressive, and compulsive personality types? Generally, the patient's defence structure should be adequate to preserve a hold on reality, should be balanced, and should not include too large a component of 'primitive' defences such as projection where all personal faults are thought to be the faults of others, or profound denial of external reality. The subject of defence mechanisms is particularly well described by Brenner (1957).

Conscience (superego)

An over-strict or punitive conscience in a psychotherapy patient tends to lead to problems in capitalizing on therapeutic gains; any progress is a signal for guilt and self-punishment. A repeated vicious circle of gains and losses may occur, with recurrence of symptoms and to one phenomenon in particular, the negative therapeutic reaction. This develops when the threat of termination is so intolerable that the patient relapses. In assessment one looks for a conscience structure that allows the person to act in a way governed by normal 'guide-lines' (i.e. socially acceptable behaviour) but does not lead to excessive guilt. Guilt is not a difficult concept for potential patients to grasp and a direct question like 'do you tend to suffer from excessive feelings of guilt?' will usually produce a discussion upon which a decision about suitability can be made.

Relationships

These are the fourth important dimension for assessment. Does the patient have the capacity, as shown by his discussion of relationships with parents, friends, spouse, lover, or children, to form relationships with both sexes from which he can receive and give affection. Concern with, rather than dependence on, others is particularly looked for. Again this is not a difficult area to asses—compare the extremes of non-existent relationships in the psychopathic or schizoid personality with the spectrum of more 'normal', average or appropriate human relationships.

The higher the patient's rating in these assessment areas the better his prospects for long-term therapy. Further, and most important, assessment is extended into the next phase of the start of psychotherapy.

Starting psychotherapy

The phase of starting psychotherapy has been modified more than any other in recent years. It is of course vital: to make the obvious point, no one can help a patient who attends only for the diagnostic and assessment sessions and then fails to enter treatment proper.

Preparation for therapy

Patients need to be encouraged into therapy, coaxed sometimes; certainly they require the necessary information to decide about it, why the therapist considers therapy necessary, and what it involves in time and expense. Attitudes reflected in such phrases as unconditional positive regard, warmth, and empathy should be expressed by the therapist and an emotion like hope instilled into the patient; the therapist should feel he wants to help and that he can. That careful attention needs to be paid to this preparatory phase is now accepted by most therapists. A therapist must conduct this preparation *in his own way*. While the ground rules are clear, he must be himself, not act the part of 'the therapist' or of someone else being a therapist. Styles of therapy (Luborsky, Singer, and Luborsky 1975) and of therapist (Rice, Gurman, and Razin 1974; Staples, Sloane, Whipple, Cristol, and Yorkston 1975) obviously vary. Therapy induction procedures must therefore be developed and adopted by therapists to suit their own style and to the different patients they treat. For example, some patients need a challenge, others persuasion, when starting therapy. This has been referred to previously and, with selected patients, the challenge may be extreme as in prokaletic therapy.

The therapeutic contract

The arrangements—both general and specific, partly fixed and partly negotiable—made between therapist and client constitute the therapeutic contract. Flexibility is the key word. The only fixed, or relatively fixed, components to the contract are the initial logistics: times, length, and frequency of sessions. Even these may be modified later but they should be agreed upon at least for a specified period; therapist's and patient's lives need some framework. Throughout therapy, any alterations should, so far a possible, not be made on impulse but should be thoroughly discussed and worked through. This allows the time to understand the full implications of change in terms of the patient's personality, his problems, his lifesituation, his relation with the therapist (transference), or whatever else is relevant, and may contribute to the patient's insight.

Goals of therapy

Setting goals is a controversial subject. One advantage of long-term therapy is that a relatively leisurely attitude can be taken to the task compared, for example, with crisis intervention. Broad objectives should be discussed like resolution of symptoms or increased work satisfaction, but where basic personality change is an aim it can often not be seen clearly either by patient or therapist during the early stage of treatment. Establishment of goals becomes part of the continuously negotiable contract. Malan (1976) and Sifneos (1968, 1969) writing of brief psychotherapy suggest that a clear focus on specified goals is mandatory. The disagreement, if that is what it is, may relate to the terms brief and long-term psychotherapy: in the latter one has ample time to set goals and to add to, or modify them, if necessary.

Trial of psychotherapy

Most patients can be allocated fairly easily into two groups: those unlikely to benefit from long-term psychotherapy (although they may benefit from some other approach and should be guided towards it) and those that probably will. A third group of patients exists in which assessment leads only to a tentative decision: here a trial of treatment may be agreed on between patient and therapist. This usually involves 3–6 sessions, after which the question of suitability becomes clearer. Often professional patients (doctors, social workers, teachers, students) are particularly difficult to assess: their background and training encourages them not only to be clear about what sort of treatment they would like, but also to put on their best face in the preliminary interviews. They may know, for example, that to express motivation is wanted and do this verbally to manipulate the immediate situation, although genuine and sustained motivation is lacking.

Significant others

Psychoanalysis has traditionally treated the patient alone with the argument that the changes he achieves will lead to appropriate changes in those around him. In recent years, however, as more interest has focused on marital and family therapy it has become clear that one ignores significant other persons in the patient's life at great peril to the future of the therapy itself and to the future of the patient's relationships, particularly with his spouse and children. There are, therefore, ethical, as well as clinical, issues involved (Crown 1977). Should we alter a patient's intimate relationships without at least being aware of what we are doing and taking appropriate caution? I am in no doubt that significant others, usually the spouse or other partner, should participate in any important decision-making in therapy. This may involve interviews and discussions in the early stages of assessment—often, incidentally, helpful in its own right—so that everyone knows what is entailed. Full participation of relevant people in this way is a helpful adjunct to treatment by discouraging any possible sabotage by them and promoting their co-operation. The therapist's responsibility may involve helping the spouse or significant other to obtain treatment in his or her own right if this should prove necessary; if, for example, changes in the designated patient prove too difficult for the partner to tolerate reasonably.

Any questions?

At the end of the assessment period the patient should be encouraged to ask questions of the therapist. Formal psychoanalysis forbids this; it assumes, perhaps correctly, that people entering this form of treatment know what to expect. Now that the aim of the psychotherapies is to reach a far broader segment of the social spectrum than hitherto, therapists will find that potential patients are not always aware of certain things they wish to know, and should know; they should be genuinely encouraged to ask.

Therapeutic Strategies

Free association

Long-term psychotherapy, although it now tends to take place in a more informal atmosphere, the patient usually sitting in a chair rather than lying on a couch, still uses, so far as this is possible, Freud's fundamental rule that the patient should try and say everything that comes into his mind without self-control or censure. This is of course an ideal not truly accomplishable; the mind does not function as a computer programmed to draw at random from its stores of memories and emotions. Some patients can however approach this ideal and soon learn to do so. In any event, the basic principle remains: when therapy actually starts the patient does the major work—as he sees it; the therapist accepts the material presented by the patient as primary data which say something of significance about the patient and his problems.

The first psychotherapy session

In a sense this is the second stage of the preparation process with the patient looking more deeply into therapy. It is important that the therapist be both careful and helpful. It seems pointless to make the first session an agony for a patient who is too tense to say anything that 'comes into his mind'. If a patient is so tense it is both helpful and human to adopt a simple strategem like taking an obvious part of his history and suggesting that he may like to talk about this. Most people will respond with relief and gratitude whether or not they actually go ahead and talk about what has been suggested. Later they will need this help less and less often. Some articulate and sophisticated patients need no help to begin; less sophisticated, perhaps less educated, often working-class patients, may need considerable help and it should be given willingly. (The supposed limitations of doing long—term psychotherapy with working-class patients have been spelled out and perhaps exaggerated in the United States (e.g Garfield 1971).) Attention should be paid particularly to any communication difficulties by, for example, using concrete rather than abstract terms (tension rather than anxiety) and assisting the working-class patient to learn how to function effectively in the psychotherapy situation. In principle, nothing different is involved than in teaching a person how to cope with any other unfamiliar situation such as a job interview. The 'analytic honeymoon' should be a reasonable period for the patient, one for him and his therapist to learn how to work together and a little about each other's personalities.

After this, progress inevitably becomes more difficult; in terms of psychoanalytic theory resistances or unconscious blocks to clinical progress emerge and, in order to overcome these, therapeutic strategies have been formulated. As the topic is immense, only simple guidance can be given in this chapter with further references for the systematic reader. There are five main interventions or strategies: clarification, linking, reflection, interpretation, and confrontation.

Clarification

Clarification is a common therapist activity: if unclear about what a patient is saying, ask. Patients' lives are complex; the initial history obtained during assessment covers only a tiny fragment. As facts emerge it will be necessary from time to time to seek further explanation or clarification. An example would be a name mentioned for the first time with little elaboration. There is only one guiding rule—if unsure, ask. This applies particularly to patients from another culture: if the therapist does not for example know about marital or family customs in Trinidad or Bombay he simply asks. Or to patients with a technical expertise with which the therapist is unfamiliar, e.g. instrumental technique in a professional musician where this is relevant to his problem. Another use of clarification, described by Kernberg (1977), is to detect a patient who may be more seriously ill than the therapist has suspected: unclear speech may reflect unclear thought. Unclear thought may in its turn

reflect neurotic anxiety or represent schizophrenic thought disorder
and thus point to an unsuspected psychosis. As a generalization,
when challenged to clarify, a neurotic does so whereas a schizophrenic's thinking may be thrown further into disarray.

Linking

A therapist often helps the patient by explicating links that as an outsider he has noted but the patient has missed. These links may be
between aspects of current feelings and behaviour (e.g. at work and
at home) or between past and present experiences (e.g. attitude to
parents and employer) or, most importantly, between past, present,
and future (aspirations for example). The future is in the
present—many conflicts and difficulties relate to expectations,
ambitions, plans, or hopes.

Reflecting

Reflecting is a basic technique of all therapies derived from Rogerian
Client-centred Therapy (see Murray 1970). Its essence is that a
problem or situation presented by the patient is sifted through the
therapist's mind, drawing on his experience, and is reflected back to
the patient in a way that makes the problem or situation clearer.
Even simple reflective techniques can be immensely helpful. For
example, in a patient faced with a career decision the therapist
comments: 'it seems to me that this conflict is between what you
want to do and what you feel you should do'. The chief feature of
reflecting is that nothing is added to, or taken from, what is
produced by the patient. Nor is understanding of a different order
placed on the patient's thoughts as might be the case in interpreting
unconscious motives.

Interpretation

Interpretation, a technique derived from psychoanalysis, is an
attempt to make unconscious motives, attitudes, and feelings
conscious in order that the patient can learn more about himself.
Insight is a fundamental way in which psychotherapy leads to
personal change (Strupp 1975; Crown 1973), and interpretations, if
successful, should increase this insight. Interpreting applies to any

facet of apparently unconscious behaviour that the therapist observes and thinks may be important. Any manoeuvre that the patient uses in order apparently to avoid the discussion of problem areas, e.g. claiming that he is too busy to attend sessions, or of intrapsychic conflicts, e.g. a family conflict of earlier life, should be interpreted. To deal with the latter may involve interpretation in four areas: transference, defences, conscience, and dreams.

The need to interpret the transference, particularly feelings the patient has about the therapist as reflecting his early feelings about family members, is stressed by Malan. A helpful paper by Offenkrantz and Tobin (1974) spells out four conditions under which the transference should be interpreted: when the patient shows undue emotion with no obvious cause within the therapeutic situation and particularly if this occurs repeatedly; when the flow of associations in the patient becomes blocked; when the therapist considers it likely that a transference interpretation will increase a patient's insight and understanding; and when the link between infantile attitudes to important figures in the past and attitudes to the therapist are very close to the patient's conscious awareness.

Characteristic defence mechanisms also need interpreting when they arise. For example, projection of feelings onto others, denial of one's feelings of the reality of a situation, intellectualizing, and rationalizing away the unconscious roots of behaviour and attitudes. Defence mechanisms are well discussed by Brenner (1957).

Conscience (superego) manifestations like excessive guilt need interpretation in an effort to discover their source and to modify their harmful effects. Dreams usually reflect both current preoccupations and problems, and earlier conflicts. The patient should with appropriate therapist interpretation learn to decode a dream as experienced (manifest content) so as to understand its underlying meaning (latent content).

An interpretation is a hypothesis to account for a certain attitude, emotion, or aspect of behaviour: if accurate there should be a change in the patient towards increased insight, modified attitude or emotion, or more effective behaviour; if inaccurate there will be no effect. Sometimes the therapist may give a 'correct' interpretation early in treatment but which is rejected by the patient only for the same interpretation to 'click' later (Balint, Ornstein, and Balint 1972). This is not unlike the increasing insight that comes from repeated reading of a complex novel or listening to a piece of music. The main guideline is—interpret when you think it is appropriate; do not either be put off by the patient's negative response or, conversely, be too gratified by his ready acceptance of your wisdom. Too ready acceptance, compliance (Blackwell 1976), may itself be a defence and need further interpretation. The only way to judge the effectiveness of interpretations is via the general progress or otherwise of therapy.

Confrontation

Periodically patients need to be confronted with the consequences of their actions. Confrontation is basically a challenge: thus, for example, a patient who jeopardizes his therapy by constant and repeated lateness may need to be faced with the fact that the effectiveness of treatment is rendered null and void; the therapist's time could better be given to another patient. In general it is better to use interpretation before resorting to confrontation.

Acting out is a special problem that may need both interpretation and, later, confrontation. Acting out reflects a patient's failure to acknowledge and to face up to his psychological problems and anxieties; instead, a course of action, often self-destructive, is taken. Hence the difficulty of dealing with impulsiveness in psychotherapy: an alcoholic, for example, at the first sign of an increase in his anxiety may go out on a binge to alleviate this. Attempted suicide, self-mutilation, reckless driving, relationship-threatening behaviour, and unnecessary challenges to supervisors risking dismissal, are common examples of acting out for which confrontation may be necessary.

Managing the unsuitable patient

The patient suitable for psychotherapy has already been discussed. Sometimes, due to poor selection by the therapist or, with therapists in training, by a supervisor, a patient gradually reveals himself as unsuitable for long-term psychotherapy—perhaps because he is impulsive, paranoid, histrionic with gross acting out, or holds intense religious or political convictions. Management includes altering the basic therapeutic approach: decreasing the frequency of sessions; using more direct support and less interpretation of unconscious motives, using less reconstruction of the past; placing greater emphasis on the present reality, e.g. jobs and relationships; and becoming less opaque, more transparent. Although a difficult situation for the inexperienced therapist these strategies are often helpful.

Finishing therapy

Positive and negative reasons for termination

There are positive and negative reasons for finishing therapy. A positive reason is the feeling in both patient and therapist that as much has been achieved as is likely to be achieved—not necessarily of course all changes considered desirable initially—and that an agreed time for termination should be reached. Patients usually evaluate their progress by using some sort of subjective global rating of how they feel about themselves, but therapists should train themselves in the demanding self-discipline of making a systematic assessment: symptom relief and personality change, the latter divided into work, social, and sexual areas. If a research programme is being undertaken then standardized ratings or questionnaires may be used.

The termination process is not difficult provided common sense and human kindness are observed. When it is clear to patient and therapist that termination is appropriate the patient's own pace should be considered: some like a few more sessions, most aim for a readily identifiable date such as the summer or Easter or Christmas break. A negative therapeutic reaction, as discussed earlier, may occur leading to apparent return of symptoms and loss of progress but analysis and discussion of the reasons for this are usually effective.

Negative reasons for breaking-off treatment may be situational (e.g. a patient's job transferred to another part of the country) or as summed up in the term 'therapeutic failure'. In the case of the latter the therapist should try to ascertain where the problem lies: the patient's symptoms or personality, the therapist's personality, the patient–therapist realationship, or an incorrectly chosen modality of treatment. From this assessment it is desirable to help the patient to adopt the next course of action: no therapy, a different sort of treatment, or similar treatment with another therapist. Although these analyses are painful for both therapist and patient they tend to lead to further growth and development in both.

Further treatment

Further treatment with the same therapist is always a possible course of action. The patient should be told in such a way: that he knows that it will be possible at a later stage if it proves necessary; that a new therapeutic contract will then be negotiated; and that further treatment is neither expected nor forbidden by the therapist. Generally only a minority of patients return, but all feel grateful and relieved to know that they can do so if they wish. If a therapist knows he will not be available, a colleague's name can be given to the patient whom he can contact, or information about a suitable clinic can be provided.

Socializing with patients

Every therapist tries this once! It is an unrewarding practice mainly because in long-term psychotherapy the therapeutic relationship is predominantly one-sided, and the strange, intense-but-distant relationship of psychotherapy does not mix with ordinary friendship in which people are basically equal. Little more needs to be said of this—therapists must establish their own standards and values (Crown 1977).

Problems for the therapist

I suggested earlier that therapists should 'be themselves' and learn to develop their own therapeutic style. This is so but certain problems emerge and three of these need to be discussed: counter-transference, activity–passivity, and opaqueness–transparency.

Counter-transference

Counter-transference is an extension of the transference concept and refers to the attitudes that a therapist develops to his patients during therapy and that reflect his own feelings and attitudes to important persons in his life, past and present. A range of powerful emotions may be aroused: tenderness, dislike, anger, frustration, fear, insecurity, homosexual; how else could it be? Therapists are human beings and have human feelings. This is another way in which the classical psychoanalytic notion of the therapist as a mirror reflecting the patient's feelings, although partly true, needs considerable modification.

The keys to coping with counter-transference are firstly to be aware of it, neither to deny nor act on it. If one does behave inappropriately—for example, by getting unreasonably angry—a simple apology is appropriate; after all psychotherapy, whatever else it is, is also a *social* interaction (Argyle 1967) so that accepted social conventions are appropriate. Secondly, the therapist should never act out his counter-transference feelings. This is particularly important in relation to sexual feelings: no patient's sexual problem was ever solved by overt sexuality with the therapist (Kardener 1974). Long-term psychotherapy tends to facilitate the emergence of counter-transference feelings because the therapist–patient relationship is intense and extends over a lengthy period. Just as the therapist encourages the patient to analyse his feelings in the transference, so the therapist must, to himself, be prepared to look at his own counter-transference. The advantange of long-term therapy is that there is no rush: if in doubt do nothing, think about the problem between sessions and then take the appropriate steps. Counter-transference feelings may also need systematic observation and analysis because they provide a clue to the patient's psychopathology. If a patient has a persistent need to denigrate his therapist, this need will be experienced in the counter-transference, the therapist feeling angry because he is under-valued. This feeling may usefully be fed back to the patient to help him to understand an aspect of his relationships with others both in the remote past and in the present.

Therapist activity–passivity

Activity–passivity as a dimension of personality, 'personal tempo' (Eysenck 1947), may well exist as a basic constitutional attribute. Common observation of therapists, no matter the school they belong to, suggests that they differ markedly in this respect and, once again every therapist has to come to terms with the sort of person he is. Training is also relevant: certain patients may be 'switched-off' by a highly active therapist while others feel threatened by a therapist who assumes too passive and analytic a role. Therapists must learn to know their own personality and train themselves to adapt appropriately to different patients.

Therapist transparency–opaqueness

This dimension refers to how a patient perceives the therapist

(Yalom 1975): theoretically the dimension could stretch from a pure fantasy-figure, totally opaque, upon which he can project his own feelings and attitudes, through to a friend, openly revealing of himself. Therapists, in fact, vary from the classically opaque psychoanalyst to the emotionally involved and transparent encounter group leader. Although transparent–opaqueness is associated with activity–passivity (it would be extremely difficult for an active therapist to remain opaque), they are not the same thing: a therapist who is highly active may discipline himself to work so closely with material from the patient that he reveals little of himself and remains relatively opaque.

Once again the only guide-lines possible in psychotherapy are to be aware of the extremes and to avoid them and to recognize the particular needs of patients. Analogy, metaphor, humour, anecdotes, personalized expressions of caring or of sorrow for a patient's disappointment, loss or failure or of pleasure at his success—these and many other aspects of therapist-transparency can be helpful at appropriate times. Sensitivity and appropriate control can only be learned with experience.

Training

Training is too big a topic to be more than hinted at here; it is ably discussed by Pines (1974). Therapists need three dimensions to their training: clinical practice under supervision, theoretical reading and instruction, and opportunity for personal growth. Several different types of patient should ideally be treated, particularly a patient with neurotic symptoms and one with a disordered personality. Patients with sexual problems are an important third possibility. Supervision needs vary—individual supervision seems the most effective and helpful to the majority of trainees while group supervision and discussion may be preferred by some. However other trainees feel inhibited by the presence of peers if they feel they have made mistakes. Supervision should be regular even if not necessarily frequent—at least every two weeks, preferably once a week.

Theoretical instruction is difficult to outline here: a brief list of recommended further reading is appended to this chapter. The Royal College of Psychiatrists has a regularly updated reading list (Kendell and Smith 1977) in which the psychotherapy literature has been carefully chosen. In addition the opportunity to discuss reading and other teaching material in tutorial-size groups is helpful for many. As yet only a few centres use audio-visual aids (one-way screens, videotape, films) in teaching psychotherapy but the opportunity for trainees to see both themselves at work as well as experienced therapists is worthwhile.

A thorny question is what opportunity, if any, should there be in the nature of personal growth? This must vary according to the needs of trainees and includes personal psychoanalysis or other form of psychotherapy, a group experience, either therapeutic or T-group, or encounter. In Balint-type training, opportunity for personal growth is combined with and based on discussion of patients' case material. In order to carry out effective long-term psychotherapy without too much emotional cost to the trainee-therapist, more rather than less personal psychotherapy is probably sensible.

Conclusion

All the psychotherapies, including psychoanalytically-oriented psychotherapy, are limited in the degree to which they are capable of modifying man's behaviour. Every psychotherapy needs, through research, to explore its strengths and its weaknesses. What *really* is important: a particular therapy, the therapist, the patient's personality, the patient's complaint, or the interaction between these? Clarifying the answers to these questions is the overall research task for the next decade. A simple account of problems and strategies is that of Crown (1981).

Psychoanalytically-oriented theory chiefly needs to reformulate its 'economic' principle so as to replace outmoded 'energy' concepts with concepts expressed in terms of learning, information theory, and contemporary neurophysiology. Long-term individual psychotherapy must begin to use observational techniques such as videotaped interviews to validate (or refute) theoretical constructs like transference, resistance, defence, and interpretation. From this will come increased understanding of the psychotherapeutic process and more precise demonstration of the criteria of cure, particularly evidence of personality change.

Summary

This chapter has focused on once-weekly, long-term psychotherapy whose aims are symptomatic relief and personality change. I have discussed the background of such treatment both within and outside psychoanalysis and the gradual change of emphasis towards a more flexible technique particularly in terms of the induction process into therapy and the principle of the continuously negotiated and re-negotiated therapeutic contract. Criteria of assessment have been outlined: positive features in the patient include his 'motivation' and 'desire to change'; particularly unsuitable are patients with paranoid traits, impulsiveness, and an overall pessimistic attitude to life. Research criteria for selection have been discussed particularly demographic and personality qualities in the patient, with some note of factors in the therapist and in the therapist–patient relationship. Therapist issues such as counter-transference, activity–passivity, and transparency–opaqueness have been examined as have his thera-peutic strategies— clarification, linking, reflecting, interpreting, and confrontation. The chapter ends with an account of the criteria for termination and how to do it, and with a section on training.

References

Aichorn, A. (1935). *Wayward youth.* Viking, New York.

Alexander, F. (1957). *Psychoanalysis and psychotherapy.* Allen and Unwin, London.

Argyle, M. (1967). *The psychology of interpersonal behaviour.* Penguin, Harmondsworth.

——, Bryant, B., and Trower, P. (1974). Social skills training and psycho-therapy, *Psychol. Med.* **4**, 435–43.

Balint, M., Ornstein, P., and Balint, E. (1972). *Focal psychotherapy.* Tavistock, London.

Bandura, A. (1969). *Principles of behavioral modification.* Holt, Rinehart and Winston, New York.

Barron, F. (1953). An ego-strength scale which predicts response to psycho-therapy, *J. consult. Psychol.* **17**, 327–33.

Bergin, A. E. and Strupp, H. H. (1972). *Changing frontiers in the science of psychotherapy.* Aldine, New York.

Blackwell, B. (1976). Treatment adherence, *Br. J. Psychiat.* **129**, 513–31.

Brenner, C. (1957). *An elementary texbook of psychoanalysis.* Inter-national Universities Press, New York.

Brown, J. A. C. (1961). *Freud and the post-Freudians.* Penguin, Harmondsworth.

Bugental, J. F. T. (1967). *Challenges of humanistic psychology.* McGraw-Hill, New York.

Crown, S. (1973). Psychotherapy, *Br. J. hosp. Med.* **9**, 355–62.

—— (ed.) (1976*a*). *Psychosexual problems.* Academic Press, London.

—— (1976*b*). Marital breakdown: epidemiology and psychotherapy. In

Recent advances in clinical psychiatry (ed. K. Granville-Grossman). Churchill Livingstone, Edinburgh.

—— (1977). Psychotherapy. In *Dictionary of medical ethics* (eds A. S. Duncan, G. R. Dunstan, and R. B. Welbourn). Darton, Longman and Todd, London.

—— (1981). Psychotherapy research today, *Br. J. Hosp. Med.* **25**, 492–501.

Entwistle, N. and Wilson, J. (1977). *Degrees of excellence: the academic achievement game.* Hodder and Stoughton, London.

Erikson, E. H. (1959). Growth and crises of the healthy personality. In *Personality* (eds R. S. Lazarus and E. M. Opton). Penguin, Harmondsworth.

—— (1965). *Childhood and society.* Penguin, Harmondsworth.

Eysenck, H. J. (1947). *Dimensions of personality.* Kegan Paul, London.

—— (1952). The effects of psychotherapy: an evaluation, *J. consult. psychol.* **16**, 319–24.

Frank, J. D. (1973). *Persuasion and healing.* Johns Hopkins University Press, Baltimore, Md.

—— (1974). Therapeutic components of psychotherapy. A 25-year progress report of research, *J. nerv. ment. Dis.* **159**, 325–42.

Freud, S. (1976). *Two short accounts of psychoanalysis.* Penguin, Harmondsworth.

Garfield, S. L. (1971). Research on client variables in psychotherapy. In *Handbook of psychotherapy and behavior change: an empirical analysis* (eds A. E. Bergin and S. L. Garfield). Wiley, New York.

Goffman, E. (1972). The neglected situation. In *Language and social context* (ed. P. Giglioli). Penguin, Harmondsworth.

Gottschalk, L. A. and Auerbach, A. H. (1966). *Methods of research in psychotherapy.* Appleton-Century-Crofts, New York.

Groddeck, G. (1977). *The meaning of illness.* International Universities Press, New York.

Gurman, A. S. and Kniskern, D. P. (1978). Research on marital and family therapy: progress, perspective and prospect. In *Handbook of psychotherapy and behavior change: an empirical analysis* 2nd edn (eds S. L. Garfield and A. E. Bergin). Wiley, New York.

Hartocollis, P. (ed.) (1977). *Borderline personality disorders: the concept, the syndrome, the patient.* International Universities Press, New York.

Hudson, L. (1967). *Contrary imaginations.* Penguin, Harmondsworth.

Hughes, A. (1974). Contributions of Melanie Klein to psychoanalytic technique. In *Psychotherapy today* (ed. V. Varma). Constable, London.

James, M. (ed.) (1977). *Techniques in transactional analysis.* Addison-Wesley, Reading, Mass.

Kardener, S. H. (1974). Sex and the physician-patient relationship, *Am. J. Psychiat.* **131**, 1134–6.

Kendell, R. E. and Smith, A. C. (1977). *Reading list in psychiatry* (4th edn). Royal College of Psychiatrists, London. Also Psychotherapy (1982). London.

52 An introduction to the psychotherapies

Kernberg, O. F. (1977). The structural diagnosis of borderline personality organization. In *Borderline personality disorders* (ed. P. Hartocollis). International Universities Press, New York.

Lipowski, Z. J. (1975). Physical illness, the patient and his environment: psychosocial foundation of medicine. In *American handbook of psychiatry* (ed. S. Arieti) Vol. 4. Basic Books, New York.

Luborsky, L., Chandler, M., Auerbach, A. H., Cohen, J., and Bachrach, H. M. (1971). Factors influencing outcome of psychotherapy: a review of quantitative research. *Psychol. Bull.* **75**, 145–85.

——, Singer, B., and Luborsky, L. (1975). Comparative studies of psychotherapy, *Archs gen. Psychiat.* **32**, 995–1008.

—— and Spence, D. P. (1971). Quantitative research on psychoanalytic therapy. In *Handbook of psychotherapy and behavior change: an empirical analysis* (eds A. E. Bergin and S. L. Garfield). Wiley, New York.

Lucas, C. J., Crown, S., Stringer, P., and Supramanium, S. (1976). Further observations on study difficulty in university students, including 'syllabus boundness', *Br. J. Psychiat.* **129**, 598–603.

Malan, D. (1963). *A study of brief psychotherapy*. Tavistock, London.

—— (1973). The outcome problem in psychotherapy research. A historical review, *Archs gen. Psychiat.* **29**, 719–29.

—— (1975). Psychoanalytic brief psychotherapy and scientific method. In *Issues and approaches in the psychological therapies* (ed. D. Bannister). Wiley, London.

—— (1976). *The frontier of brief psychotherapy: an example of the convergence of research and clinical practice*. Plenum Press, New York.

——, Bacal, H. A., Heath, E. S., and Balfour, F. (1968). A study of psychodynamic chances in untreated neurotic patients. I. *Br. J. Psychiat.* **114**, 525–51.

——, Heath, E. S., Bacal, H. A., and Balfour, F. (1975). Psychodynamic changes in untreated neurotic patients. II. Apparently genuine improvements. *Archs gen. Psychiat.* **32**, 110–26.

Marteau, L. (1976). Encounter and the new therapies. *Br. J. hosp. Med.* **15**, 257–65.

Meltzoff, J. and Kornreich, M. (1970). *Research in psychotherapy*. Atherton Press, New York.

Murray, D. (1970). Client-centred therapy. In *Four psychotherapies* (ed. L. Hersher). Butterworths, London.

Nemiah, J. C., Freyberger, H., and Sifneos, P. E. (1976). Alexythymia: a view of the psychosomatic process. In *Modern trends in psychosomatic medicine* (ed. O. W. Hill) Vol. 3. Butterworths, London.

Offenkrantz, W. and Tobin, A. (1974). Psychoanalytic psychotherapy, *Archs gen. Psychiat.* **30**, 593–606.

Parlett, M. R. (1969). The syllabus-bound student. In *The ecology of human intelligence* (ed. L. Hudson). Penguin, Harmondsworth.

Parloff, M. B., Kelman, H. C., and Frank, J. D. (1954). Comfort, effectiveness and self-awareness as criteria of improvement in psychotherapy, *Am. J. Psychiat.* **111**, 343–51.

Pines, M. (1974). Training in dynamic aspects of psychotherapy. In *Psychotherapy today* (ed. V. Varma). Constable, London.

Rice, D. G., Gurman, A. S., and Razin, A. M. (1974). Therapist sex, style and theoretical orientation, *J. nerv. ment. Dis.* **159**, 413–21.

Rubenstein, D. and Alanen, Y. O. (1972). *Psychotherapy of schizophrenia.* Exerpta Medica, Amsterdam.

Rycroft, C. (1972). *A critical dictionary of psychoanalysis.* Penguin, Harmondsworth.

Segal, H. (1964). *Introduction to the work of Melanie Klein.* Heinemann, London.

Sifneos, P. E. (1968). Learning to solve emotional problems: a controlled study of short-term anxiety-provoking psychotherapy. In *The role of learning in psychotherapy* (ed. R. Porter). Churchill, London.

—— (1969). Short-term, anxiety-provoking psychotherapy: an emotional problem-solving technique, *Semin Psychiat.* **1**, 389–98.

Skynner, A. C. R. (1976). *One flesh, separate persons. Principles of family and marital psychotherapy.* Constable, London.

Staples, F. R., Sloane, R. B., Whipple, K., Cristol, A. H., and Yorkston, N. J. (1975). Differences between behaviour therapists and psychotherapists, *Archs gen. Psychiat.* **32**, 1517–22.

Strupp, H. H. (1975). Psychoanalysis, 'focal psychotherapy', and the nature of the therapeutic influence, *Archs gen. Psychiat.* **32**, 127–35.

Taylor, F. K. (1969). Prokaletic measures derived from psychoanalytic technique, *Br. J. Psychiat.* **115**, 407–19.

Yalom, I. D. (1975). *The theory and practice of group psychotherapy.* Basic Books, New York.

——, Bond, G., Bloch. S., and Zimmerman, E. (1977). The impact of a weekend group experience on individual therapy, *Archs gen. Psychiat.* **34**, 399–415.

Recommended reading

Bannister, D. (ed.) (1975). *Issues and approaches in the psychological therapies.* Wiley, London. (Interesting, short comparative accounts of many of the psychotherapies.)

Brenner, C. (1957). *An elementary textbook of psychoanalysis.* International Universities Press, New York. (Includes a clear account of ego defences.)

Freud, S. (1974). *Introductory lectures on psychoanalysis.* Penguin, Harmondsworth. (The most straightforward approach to psychoanalysis.)

Kernberg, O. F. (1977). The structural diagnosis of borderline personality organization. In *Borderline personality disorders* (ed. P. Hartocollis). International Universities Press, New York. (Essential reading on technique for the more experienced psychotherapist.)

Offenkrantz, W. and Tobin, A. (1974). Psychoanalytic psychotherapy, *Archs gen. Psychiat.* **30**, 593–606. (For transference interpretation—when and how to do it.)

Porter, R. (ed.) (1968) *The role of learning in psychotherapy.* Churchill, London. (Discusses the relevance of learning to all psychotherapy.)

Rycroft, C. (1972). *A critical dictionary of psychoanalysis.* Penguin, Harmondsworth. (A useful reference book.)

Sandler, J., Dare, C., and Holder, A. (1973). *The patient and the analyst.* Allen and Unwin, London. (Useful discussion of all psycho-analytically-based interventions relevant to long-term psychotherapy.)

3

Brief focal psychotherapy
Bernard Rosen

Brief focal psychotherapy has come into its own in recent years and brought into question the optimal duration of psychodynamically oriented treatment. In this chapter Rosen draws our attention to the central importance of this time-limited approach. After providing a brief historical background he defines brief therapy and highlights its chief features—its brevity, the emphasis on selecting a focus on which to work, and the critical aspect of termination. Attention is then given to selection. The typical process of treatment is described in terms of three phases—beginning (assessment, preparation, and negotiation of a contract), the active phase, and termination. Typical problems that are encountered in treatment are discussed and the chapter concludes with brief sections on effectiveness and training.

If one reads many of the classic books and papers in psychotherapy, one will come away with the impression that psychotherapy is a time-consuming treatment, lasting months and sometimes years. Patients are often expected to attend at least weekly, frequently more than this, and one reads about issues which could occur only in a lengthy period of therapy, such as the effect on it of enforced breaks and vacations.

Yet in practice it seems quite likely that this is not the case. As Butcher and Koss (1978) point out, 'Most psychotherapeutic contacts, whether or not they initially were planned to be, turn out to be brief ones.' The large scale surveys they reported on suggested that at least 50 per cent of patients terminated their contacts within eight sessions, the most recent survey of 979 000 patients found an average of 4.7 contacts per patient with therapists.

What are the reasons for this? It may be, as Butcher and Koss suggest, that at least some treatments were originally planned to be brief. Some patients may have been inappropriately selected for psychotherapy or found it unhelpful. But I suspect that many patients did find their therapy useful and obtained the amount of help they required quite quickly—more quickly perhaps than their therapists would have expected.

Brief psychotheraphy has developed partly because some therapists became aware that patients can change more rapidly than was once thought possible, and partly because longer term approaches are really not feasible for most patients or therapists. This is because long-term psychotherapy is time (and often financially) consuming and may cause problems through its disruption of the patient's day to day life. Also most therapists, working in public health services, are unable to afford the time for long-term therapy. As a result it often becomes the treatment of a privileged and select few. Yet it seems that the demand for psychotherapy greatly exceeds the supply available at present (Wing and Wing 1970; Wolff 1973).

This chapter describes the development of brief psychotherapy and some of the specific concepts and techniques that have become associated with it. It is concerned with the amount of help that can be offered in a limited period of time to patients who are suitable for psychotherapy. It also reports some of the research done in the area which strongly suggests that many patients who are offered long-term psychotherapy could, equally effectively, be treated by brief therapy. It is not intended as a 'cookbook'. Nevertheless, over recent years, a large growth of brief therapies has occurred, and from them it is possible to distill some common features and principles which are reasonably easily learnt and applied.

Background

It might be thought from what has been said thus far that brief psychotherapy is a late development in the field of psychotherapy. In one sense this is true, but it is worth remembering that Freud's reputation developed partly through his success in quickly relieving symptoms that had often been present for a considerable time and had proved resistant to other therapeutic approaches.

Freud's early cases (Freud and Breuer 1974) mostly received treatment over weeks or months. Interestingly, it was Freud's new active technique of catharsis which appeared to be associated with more rapid improvement. Good examples are those of Miss Lucy R., treated in nine weeks, Fraulein Elizabeth Von R., between three to four months (Freud and Breuer 1974), and the conductor Bruno Walter who was cured in six sessions. He had developed a paralysis of his conducting arm after the birth of his first child (Sterba 1951). However 'Dora' (Freud 1977), another of his early successes and treated in three months, revealed a phenomenon that was to result in the eventual lengthening of psychoanalysis to the several years that are now commonplace. Freud's recognition of transference during her analysis paved the way for a radical new theory of psychopathology and with it an increasing concern with the analysis of the therapeutic relationship itself rather than repressed psychic content. Malan (1963) has drawn attention to the 'lengthening' factors associated with the development of psychotherapy.

By the end of the First World War, psychoanalysis had already become a lengthy process. Ferenczi (1920) made an attempt to counter this with the advocacy of an 'active' technique. This involved the therapist adopting a more personally involved and confronting role with his patients, even to the extent of touching and holding in an effort to reverse the effects of earlier parental rejection. In 1925 Ferenczi and Rank published an influential restatement of psychoanalytic technique, particularly drawing attention to the concept of acting out, in this context covering the propensity of patients to express their unconscious impulses in action. They suggested that analysis of this behaviour did not require an analysis of early experiences but could be understood through an examination of the therapeutic relationship. This early emphasis of the 'here and now' was important for the development of brief psychotherapy. Rank (1945) made a further major contribution by setting a time limit on therapy at its onset and by recognizing the importance of termination. Ferenczi had earlier suggested that treatment could be completed in six weeks. The setting of a time limit also led Rank to consider the associated processes of motivation and individuation—this referring to the development of an independent self. Both processes have become key issues for later therapists and researchers.

The other important influence on brief therapy was that of Alexander and French (1946). Like Rank they suggested the need to concentrate on current issues, on understanding current personal functioning rather than infantile memories, and, crucially, the need to adopt a flexible, empirical approach to treatment. They considered a central therapeutic factor to be the 'corrective emotional experience'. This occurs during therapy when the patient is made aware of unconscious fantasies which are determining his current attitudes and behaviour through a confrontation with his actual experiences in therapy. Alexander (1963) also warned against allowing the patient to regress to 'preconscious early infantile material as a manoevre to evade the essential pathogenic conflicts'.

The work of Alexander and French was a major spur to the development of brief psychodynamic psychotherapies. Thereafter a number of theoretical and technical approaches have been described. Perhaps the major ones are those by Deutch (1949), Malan (1963, 1976a, 1976b), Bellak and Small (1965), Gillman (1965), McGuire (1965a; 1965b), Wolberg (1965), Sifneos (1967), Barten (1971), Balint, Ornstein, and Balint (1972), and Mann (1973). More recently Davanloo (1980) has described some further developments.

This account of the evolution of brief therapy would not be complete without mention of the influence of behavioural psychotherapy. Alexander (1963) among others realized that behavioural and psychodynamic forms of therapy had much in common, and indeed brief psychotherapy would seem to be a useful meeting point for them. Most, though not all, behavioural techniques are applied over short periods of time. But as Gelder points out (see Chapter 6), the particular contribution of behaviour therapy is its approach to the definition of problems, which is conceptually not far removed from the identification of a 'focus' in brief psychodynamic therapy. More recent developments in behavioural therapy, particularly the cognitive approach, have further bridged the gap between behavioural and psychodynamic schools. An excellent example of this is provided by Beck (1976).

Definition

It will already be obvious that no single theoretical model of brief psychotherapy exists. Indeed, it would be more accurate to talk of the 'brief psychotherapies'. Like psychotherapy in general, there are at least three major approaches: psychodynamic, cognitive-behavioural, and client-centred (and their various combinations). In addition brief psychotherapy has been applied in several contexts including the individual, group, and family. Clearly, this burgeoning field cannot be dealt with in detail in this chapter. The remainder of the chapter is concerned largely with general principles and with brief *individual psychodynamic* psychotherapy in particular as this approach is the most widely used and documented.

Brief focal psychotherapy utilizes many of the principles and techniques of longer term psychodynamic therapies. Therapists make use of the therapeutic relationship in understanding the patient and in effecting change. The therapist makes sense of the patient's problems in terms of unconscious conflict. However, the two cardinal features of this approach are the adoption of a time limit to therapy and the identification at the outset of a problem (or set of problems) which forms the focus of treatment. Other problems are either deliberately disregarded or related to the chosen focus.

Brief psychotherapy should be distinguished from crisis intervention although it is often not possible to separate them strictly. In general, crisis intervention is shorter, involves more directives from the therapist, and concentrates on the reduction of arousal rather than its mobilization. Sifneos (1972) has referred to the last as 'Anxiety Suppressive Therapy'. One would also anticipate that the problem that has led to a search for help is perceived as more threatening and immediate by those receiving crisis intervention compared with those in brief psychotherapy.

Features of brief psychotherapy

(1) *Time in therapy*

What distinguishes brief therapy from longer term approaches appears not to be time in therapy itself, but the expectation that it will be limited. A number of variations of this aspect have evolved. In the first, a time limit is a basic feature of the therapist's work and influences the conduct of therapy but the limit is not communicated directly to the patient. The second and probably the most popular approach is to set explicitly the number of sessions at the outset of treatment. This has been advocated particularly by Mann (1973) who describes how therapist and patient plan detailed arrangements of treatment during their first meeting. The third approach (Wolberg 1965 and Sifneos 1972) appears to be less specific although the patient is told that therapy will be limited in time.

An associated question is how long therapy will last. The literature is confusing here, the variation in the numbers of sessions ranging from one to 200 sessions (Small 1971)! Brevity is clearly a relative phenomenon. In their review, Butcher and Koss (1978) placed practitioners in three categories in terms of duration—one to six sessions, up to 25 sessions, and up to 40 sessions. One might expect that this considerable variation would affect what happens during treatment and after. At present, we know precious little about this matter. Obviously, the selection of patients, another poorly defined area in psychotherapy, should influence the period of time decided upon as should the goals set by the therapist. However, there is little evidence pointing to an optimum number of sessions even with careful consideration of selection and therapeutic aims.

Furthermore, common sense suggests that patients require different lengths of time for improvement to occur and for this reason my own practice has increasingly been to determine the time allocated according to such factors as severity and motivation. Thus, I offer most patients between six and 16 sessions of one hour each, on a weekly basis.

To continue in this empirical vein, another relevant question is whether length and frequency of individual sessions should vary. Almost all contributors to the literature on this issue describe weekly sessions, mostly of the '50 minute hour' variety. However, Barten (1965) has limited each session to 15 minutes; by contrast Roth, Bierenbaum, and Garfield (1969) have described a single, 10-hour session, a somewhat unrealistic schedule for most therapists. Lorr, McNair, Michaux, and Raskin (1962) studied frequency of sessions in relation to outcome by assigning patients to once-weekly, twice-weekly, or six-weekly treatment conditions. No difference in outcome was found between the three groups. A different approach was used by Bierenbaum, Nichols and Schwartz (1976) who varied both length of sessions and their frequency so that overall time in treatment was similar. Their results suggest that frequent and shorter sessions result in the greatest relief of anxiety. However, weekly, one-hour sessions were associated with greater emotional cartharsis, symptom reduction, and patient satisfaction.

The Bierenbaum work is promising in that it points to the possibility of planning therapy to suit the specific patient, a matter of obvious concern in the selection of patients for psychotherapy.

(2) *The selection of a focus in treatment*

The most characteristic feature of brief psychotherapy is the identification of a focus for treatment. This occurs at the outset but most practitioners agree on the importance of maintaining the focus throughout treatment. The emphasis on a focus has helped to establish brief psychotherapy as a meeting point between psychodynamic and behavioural approaches.

The means of identifying a focus is not always obvious. There is general agreement th'at the problem to be worked at should be reasonably circumscribed, but this is not to say that it is totally distinct from other problems which may not be part of the selected focus. The problem does not necessarily have to be one which developed recently although it should be playing a significant part in the patient's current difficulties and distress. The problem is inevitably viewed differently by therapists of different theoretical schools but the following points apply in general.

(a) *The problem can be operationally defined*, i.e. it affects the individual and his relationship with his environment in a number of specific ways. Furthermore, the problem can be seen to have one or more causes, a developmental history, and certain consequences in specific circumstances. The problem should also be amenable to modification using techniques derived from the therapist's theoretical framework. These features appear to apply even though the nature of the problem focused upon may vary considerably. Thus, Mann (1973) tends to select problems that reflect difficulties in achieving emotional independence. Malan (1976*b*) identifies an important unconscious psychological conflict of which the patient can be readily made aware, and which is usually related to the Oedipal phase of development.

(b) *There is agreement between therapist and patient about the nature of the problem*, i.e. the problem can be conceptualized in such a way that it has meaning for both patient and therapist. In order to achieve this, the therapist must adopt a form of language of feelings and understanding which encompasses both his own and the patient's views of the problems. Two processes are involved in treatment itself. Firstly, in his exploration of the patient's difficulties, the therapist helps to create a sense of meaning and order out of chaos. Secondly, the therapist, in doing so, translates his own concepts into language understandable to the patient. These two processes involve delicate negotiation over different, and sometimes conflicting, value systems so that a basis for a therapeutic alliance can be created (Lazare Ewenthal, and Wasserman, 1975).

(c) *The problem is soluble within the period of time allocated to treatment.* This point applies particularly to a situation where therapy is strictly time-limited, but it should always be considered in the selection of any problem. There are no clear guide-lines unfortunately; effective determination and statement of the problem in the context of this criterion is a matter mostly of experience. My own practice, therefore, is to spend a longer period on the assessment phase in order to select a problem which is realistically amenable to some solution within a relatively brief period.

(3) *Therapeutic techniques*

As has been noted previously, brief psychotherapy does not represent a unitary approach but encompasses a range of models of treatment which have in common the feature of brevity, and the delineation of a focus upon which to work. In these respects it is clear that behavioural and client-centred principles have influenced the psychodynamic approach. The traditional therapist's stance in psychoanalytically-oriented treatment of relative passivity and reflectiveness provides a relatively non-threatening 'holding' environment which allows a therapeutic relationship, encompassing a dimension of transference, to develop over an extended period of time. By contrast, practitioners of brief psychotherapy stress the need for a more active approach.

(a) *The therapeutic relationship* A principal aim in brief therapy is to create rapidly a trusting, safe therapeutic environment that does not foster dependency on the therapist. This is by no means always an easy task; it involves an active listening 'stance' on the part of the therapist and his determination not to deviate unduly from the agreed focus. Whatever their theoretical persuasion, most therapists appear to be more directive than is the custom in long-term therapy (Butcher and Koss 1978). This varies from prescribing behavioural tasks (Rosen 1979) to the selective attention to specific unresolved conflicts (Sifneos 1972).

(b) *Transference* This is a concept central to the practice of psychodynamic psychotherapy although it has undergone a number of changes in meaning (Sandler, Dare, and Holder 1970) and in application. It is generally agreed to refer to those aspects of the therapeutic relationship which reflect and impinge on the patient's (often) unexpressed fantasies, conflicts, and expectations. The understanding of the process of transference distinguishes psychodynamic psychotherapies from other forms of treatment but the attention paid to it varies according to the length and aims of therapy. In psychoanalysis, for example, the development of the patient and his problems from an early age are analysed through the transference ('transference neurosis'). In brief focal psychotherapy, the immediate aims are necessarily more limited and a number of themes on transference emerge from writers in this field. Gillman (1965) stresses the need to foster a positive transference in the patient. A similar point is made by McGuire (1965*b*) and Sifneos (1967) who both warn against the development of a transference neurosis, since such a process of regression is antithetical to the chief principles of therapy. Malan (1963) notes that the early development of transference and its interpretation to the patient has a positive bearing on outcome. There is also a suggestion that the interpretation of less positive aspects of transference may be of value, particularly in the termination phase of therapy. Mann (1973) whose special focus is separation–individuation (i.e. the process of establishing an independent self), highlights with his patient the anxiety and frustration of termination, as he sees mature emotional development as being closely related to a realistic view of time limits. It seems that sensitive attention to transference phenomena enhances the therapeutic relationship. As I have already noted elsewhere (Rosen 1978), however, a careful balance must be drawn between facilitating a trusting relationship through interpretation of transference aspects and the undesirable development of a collusion with the patient in which the realities of the time limit and the focus set are neglected.

(c) *Interventions* Considerable differences of opinion exist among practitioners of brief therapy about the kind and direction of therapeutic interventions. Unfortunately research does not provide clear answers to this issue. It seems likely that in brief therapy, as in longer term therapies, beneficial change can occur as a result of so-called 'non-specific' factors. This point is made by Wolff (1971) who distinguishes between the 'being with' and 'doing to' components of psychotherapy and suggests that factors other than explicit interventions by the therapist may be useful. These include his personal qualities and the 'match' between the patient and himself (Strupp 1980).

However, writers and researchers in brief therapy have suggested some specific guide-lines for interventions. Malan (1963, 1976*b*) has emphasized the importance of making interpretations early in treatment but that these should be limited in number. This was also noted by Sloane *et al.* (1975) who found greater improvement in patients when their therapists used fewer clarifying and interpreting statements. Malan (1976*a*) has also suggested that interpretations related to the transference are of greater value than those which are concerned, say, with explaining the effect of previous life events. The intensity of the therapist's interventions and, in particular, how confronting he is form the basis of Sifneos's (1967) definition of two types of brief therapy, namely anxiety-suppressive and anxiety-provoking. Similarly, Nichols (1974) compared a cathartic approach aimed at producing a high level of emotional arousal with a more traditional, analytic approach. In two groups of university students, he found that the emotionally-aroused group showed more improvement after nine sessions on measures of behavioural goals and personal satisfaction. Another view is offered by McGuire (1965*b*): 'Interpretations are made with the idea of consolidating what has already been perceptually ordered, learned and uncovered in therapy, and not to broaden the area of inquiry or to foster further uncovering.'

My own approach is probably representative of many brief therapists. Interpretations are initiated at a 'here and now' level and are used to achieve the following goals:

   (i) to maintain an optimum level of arousal within the therapy session;
  (ii) to deal with feelings towards the therapist which might impair progress;
 (iii) to draw attention to issues involved in termination; and
  (iv) to illuminate the patient's difficulties and successes in his day to day life.

Selection

The selection of patients for various forms of brief psychotherapy is most problematic. An extensive reading of the literature and considerable experience in this field has not helped me to reach any definitive decisions about who is most likely to benefit. Brief psychotherapy, like all major forms of psychotherapy, has been applied to a vast range of psychological problems. Research findings on outcome ought to be helpful but in practice only give broad and often unspecific guide-lines. The excellent review by Luborsky, Singer, and Luborsky (1975) suggests similar success rates for brief and long-term psychotherapies. Yet, the studies cited involve diverse groups of patients, non-standardized treatments and, of course, therapists of different shades of opinion, experience, and personality. It appears as if many of the criteria employed for selection for brief psychotherapy have been derived from long-term psychotherapy and tend to be used in order to exclude 'unsatisfactory' patients rather than to give specific indications for inclusion.

My own practice within the British National Health Service involves referrals largely composed of working and lower middle-class patients. Most of them have previously received other forms of psychiatric treatment (usually medication) and may have been previously admitted to hospital. They may be unfamiliar with the process of psychotherapy or have idiosyncratic views about it. These referrals are probably typical of the clinical population at large, and in particular what most of us in the helping professions will experience. Although my own selection criteria differ from those used by the typical psychotherapist in private practice, they are likely to be relevant to a wider range of clinical settings.

(a) *The diagnosis* The following conditions are *not* suitable for treatment by brief psychotherapy: organic psychoses, schizophrenia, affective psychoses, alcoholism, and drug addiction.

The following are probably best treated by *behavioural psychotherapy* but brief psychotherapy may be useful as an adjunct: phobic disorders (including agoraphobia), obsessive–compulsive neurosis, sexual disorders including sexual dysfunction and sexual paraphilias.

Brief psychotherapy should be considered as the *primary* approach in: anxiety states, depressive reactions, and personality disorders. By definition the latter are long-standing developmental disorders. Brief therapy clearly will not effect major personality change but can provide short-term focused help. This seems to be helpful for patients who have considerable needs and problems but whose personality makes a long-term therapeutic relationship difficult to sustain. The personality disorders to which this approach is applicable are classified in the International Classification of Disorders (ICD 9), in particular the Anankastic (Obsessional), Hysterical, and Asthenic.

(b) *Type of problem* As has been mentioned earlier, the definition of problems lies at the heart of brief psychotherapy. Problems which can be conceptualized within both the patient's and therapist's frames of reference are more likely to respond. It is important to distinguish between problems which are directly related to the reasons for the patient seeking help and others which may be present but not causally related to the patient's requests for help. Thus, bereavement may or may not be a problem as defined here. Most therapists suggest that problems of recent onset are likely to respond better (Butcher and Koss 1978). This appeals to common sense, but it should be noted that Malan (1976*b*) did not find an association between time of onset and improvement in his outcome studies. With regard to the category of problems, it is clear that those susceptible to change as a result of initiatives taken by the patient are most suitable. For example, problems that involve potentially resolvable conflicts and maladaptive responses are most likely to respond. Problems over which patients have little control, such as unemployment and poverty, are in themselves not treatable by brief therapy.

Brief psychotherapy has also been employed in treating psychiatric symptoms associated with physical illness and its medical or surgical treatment. The interested readers is recommended to the outstanding studies by Balint and Balint (1961) and Balint (1964).

(c) *Features of the patient and of the therapist* Rogowski (1982) suggests in an excellent review of brief psychotherapy that patients who do well show the following features:

(i)   they function reasonaly well in their social relationships, e.g. work, leisure;

(ii) they have shown evidence of being able to establish interpersonal relationships;

(iii) they are psychologically-minded, i.e. they can think in psychological terms; and

(iv) they are able to experience and express feelings as well as to tolerate them.

To this list may be added a fifth factor, one that Malan (1976*b*) considers the most important of all—the motivation of the patient to change. Since all these criteria are also commonly applied in the selection of patients for long-term psychodynamic therapy, it is difficult to determine whether the criteria have any specificity. They are also not dissimilar to the so called YAVIS syndrome (youthful, attractive, verbal, intelligent, and successful), described by Schofield (1964) to denote the pattern of qualities in the patient that therapists find appealing and often use as positive criteria in their assessment.

Likewise, there do not appear to be features of the therapist which help to distinguish brief and long-term selection. The considerable literature on the relationship between desirable qualities and outcome pertains to therapy of all forms (Parloff, Waskow, and Wolfe 1978).

Recently efforts have been made to match patients and therapists on a number of factors (Parloff *et al.* 1978), with varying degrees of success. This is an important exercise as match or mismatch appears to be a significant reason for success or failure in psychotherapy (Strupp 1978). However, at present, it is not possible to formulate guide-lines about the matching of specific patient and therapist characteristics.

In view of our current state of knowledge about selection, it is wiser to err on the side of overinclusion rather than exclusion. Even patients with 'undesirable' criteria can, in my experience, be helped substantially if the patient's initial expectations of what treatment will provide and problem definition are realistically attended to at the beginning of therapy.

Process of brief psychotherapy

In this section I can generalize only about the process of treatment. With many different techniques available one might anticipate that the process will vary accordingly. For example, therapies in which the date of termination is fixed at the outset are likely to differ in certain respects compared with those that do not make the time limit explicit. However, most clinicians agree that any brief therapy will go through a number of phases. These phases tend to be more pronounced in brief than long-term therapy. I have reduced them to three for simplicity's sake, but it should be borne in mind that there is not always a clear dividing line between them.

(1) The initial phase

This phase usually lasts up to three sessions and involves the following tasks.

(a) *Assessment*

Therapist and patient delineate the patient's problems along the lines already discussed. Inevitably this goes hand in hand with a consideration of the patient's development particularly life events related to current and past problems and coping strategies including previous patterns of response to stress and reactions to current problems. The therapist will also want to gain an idea of unaffected areas of the patient's life, in particular his capacity to maintain family and social relationships and the effect of the problem on work and on leisure pursuits. An effort should be made to determine the patient's level of motivation, remembering that a sense of demoralization and of failure may well influence it. It is also worth noting that almost all patients who seek help wish to change but at another level seek to maintain the *status quo*. This ambivalence to change lies at the heart of the concept of resistance and is one of the major challenges to the therapist. Motivation is a delicate flower; my own experience, along with many others, suggests that it will vary according to the patient's present state and the vicissitudes of therapy itself.

Another important aspect of assessment is the patient's sense of self-esteem and in particular how he appraises his own strengths. This self-evaluation provides an idea of the possible difficulties that may crop up in therapy. Further, useful information will be obtained by exploring the patient's relationships with previous helpers including the general practioner, other psychotherapists, and friends. Uncritical adulation or dismissal of them is often a useful indication of potential difficulties in help-seeking relationships including the present one.

Finally, it is important to obtain an idea of the patient's 'style of thinking'. The term 'psychological-mindedness' is used to describe the capacity to recognize and verbalize feelings, to utilize psychological concepts such as conflict, and to develop insight. This is commonly regarded as a valuable selection factor for psychodynamic psychotherapy. My experience however is that it is often related to issues of like/dislike between therapist and patient and their respective social and cultural backgrounds. One way of assessing the patient's psychological-mindedness is through the therapeutic relationship which can be gently explored even at an early stage in treatment. The exploration should also include an enquiry into the patient's initial understanding of psychotherapy, what he is hoping it will achieve, and the way he expects the therapist and patient to be involved. For example, some patients think of psychotherapy rather like surgery in which the patient plays a passive role and the therapist does the active 'work'. Others think of it as a highly emotionally charged experience in which they will be expected to give vent to powerful and frightening feelings.

(b) *Preparation*

During the first phase it is essential to prepare the patient for what will follow. In a well-known study, Hoehn-Saric, Frank, Imber, Nash, Stone and Battle (1964) demonstrated that patients who were prepared systematically for therapy by a 'role-induction interview' did significantly better than control patients. The researchers gave information about the therapeutic process and the behaviour required of both patient and therapist. Preparation involves a careful explanation of some of the feelings that may emerge in therapy. In this way I try to prepare patients for the development of transference which can be a confusing or even alarming experience. It is also necessary to define the limits of therapy. The focal nature of treatment should be emphasized and it should be understood that some problems may not be dealt with. (In fact, follow-up studies of brief psychotherapy have found a 'snowball' effect with improvement continuing after treatment has finished.)

(c) *The therapeutic contract*

There is no clear dividing line between establishing a therapeutic contract and preparation. The essence is an agreement between patient and therapist about the problems to be tackled and associated goals in terms which are understandable and acceptable to the patient. The therapist should have formed an operational hypothesis based on his understanding of the psychodynamic basis of the problem, its development, and current expression. An agreement is also needed regarding the number of sessions and their frequency, even if an exact time limit is not specified.

(2) The phase of activity

This phase constitutes most of the sessions but is difficult to describe in detail because what happens obviously depends on the specific techniques employed. In general it consists of further exploration and reworking of the problem and its ramifications, particularly involving the therapeutic relationship itself. Whatever technique is involved, it is common to see a certain pattern of responses in the patient. In effective treatment the early part of the phase is marked by a renewal of hope and an improvement in self-esteem. The patient works diligently at self-examination and at achieving the goals set. Important insights may be obtained accompanied by tentative experimentation with new, more adaptive behaviour. There is often a sense of hope, even excitment about the sessions. The inexperienced therapist may conclude that the problem has been resolved and that the number of sessions can be reduced. This is almost always a mistake.

Two events may occur. In the first, after a period of improvement the patient suddenly relapses. The original problem reasserts itself. This may lead the patient (and possibly the therapist too) to feel that whatever gains occurred were illusory and that the problem is essentially immutable. Some therapists interpret this event as evidence of a 'transference cure', that is, the initial improvement was due to the patient's desire to please the therapist or constituted a 'flight into health'—improvement occurring in order to avoid the feared consequences of 'forbidden' unconscious material being uncovered later. These processes may well be operative but it is still important not to lose sight of the actual change that has taken place. Sudden relapse, particularly after the rediscovery of hope, can deal a serious blow to the patient's self-esteem and must be handled with great care. Paradoxically, in my experience, relapse during therapy is frequently associated with a better long-term outcome. This may be because re-encountering previous difficulties allows the patient to rehearse new approaches, insights, and techniques of problem-solving that developed during the earlier part of therapy.

(3) The phase of termination

Termination may become an important issue at any time during therapy. I have frequently encountered patients with whom it became the central issue in the very first session. More usually, however, it develops later, about half-way through treatment and beyond. Whether the patient raises the issue or not, it is vital that the therapist deals with it. In my own practice, if the matter has not been broached directly by the patient by the time say two-thirds of the programme has been completed, then the therapist must do so.

Termination in brief psychotherapy is a key issue. It is normally associated with an experience of anxiety which the patient may communicate directly. Sometimes, however. the therapist may be alerted to this anxiety by a variety of developments such as a return of symptoms, an apparent intensification of the original problem, or by the complaint of new problems.

The patient may also introduce new themes, often related to early childhood experience, in an unconscious attempt to ward off the impending separation from his therapist. Conversely, the patient may demonstrate additional improvement, evidence of new plans, and increased energy. He may suggest termination earlier than planned. This often conceals considerable anxiety about loss and separation and should be resisted. The therapist may find that therapy becomes disrupted. The patient may miss a session for the most 'understandable' of reasons. There may be 'unavoidable' problems about the timing of sessions. During sessions, the patient may be more anxious and may seem to lose motivation. He may become depressed, critical, or angry. Occasionally he may 'idealize' the therapist and the treatment.

Termination presents considerable problems for the therapist as well as for the patient. The therapist, even when experienced, rediscovers his own separation anxieties and has to withstand and contain the difficulties of the patient. The therapist must face the possibility of failure of treatment with possible criticism, actual or implied, of himself. In dealing with this phase, it is important to remember that termination is a normal and necessary event. Its successful negotiation may be of enormous long-term benefit even though it can be a painful experience at the time. This is not to suggest that all patients will experience difficulties with termination to the same extent. During this phase it is important that the therapist not lose sight of the original focus of treatment; indeed, he may need to reaffirm it. At this time the main therapeutic task is to integrate the focus and the process of termination. Commonly, in fact, the original focus is related to termination issues. These include feelings of loss and the patient's reaction to them, anxiety about the future, and concern about the patient's sense of worth.

The therapist should be aware of two common pitfalls at this stage:

(i) the patient's progress has been so satisfactory that the therapist is seduced into expanding the original goal of therapy; and

(ii) the goal has only been partially achieved. In this event, the therapist needs to decide whether further sessions are likely to make a substantial difference or whether his own anxiety is influencing his perception of the situation.

Problems encountered in therapy

Some of the problems encountered in selection and in termination have already been mentioned. Overall the chief problem of brief therapy lies in its brevity. Implicit in treatment are the aims of rapid change and restriction of the patient's dependency on the therapist. By contrast, all long-term psychodynamic therapies foster and utilize the latter. Brief therapy is more challenging both to the patient, and to the therapist who is required to assess repeatedly a changing therapeutic environment. Inevitably, he has to ask whether some patients require longer forms of therapy in preference to brief therapy; I will return to this point in the section on effectiveness. In view of the brevity, the therapist must also make a judgement about the need for further contact in the future, either follow up or additional therapy.

Therapists differ in their attitude to follow up. Mann (1973) for example does not see his patients after the end of treatment on the grounds that to do so would create difficulty for them in dealing with the issue of separation. On the other hand, research-minded therapists find it virtually impossible not to review their patients' progress. Working within a public health service in which responsibility is assumed for the mental health of a community also makes some form of follow up desirable. My experience suggests that reasonably planned follow-up appointments (between two and six months) do not undermine the effects of therapy.

In some cases follow up has a positive value. Not all patients are able to separate successfully after a short but intense therapeutic experience; for them a reasonable plan is to offer a number of appointments (usually between three and four) with extended intervals between them, and arranged in advance. The therapist may also offer such a series of sessions with the understanding that the patient may, if he wishes, cancel them as the time approaches. This compromise looks well with a patient who is struggling with a fragile sense of independence.

A further problem concerns patients who relapse or seek help for a new problem. Failures or partial successes do not feature prominently in the writings of psychotherapists, but this issue is obviously of great relevance. Common experience indicates that a proportion of patients are bound to relapse. Obviously, if one employs rigid exclusion criteria, the proportion will be reduced. The decision about what to do then clearly involves an understanding of the reasons for the relapse, the circumstances in which it has occurred, and the gains made in the original therapy. Some patients paradoxically return for help after realizing their goals in therapy. One patient, for example, with problems of making intimate relationships completed a course of time-limited therapy. He improved sufficiently to seek out a mate whom he subsequently married. All was well until he became depressed following the birth of their first child. In this case he was offered a further course of brief therapy in which a new focus was identified, a difficulty in adapting to his new-found role as father. This case illustrates a further problem encountered in brief therapy. The therapist must decide whether, even if the goals of therapy have been achieved, further therapy is indicated. In forming a view on this matter, it is worth considering the following. Firstly, as mentioned earlier, patients often continue to improve, and sometimes in unpredictable ways, after the end of therapy. Secondly, it is difficult to form a prognosis at this point and one may be most surprised by the future course of events. Thirdly, a number of patients appear to gain strength from the knowledge that the therapist shows confidence in them to end treatment.

In the light of these considerations, a 'wait and see' policy is most apt. If a patient returns and has been helped by the first course of therapy it seems reasonable to offer another. This approach is probably more helpful (and realistic) than extending treatment indefintely.

Effectiveness

Is brief psychotherapy an effective method of treatment, and if so, why? A number of studies with reasonably acceptable methodology suggests that it is indeed of value. Malan (1963) studied 21 patients treated by skilled and experienced therapists. A positive outcome was reported in many cases and substantial improvement endured after the end of therapy. Sifneos (1972), Stewart (1972), and Frank (1974) confirm these results. Comparing brief with long-term therapy, the overwhelming weight of evidence suggests that they are equally effective. Shlien, Mosak, and Dreikurs (1962) for instance found that brief therapy was not only as effective as long-term treatment but more efficient with improvement taking place at an earlier point.

The lack of obvious advantages in terms of outcome of long-term over brief therapy has led Strupp (1978), a distinguished commentator and researcher in psychotherapy, to state: 'Short-term therapy should be the treatment of choice for practically all patients. On the basis of many reports, about two-thirds of patients will respond positively to such interventions; the remaining one-third can be continued if this seems indicated, referred elsewhere, or judged to be beyond currently available therapeutic efforts.'

Several studies have compared brief and behavioural therapies. The best known of these is by Sloane and his colleagues (1975). In a well-designed and well-executed investigation, they found remarkably few differences between the two forms of treatment. Although, behaviour therapy seemed to result in lower scores on target symptoms at a one-year follow up, by two years there was little difference between the groups.

Why is brief psychotherapy effective? Perhaps there are clues from the work of Jerome Frank, a doyen of psychotherapy research in the USA. In 1974 he published a review of 25 years of research done in his unit which indicated that, regardless of the type or duration of therapy, subjective symptoms improved in large part through the promotion of hope. It is likely that a time limit contributes to this promotion of hope and this could be associated with a therapist who—because he is more active than his counterpart in long-term therapy—is likely to convey a greater sense of enthusiasm. Malan (1963) has indeed argued that improvement is related in part to the level of therapist enthusiasm.

A further effect of brevity is that it may act as a pressure towards change. Evidence for this is suggested by Shlien *et al.*'s study (1962) which found that patients in time-limited therapy (20 sessions) reported greater improvement by the end of seven sessions than patients in a time-unlimited form of treatment. Another feature of brief therapy, namely its structured format may also be relevant. For instance, a number of studies have demonstrated conclusively that preparing patients for brief psychotherapy enhances outcome, perhaps by enabling them to appreciate what treatment will entail (McCaskill and McCaskill 1983).

Lastly, the relatively structured approach to therapy, the definition of a clear focus, and the expectation of change may well be helpful to the patient who presents in a state of chaos and with a sense of helplessness. Support for this view is provided by the work of Seligman (1975) who has demonstrated a relationship between helplessness, depression, and anxiety.

Training

A number of training and supervisory models in brief psychotherapy are used, but at the present time there is insufficient evidence to suggest that there is an overall advantage for any particular approach. There are probably advantages to supervision (of cases) in groups. Some purists would suggest that because of the particular therapeutic demands of brief psychotherapy, it is best taught after training in long-term work. My own supervisory experience would not support this view; on the contrary, brief therapy with its emphasis on problem identification and goal determination provides a useful learning structure for novice therapists. In fact, more problems may arise with experienced long-term therapists who sometimes have difficulty in limiting themselves to a focus and in responding to the rapid changes that are so much a feature of a brief programme.

Training in brief therapy also lends itself to recently developed supervisory techniques. Notable amongst those is the use of audio and, particularly, video feedback. These are powerful confrontation media which appear to stimulate rapid learning and self-discovery. They can be allied with role-play techniques, particularly useful for developing skill in interviewing, assessment of problems and defining a focus.

Conclusion

Brief psychotherapy is an efficient and cost-effective treatment which has made it possible to offer help to a greater number and to a wider range of patients than long-term psychotherapy. It is also a convenient meeting point for several contemporary models of treatment and should thus appeal to a therapist who values eclectism and empiricism. It is particularly suited to the therapist working within a public health service faced with a wide range of responsibilities and who, therefore, has only limited resources to offer individual patients.

Although there are several distinct features of brief therapy, it has much in common with long-term therapies and for this reason has proved useful as a research tool. Much of our understanding of therapeutic processes has been derived from studies of brief psychotherapy. It has also made it possible to measure and compare outcomes with other approaches. In such comparisons brief psychotherapy shows up very favourably and particularly so with longer term therapies. In a cost-conscious world, brief psychotherapy will undoubtedly become a first-line treatment for a large proportion of patients who require psychological help.

References

Alexander, F. (1963). The dynamics of psychotherapy in the light of learning theory. *Am. J. Psychiat.* **120**, 440–3.
—— and French, T. (1946). *Psychoanalytic therapy. Principles and application.* Ronald Press, New York.
Balint, M. and Balint, E. (1961). *Psychotherapeutic techniques in medicine.* Tavistock, London.
—— (1964). *The doctor, his patient and the illness.* Pitman, London.
—— Ornstein, P. and Balint E. (1972). *Focal psychotherapy.* Tavistock, London.
Barten, H. H. (1965). The 15-minute hour. Brief therapy in a military setting. *Am. J. Psychiat.* **122**, 565–7.
—— (1971). *Brief therapies.* Behavioural Publications, New York.
Beck, A. T. (1976). *Cognitive therapy and the emotional disorders.* International Universities Press, New York.
Bellak, L. and Small, L. (1965). *Emergency psychotherapy and brief psychotherapy.* Grune & Stratton, New York.
Bierenbaum, H., Nichols, M. P., and Schwartz, A. J. (1976). Effects of varying session length and frequency in brief emotive psychotherapy. *J. consult. clin. Psychol.* **94**, 790–8.
Butcher, J. N. and Koss, M. P. (1978). Research on brief and crisis oriented therapies. In *Handbook of psychotherapy and behaviour change: an empirical analysis*, 2nd edn (eds Garfield, S. L. and Bergin, A. E.). Wiley, New York.
Davanloo, H. (ed.) (1980). *Short term dynamic psychotherapy.* Aronson, New York.
Deutch, F. (1949). *Applied psychoanalysis. Selected lectures on psychotherapy.* Grune & Stratton, New York.
Ferenczi, S. (1920). The further development of an active therapy in psychoanalysis. In *Further contributions to the theory and technique of psychoanalysis.* Hogarth, London.
—— and Rank, O. (1925). The development of psychoanalysis. *J. nerv. ment. Dis* , Monograph No. 40.
Frank, J. D. (1974). Therapeutic components of psychotherapy. A 25-year progress report of research, *J. nerv. ment. Dis.* **159**, 325–42.
Freud, S. (1977). *Case histories. 'Dora' and 'Little Hans'.* Pelican Freud Library, Penguin, Harmondsworth.
—— and Breuer, J. (1974). *Studies on hysteria.* Pelican Freud Library, Penguin, Harmonsworth.

Gillman, R. D. (1965). Brief psychotherapy: a psychoanalytic view, *Am. J. Psychiat.* **122**, 601–11.

Hoehn-Saric, R., Frank, J. D. Imber, S. D., Nash, E. H., Stone, A. R., and Battle, C. C. (1964). Systematic preparation of patients for psychotherapy. 1. Effects on therapy behaviour and outcome, *J. psychiat. Res.* **2**, 267–81.

Lazare, A., Ewenthal, S., and Wasserman, L. (1975). The customer approach to patienthood. Attending to patient requests in a walk-in clinic, *Archs gen. Psychiat.* **32**, 553–8.

Lorr M., McNair, D. M., Michaux, W. W., and Raskin, A. (1962). Frequency of treatment and change in psychotherapy, *J. abnorm. soc. Psychol.* **64**, 281–92.

Luborsky, L., Singer, B., and Luborsky, (1975). Comparative studies of psychotherapy. Is it true that 'Everyone has won and all must have prizes'? *Arch. Gen. Psychiat.* **32**, 995–1008.

McCaskill, N. D. and McCaskill, A. (1983). Preparing patients for psychotherapy, *Br. J. clin. soc. Psychiat.* **2**, 80–4.

McGuire, M. T. (1965*a*). The process of short term insight psychotherapy. I. Process and variables, *J. nerv. ment. Dis.* **141** 83–94.

—— (1965*b*). The process of short term insight psychotherapy. II. Content, expectation and structure, *J. nerv. ment. Dis* **141**, 219–31.

Malan, D. H. (1963). *A study of brief psychotherapy.* Social Science Paperbacks, London.

—— (1976*a*). *Frontier of brief psychotherapy.* Plenum, New York.

—— (1976*b*). *Towards the validation of dynamic psychotherapy.* A replication. Plenum, New York.

Mann, J. (1973). *Time-limited psychotherapy.* Harvard University Press, Cambridge, Mass.

Marmor, J. (1979). Short-term dynamic psychotherapy, *Am. J. Psychiat.* **136**, 149–55.

Nichols, M. P. (1974). Outcome of brief cathartic psychotherapy, *J. consult. clin. Psychol.* **42**, 403–10.

Parloff, M. B., Waskow, I. E., and Wolfe, B. E., (1978). Research on therapist variables in relation to process and outcome. In *Handbook of psychotherapy and behaviour change: an empirical analysis* (eds Garfield, S. L. and Bergin, A. E.) Wiley, New York.

Rank, O. (1945). *Will therapy and truth and reality.* Knopf, New York.

Rogawski, A. S. (1982). Current status of brief psychotherapy, *Bull. Menning. Clin.* **46**, 331–5.

Rosen, B. (1978). Brief psychotherapy. In *Current Themes in Psychiatry* (eds Gaind, R. and Hudson, B.) Macmillan, London.

Rosen, B. (1979). A method of structured brief psychotherapy, Br. J. med. Psychol. **52**, 157–62.

Roth, R. M., Bierenbaum, H. L., and Garfield, S. L. (1969). Massed time limit therapy, *Psychother.: Theory Res. Pract.* **6**, 54–6.

Sandler, J., Dare, C., and Holder, A. (1970). Basic psychoanalytic concepts. III. Transference, *Br. J. Psychiat.* **116**, 667–72.

Schofield, W. (1964). *Psychotherapy: the purchase of friendship*. Prentice-Hall, Englewood Cliffs, N. J.

Seligman, M. E. P. (1975). *Hopelessness: on depression, development and death*. Freeman, San Francisco.

Shlien, J. M., Mosak, H. H., and Dreikurs, R. (1962). Effects of time limits. A comparison of two psychotherapies, *J. counsel. Psychol.* **9** 31–4.

Sifneos, D. E. (1967). Two different kinds of psychotherapy of brief duration, *Am. J. Psychiat.* **123**, 1069–74.

—— (1972). *Short-term psychotherapy and emotional crisis*. Harvard University Press, Cambridge, Mass.

Sloane, R. B., Staples, E. R., Cristol, A. H., Yorkston, N. J., and Whipple, K. (1975). *Psychotherapy versus behaviour therapy*. Harvard University Press, Cambridge, Mass.

Small, L. (1971). *The briefer psychotherapies*. Brunner/Mazel, New York.

Sterba, R. F. (1951). A case of brief psychotherapy of Sigmund Freud, *Psychoanal. Rev.* **38**, 75–80.

Stewart H. (1972). Six months, fixed-term, once weekly psychotherapy. A report on 20 cases with follow-ups, *Br. J. Psychiat.* **121**, 425–35.

Strupp, H. H. (1978). Psychotherapy research and practice: an overview. In *Handbook of Psychotherapy and behaviour change: an empirical analysis*. (eds Garfield, S. L. and Bergin). Wiley, New York.

—— (1980) Success and failure in time-limited psychotherapy: comparison I, *Archs gen. Psychiat.* **37**, 595–603.

Wing, J. K. and Wing, L. (1970). Psychotherapy and the national health service: an operational study, *Br. J. Psychiat.* **116**, 51–5.

Wolberg, L. R. (1965). *Short-term psychotherapy*. Grune and Stratton, New York.

Wolff, H. H. (1971). The therapeutic and developmental functions of psychotherapy, *Br. J. med. Psychol.* **44**, 117–30.

—— (1973). The place of psychotherapy in the district psychiatric health services. In *Policy for Action*. (eds Cawley, R. and McLachlan, G). Oxford University Press, London.

Recommended reading

Budman, S. H. (ed) (1981). *Forms of brief psychotherapy*. Guildford, New York. (A helpful compilation of major approaches to psychotherapy with chapters by important figures in the field. It also describes the application of brief psychotherapy to groups, marriages, and families.)

Davanloo, H. (ed) (1980). *Short-term dynamic psychotherapy*. Aronson, New York. (A handy volume which brings together contributions by the main figures in the field.)

Mann, J. (1973). *Time-limited psychotherapy*. Harvard University Press, Cambridge, Mass. (An excellent statement of brief psychotherapy theory with an illuminating case history in full).

McGuire, M. T. (1965*a*). The process of short term insight psychotherapy. I. Process and variables, *J. nerv. ment. Dis.* **141**, 83-94.

—— (1965*b*). The process of short term insight psychotherapy. II. Content, expectation and structure, *J. nerv. ment. Dis.* **141**, 219-31. (Good reviews of brief psychotherapy technique with particular reference to problem solving.)

Malan, D. H. (1963). *A study of brief psychotherapy*. Social Science Paperbacks, London.

—— (1976). *Frontier of brief psychotherapy*. Plenum, New York.

—— (1976). *Towards the validation of dynamic psychotherapy. A replication*. Plenum, New York. (These three books including the original classic 1963 study and the two developments published in 1976 represent the most comprehensive and empirically based versions of brief therapy.)

Sifneos, P. (1972). *Short-term psychotherapy and emotional crisis*. Harvard University Press, Cambridge, Mass. (Another very good description of aims and techniques by one of the major figures in therapy.)

4

Group psychotherapy

Sidney Bloch

The goals of long-term individual therapy discussed by Crown can also be tackled in a group format. In this chapter an eclectic model of long-term group therapy is described with special emphasis placed on therapeutic factors. Bloch covers selection, composition of the group, preparation of the patient, development of the group, and the mature-working group. An account of a segment of a session is presented to illustrate some of the points made earlier in the chapter. The final section deals with four special methods that can be incorporated into group therapy, and with training.

Human beings live, work, and play in a variety of social groups. Not surprisingly many of the emotional problems they come to experience stem from disturbed relationships within these groups. With the increasing recognition of the importance of the interpersonal factor in psychiatric theory and practice has come the rapid development in recent years of psychotherapies which have as their target problems between people rather than within the individual alone. The chapters in this volume on family, marital, and sex therapy reflect this new focus. In addition to these naturally-occurring groups the group format has also become widely used in a variety of other settings: the wards of psychiatric hospitals, the therapeutic community, the human-potential movement, the outpatient clinic, the private psychotherapist's office, and many more. Today group psychotherapy of many types is one of the most commonly used psychological treatments.

In this chapter we consider the long-term psychotherapy group composed of patients who seek symptom relief as well as some personality change. The model described is based on the interpersonal theory of psychiatry as represented by the work of Harry Stack

Sullivan (1953). A comprehensive account of this *interactional* model is to be found in Yalom (1975). A long-term group is the optimal training ground for the novice and much of what he learns there can be transfered to other group-therapy settings. Brief mention is made of other forms of group therapy at the end of the chapter, and reading recommended on them.

Background

The systematic use of groups in the practice of psychotherapy is a relatively recent development. But the healing qualities of groups have been recognized throughout history, particularly in religious practices; the shrine at Lourdes being an excellent example.

Joseph Pratt (1974), a Boston physician, is usually recognized as the father of group therapy. At the turn of the century he devised the idea of bringing together patients with tuberculosis to instruct them on medical aspects of their illness. Apart from the didactic ingredient he also promoted a group climate through which patients provided mutual support to one another. Several years later a number of American psychiatrists incorporated Pratt's ideas in their treatment of mentally ill patients. Lazell (1921) and Marsh (1974) for example both applied a similar model by forming highly structured groups of patients who were viewed as 'students' and tutored on mental ill health. This educational approach soon faded, to be replaced by the pioneering efforts of psychoanalysts to treat patients in groups. Freud (1955) himself never tried to practise group therapy but was obviously aware of the significance of group phenomena as seen in his *Group psychology and the analysis of the ego* published in 1921. Jung (1974) had a distinct bias against the use of groups in psychotherapy. He saw psychological illness as an individual experience and therefore requiring individual analysis. Adler by contrast believed in the need to consider social factors in treatment and used the group format in child guidance centres and also with alcoholics.

Several American psychoanalysts attempted to introduce their techniques into a group setting. Trigant Burrow (1974), a founder of the American Psychoanalytic Association, called his method group analysis. He felt that phenomena such as resistance and transference were as pertinent in group as in individual therapy. A group setting also had particular advantages: the patient could be helped to see that he was not unique and could derive support from fellow members; as a result his resistance would diminish and he would be prepared to take greater risks. Paul Schilder (1974) had an important influence in the 1930s, and like Burrows, applied psychoanalytic techniques to the group.

The Second World War was a spur to the growth of group therapy. It was an economical method to cope with the large patient population among the military. Some psychoanalysts who were drafted into the British army had a marked impact on clinical practice with their application of groups. The Northfield Military Hospital in particular was a major centre of innovation and there Bion (1961) and Foulkes (1946) tried out new approaches to group therapy. Bion's work later influenced therapists at the Tavistock Clinic while Foulkes was the force behind the founding of the London-based Institute of Group Analysis. Both the Tavistock and the Institute are important centres of training today.

Another key contribution, this time in the United States, was that of a group of social psychologists led by Kurt Lewin (1951). His field theory—that a person's dynamics are intimately associated with the nature of the social forces around him—was the basis for extensive research into group processes. In 1946 the State of Connecticut invited Lewin to help train community leaders in their efforts to reduce interracial tensions. In this way the T-(training) group or sensitivity-training group was born. Four years later the National Training Laboratory was formed as a centre for training in human relations and group dynamics. The idea was that participants from a variety of backgrounds such as teachers and managers in industry, could through a group workshop both experience and study group functioning and interpersonal dynamics, and as a result, act more effectively in their home setting.

A decade later the emphasis in NTL changed, particularly on the West coast, from group dynamics to personal dynamics, paralleling the swell of interest in humanistic psychology and the human-potential movement. The goals of T-groups now became greater self-awareness and personal growth. Before long the T-group had spawned the Encounter group movement, and with it, the development of the 'growth center'. Esalen in Northern California was the first such centre to be developed, in 1962, and became the prototype of an estimated 100 centres that sprang up throughout the United States during the 1960s and 1970s. Although the Encounter movement has declined in recent years, its influence on conventional group therapy is still detectable.

Selection

Indications and contra-indications

The indications for group therapy depend to a great extent on the kind of treatment offered. Obviously a self-help group like Alcoholics Anonymous (AA) will be suitable only for a specific range of people. For the type of group therapy considered in this chapter— long-term treatment whose aim is personality change—indications are less clear cut. We have so far only limited research evidence to assist us in selection, and yet the success of a group hinges critically on the patients who are chosen (Bond and Lieberman 1978). However, provisional guide-lines are available: first, there are a range of problems which can be effectively dealt with in a group setting; second, there are some desirable characteristics needed in the patient; and third, we can be reasonably confident about patients who are *unlikely* to benefit.

In addition to conventional diagnostic categories in selection, a useful approach is to consider the patient's presenting complaints and to add any pertinent dynamic problems that are free of undue inference or speculation. The following list includes the common problems which can be tackled effectively in a group:

Self-concept—lack of clear identity, low self-esteem, lack of purpose and direction.

Symptomatic—anxiety, depression, somatization, poor work or study performance, ineffective coping with stress.

Emotional—unawareness of feelings, inability to express feelings like love or anger, poor control over emotions, i.e. explosive and volatile, obsessive, i.e. controlled and rigid.

Interpersonal functioning—inability to achieve intimacy, discomfort in group situations, maladaptive interpersonal style, e.g. lack of trust, overly dependent, overly assertive, and histrionic; inability to maintain a heterosexual relationship.

There is some agreement about the *desirable characteristics* needed in the patient (see Bloch 1979 for a review of the topic of assessment for psychotherapy generally): (1) He is motivated: he wants to change, is prepared to work for it and his wish to enter the group is entirely voluntary, not the result of pressure by a relative, friend, or institution. In the process of selection, as we shall see later, setting up a series of hurdles can demonstrate a patient's level of motivation. (2) He has a particular expectational set: he has a high opinion of group therapy and does not view it as second rate or inferior to individual therapy; he believes that the group will suit his needs and prove beneficial. (3) He has sufficient psychological sophistication: although sometimes difficult to assess accurately, therapists are generally able to differentiate between prospective patients on this characteristic. As group therapy is mainly a verbal process, the patient must be able to use certain verbal and conceptual skills. He has to engage in a group process which calls for discerning self-exploration. Psychological sophistication is not however synonymous with intelligence, professional occupation or high socio-economic class. Indeed, patients from a wide range of backgrounds can be included in the same group to everyone's benefit.

Clinical experience has shown that certain patients are *unlikely to profit* from the interactional form of group treatment. It is important to note however that some of these patients may be helped by other group approaches, e.g. alcoholics in an AA group. Patients who do poorly include:

(1) *The severe depressive*—he is too withdrawn, pessimistic, and hopeless even to begin participation in a group. Efforts by the leaders and fellow members to reach him fail and result in their frustration and guilt. Unable to influence the patient, the group itself becomes dispirited. Commonly patients entering groups are mildly or moderately depressed, a reaction to their more basic problems. Such depression often lifts or at least improves after the first few months.

(2) *The acute schizophrenic*—a patient in the midst of an acute schizophrenic episode is a poor candidate. Out of contact with reality and disturbed in his thinking, he has little chance of engaging productively in the group's activities. By contrast a patient who has emerged from such an episode and is now relatively stable and with a good prognosis should be considered.

(3) *The paranoid personality*—he usually becomes alienated from the group because of his marked suspiciousness and distrustfulness.

(4) *The extreme schizoid*—the patient with marked schizoid perso-

nality traits—detachment, coldness, introversion, and hypersensitivity—cannot survive in a group which is striving to achieve open communication and intimacy. But the less severe schizoid is a good candidate since the group attempts to establish a cohesive, trusting environment in which he may feel less threatened and more prepared to risk involvement.

(4) *The drug dependent patient and the alcoholic*—this patient tends not to stick to a long-term commitment. Easily frustrated and intolerant of the anxieties intrinsic to group work, he seeks relief in the drug on which he is dependent, often with disastrous effects on the rest of the group. He tends to benefit more from a highly structured group composed entirely of patients with the same problem (Yalom, Bloch, Bond, Qualls, and Zimmerman 1978*a*).

(6) *The sociopath*—again there is a problem of long-term commitment. A low frustration threshold and a lack of a sense of responsibility to the group make both for a poor candidate and a potentially disruptive influence. The sociopath is likely to profit more from a homogeneous group, i.e. a group composed exclusively of sociopaths in which limits are set and a definite structure is provided.

(7) *The hypochondriacal type*—neurotics taken on for group therapy commonly present with somatic complaints as part of their clinical picture. The hypochondriacal patient who somatizes all his complaints and cannot be deflected from his bodily and health preoccupations does not gain from group therapy. He continues to focus on his somatic symptoms, boring and frustrating the rest of the group.

(8) *The narcissist*—completely insensitive to others, he alienates himself from the group. He claims attention for himself exclusively and cannot learn how to interact with other patients. This is in contrast to the patient who, aware of his need to get closer to others, makes efforts to communicate with, and be sensitive to fellow members.

The selection procedure

Since the fate of the group is linked so closely to the patients who constitute it, selection should be careful and methodical. Not uncommonly therapists are eager to get their group going and in their haste may generate a set of unnecessary and avoidable difficulties for themselves.

Each referred patient should be interviewed in depth on two occasions. A useful technique is to conduct an interview in which information is gathered and initial clinical impressions formed. The patient is also told about the goals and processes of the group. Before the second interview, a homework assignment is given which invoives the preparation by the patient of a list of problems he would like to tackle in treatment, the associated goals he would like to reach, and a brief biography. The effort given to these tasks serves the useful purpose of assessing motivation. The second session is used to review the written material after which the therapists can reach their decision. If the patient is selected, the therapists prepare him for the group as outlined later in the chapter. Occasionally, a third session is required.

Having accepted a patient the therapists should also prepare a problem-goal list; this will usually include the patient's list of problems as well as additional problems of a dynamic type, e.g. obsessive, passive-dependent, narcissistic, passive-aggressive, and the like. The latter will often be more inferential but should still be based on clinical evidence. They are likely to reflect interpersonal styles. Further, the therapists will find it useful to pose a question to themselves for each selected patient: what, if any, are the dangers of this patient entering the group? Will he monopolize, be silent, act as a provocateur, be moralistic? Is there any way in which these dangers can be averted or dealt with?

Composition

A patient may be suitable for treatment but not necessarily for the specific group being formed by the therapists. This raises the question of composition—should a group be balanced in a particular way or should it admit all patients assessed as likely to benefit from therapy? There is no clear answer to this issue but a few general principles are helpful in selecting a particular group. The topic is well reviewed by Melnick and Woods (1976).

Homogeneous groups, consisting of patients with similar problems, e.g. alcoholics, drug addicts, homosexuals, overweight people, are relatively easy to form as they have basically similar goals for all their members. *Heterogeneous* groups, typical of long-term therapy, require more thought regarding composition. The patients present with a variety of problems; they need a diverse 'social world' to learn about themselves and others and to try out new forms of behaviour. The group should be so constituted that opportunities for learning are optimal. For instance, a group consisting only of passive-dependent members will permit minimal scope for learning alternative ways of relating. Similarly, a unisex group will be limited in helping a patient with heterosexual difficulties.

A typical group has seven or eight members (a minimum of five seems necessary for any learning to occur while more than eight prevents the members obtaining sufficient group time for themselves) and is characterized by: an equal balance of men and women, an age range of about 20 to 50, mixed social, economic, and occupational backgrounds, and a wide assortment of clinical problems and personality types. The therapist avoids placing a patient in his group who will be obviously deviant, e.g. one woman only or a patient markedly older than the rest.

Some therapists have suggested specific guide-lines for composing a group. Bach (1954) sees a need for heterogeneity and posits the idea of each group containing a number of different roles, e.g. the leader, the timekeeper, the aggressive male. The problem with this approach is that the list of roles is infinite and bound to be arbitrary. Whitaker and Lieberman (1964) advocate the creation of a group in which patients have a wide range of problems and coping styles but are similar in their tolerance of anxiety. There are several other ways of approaching composition and the choice can be confusing. At present there is no good evidence that one method of composing a group is better than any other.

Groups may be *open or closed*. The closed group begins and ends with the same membership. For pragmatic reasons this arrangement is uncommon in long-term therapy as some patients graduate earlier than others while some patients drop out prematurely. The closed system may be appropriate for a relatively short-term group and in the case of T-groups. The open group permits members to terminate at different points and their substitution by new patients. The disadvantages are obvious: the cohesiveness of a group is threatened with each departure and arrival and the new patient must integrate into an already established structure. However these difficulties tend to be transient and the solid working group can afford both to lose members and absorb newcomers. There are advantages to the open model: the successful graduate encourages the rest of the group, both patients and therapists, while an addition is often invigorating and provides new opportunities for interpersonal learning.

Preparation

Both clinical and research evidence show the value of preparing the patient for his therapeutic experience. Most patients, new to group therapy, have anticipatory anxiety stemming from several sources: is it not inferior to individual therapy? Will I be compelled to make a confession? How can I be assured that group events will remain confidential? Will I not be affected adversely by the other patients? The concept of group therapy and the initial experience of it is often baffling and unsettling and indeed, most dropouts take place in the first three months.

This anxiety and confusion can be reduced considerably through patient preparation. It has been my practice to explore the patient's concerns and fantasies about the group and to hand out a simple document explaining how the group works, its purposes, and what is expected of him. In a second meeting the points in the document are discussed thoroughly and any misconceptions dealt with. Because of anxiety the patient may fail to assimilate the information given and there may be a need for the therapist to cover the ground repeatedly.

A controlled study examined the value of a preparatory session (Yalom, Houts, Newell, and Rand 1967). Of 60 patients selected for treatment, half were prepared in a 30 minute meeting and the other half seen for a similar period in which a clinical history was taken. The patients subsequently entered one of six groups led by therapists naïve to the nature of the experiment. A three month follow up showed that the three prepared groups interacted significantly more than the three control groups and had more faith in their therapy. Similar results have been found with the preparation of patients entering individual therapy (Hoehn-Saric, Frank, Imber, Nash, Stone, and Battle 1964; Sloane, Cristol, Pepernik, and Staples 1970).

Therapeutic factors

Despite the short history of group therapy, many theoretical schools, often contradictory and conflicting, have arisen with each claiming merit for its own approach (see Recommended Reading).

The novice is apt to become bewildered by the wide range. Fortunately there is a way of dealing with this problem: a methodical study of therapeutic factors. Given the present state of our knowledge we can reasonably conclude that certain components of group therapy are of value. Nevertheless much more research is still required in this field. For a full accout of the research that has been done see Bloch, Crouch, and Reibstein (1981) and Bloch and Crouch (1985). We should also note that therapeutic factors depend on the goals of the group and that different factors may be relevant at particular times in the life of the group.

In 1955 Corsini and Rosenberg (1955) reviewed the group therapy literature with the object of extracting statements referable to therapeutic factors. They then reduced the 300 statements they had found to nine categories. Later workers have refined these categories further (see, for example Yalom 1975 and Bloch, Reibstein, Crouch, Holroyd, and Themen 1979). What follows is a brief consideration of these factors. It should be borne in mind that the list is to some extent arbitrary and that the factors are not entirely discrete.

Group cohesiveness (acceptance)

This factor is a *sine qua non* for effective group therapy and a foundation for all other therapeutic factors. A group is cohesive when its members have a sense of belonging and of acceptance, when there is a feeling of solidarity and loyalty, and when patients are mutually supportive and the group is a source of caring. In such a setting a patient feels secure and safe: he can enjoy a continuing close contact with fellow patients and the therapists, he can take risks without disastrous repercussions, and he will not be judged, rejected, or demolished. Lest this sounds like a glorious haven we should note that cohesiveness also entails the possibility, indeed the likelihood, of negative feedback, anger, and conflict—but all expressed constructively and as a feature of caring. William Blake once said 'Opposition is true friendship'.

A substantial body of research confirms the importance and value of cohesiveness (Bloch and Crouch 1985). Groups of high cohesiveness have a better record of attendance, punctuality, member activity, and stability, and their patients are less likely to drop out prematurely. There is also evidence that patients who feel strongly identified and attached to their group benefit more from treatment (Yalom and Rand 1966).

Insight and learning from interpersonal action

Clinical observation has repeatedly shown that a patient acts in a group similarly to the way he does in his life generally. Thus the dependent, clinging woman, the explosive man, the self-centred person—all enter the group with those interpersonal behaviour patterns which have proved troublesome in their lives, and before long the same patterns are in evidence within the group.

Bill for instance had a record of broken relationships and had never achieved intimacy with men or women. Within the first few meetings, he alienated himself from his peers when he monopolized group time and incessantly grabbed attention. When deprived of the centre stage he became sulky and irritable.

Insight and learning from interpersonal action proceed along a number of steps. We can use Bill's case to illustrate the process albeit schematically for it is usually more complex than the following account conveys. But we should note that the two factors do not necessarily accompany each other. Thus, a patient may come to understand something important about himself including his behaviour, assumptions, motivations, fantasies, or unconscious thoughts. Similarly, a patient may profit from his attempt to relate constructively and adaptively within the group without preliminary acquisition of insight into the nature of the problems that relate to this attempt. First, Bill perceives that a problem exists—he relates poorly to the group members and he is not accepted by them. They begin to react to his style and inform him that they feel dominated and angered at his insensitivity. As a result they have avoided him as much as possible; engaging him will only lead to his further monopolizing of the group. Bill recognizes the group's reactions and feedback (this is not as simple as the scheme suggests since resistance in accepting feedback may render him defensive and disgruntled; weeks and sometimes months may pass before he is willing to see himself as the group sees him). He now begins to evaluate the awkward ties he has experienced with his fellow patients and comes to understand that his domineering style is responsible for the poor relationships.

At this point Bill has to commit himself to change, a major step. It is one thing to be aware of an undesirable characteristic, quite another to try to eradicate and replace it. The group plays a pivotal role here through encouragement and reinforcement of Bill's attempts to change. It applauds the risks he takes trying to relate on a new footing. On the discovery that he not only survives the experiment but is also rewarded, Bill begins to try out the new behaviour in settings beyond the group.

Need Bill also learn why he has related domineeringly in the past? Some therapists regard the learning described and the resultant understanding as sufficient for change. Others would pursue the issue further with the aim of unravelling the sources of his behaviour, usually located in early family relationships. Thus, in Bill's case unresolved sibling rivalry may emerge as the explanation and he could explore this aspect of his family history within the group. Arguments can be made for each approach. More important is the adherence to an orderly sequence of interpersonal learning as outlined above.

Universality

Before entering the group the patient commonly perceives himself as unique; he alone is burdened with problems. Universality, a potent mechanism, operates within the first few sessions. A 'we're all in the same boat' feeling soon replaces the 'I am unique' one. In one early group Peter's disclosure of shame about his masturbation was followed by all the male members sharing problems about their own sexuality. Peter soon experienced relief that he was not special in this regard. The therapist can reinforce this factor with comments like: 'It seems as if everyone shares this problem in one way or another'.

Hope

Inherent in all forms of psychotherapy is hope. The patient begins treatment with the expectation of being helped and gaining relief from his problems (Bloch, Bond, Qualls, Yalom, and Zimmerman 1976). The therapeutic factor operates during the course of therapy when he perceives that his fellow-patients show improvement and that the group can be of benefit; he, thus, gains optimism about the prospect of personal change.

Altruism

The group format facilitates, and this is one of its unique assets, mutual help, and support. The occasion frequently arises for a patient to be helpful to a fellow member. The patient has the sense of giving of himself: 'I can be useful to others and I am of value'. This is particularly useful in patients who suffer from a poor self-image.

Altruism also serves indirectly to enhance a patient's sensitivity to others and to reduce excessive self-preoccupation.

Guidance

We saw earlier that the pioneering forms of group therapy were heavily didactic—comparable to a classroom situation. Advice and information still play a role in contemporary groups but much less so. In the early meetings the therapist offers guidance to the patients who are frequently confused, hesitant, and distressed. The simple technique of clarification through information and explanation helps in lifting some of the bewilderment and so enables the patient to perceive more clearly the nature of his problems and of the treatment. Later guidance can be offered by both patients and therapists on a variety of issues. Patients commonly advise one another on how to solve problems: 'why don't you simply discuss it with your wife?' or 'you should change jobs' and the like. Although such activity reflects caring and involvement and should not therefore be undermined it usually has negligible effects. The group steadily comes to see that no easy short-cut solutions exist.

Vicarious learning

A member of a group has several potential models to learn from. Herein lies another advantage of psychotherapy using a group. Some of his achievement in therapy derives from vicarious learning. Every patient does not go through all the work needed in tackling a shared problem; he may benefit as much by noting how a peer deals with it. Further, each patient may have a quality which another wishes to emulate. For example, a passive member may attempt to model himself on a peer who is able to assert himself appropriately.

Identification is also an important mechanism in laying down desirable norms for the group. Noting that a patient takes risks, reveals personal things about himself, expresses his feelings, and survives, will encourage other patients to act similarly. The therapist of course also acts as a model but this may work both ways—a passive, reticent therapist, for example, is unlikely to generate an interactive, risk-taking group.

Catharsis and self-disclosure

This pair of factors embraces the ventilation of feelings like anger, anxiety, depression, guilt, and shame, and the disclosure of previously concealed information, often embarrassing and painful. Although the factors often occur together, they are distinguishable because of their specific therapeutic effects. Emotional arousal and release has always been considered beneficial in all forms of psychotherapy (see Chapter 1). The same is true for group therapy. But catharsis alone is of limited value unless the patient makes intellectual sense of the emotionally-laden experience. What happened when I cried so bitterly? What was the significance of the tears? What should I now do that I have a greater understanding of that experience?

Self-disclosure can encompass almost anything. The therapeutic value lies in the patient getting previously hidden material off his chest; he shares with the group something about his past, his current life, or his fantasies. Sharing is often the initial step of a process in which the patient and the group explore the relevations in depth and tackle them directly.

The group begins

Let us consider the beginning and early development of a typical group. Two co-therapists, one of each sex, have interviewed 10 referrals. Seven have been selected as suitable, four women and three men, most in their 20s and 30s, from a broad range of backgrounds, presenting various problems but all with some forms of difficulty in interpersonal relationships. They have been prepared for the experience as described earlier. The importance of confidentiality, regular attendance, and punctuality has been emphasized. The patients have also been told that although contact outside the group obviously cannot be forbidden, should it occur the members involved should inform the rest of the group about it. (Such contacts threaten cohesiveness and should always be dealt with by the group.)

The group will meet once weekly at the same time in a comfortable room for 90 minutes. It will continue for about 18 months (this varies of course) but since the group is an open one, some patients may graduate before others with new patients taking their place.

Developmental phases

A hard-working group in which the previously discussed therapeutic factors operate effectively does not arise automatically. The therapist has to guide the group through a developmental process lasting a few months. Group cohesiveness is his chief goal during this time and he lays down those norms required for the transition from an apprehensive group to one characterized by solidarity, trust, and confidence. Although each group is unique in its composition, and somewhat unpredictable in its development, clinical observation, and more systematic examination of T-groups suggest that groups pass through a number of stages before achieving maturity. The developmental pattern is not necessarily orderly: there may be to and fro movement between stages and not every patient may be in the same stage at the same time.

William Schutz's (1958) account of a group's development remains the most useful of those that have been given, many of which are in substantial agreement with one another. He mentions three basic stages:

1. *In-out*

This is the stage of dependency on the therapist. He has brought the group into existence and it is entirely reliant on him for survival. Members await guidance and instruction. They see the therapist as a knowledgeable, caring expert and want to be loved by him. Their dependency is heightened at this stage by the apparent uncertainty of the group: there is a lack of structure, no agenda, and each patient is more aware of his own personal goals than of the group's goal of evolving into a mature, cohesive social system. Because of his need to be in the group, not out, the patient is on his best behaviour. His participation is superficial, he tries to be helpful to others, for example, by giving advice and he is careful not to take any risks.

2. *Top-bottom*

This is the stage of conflict. Counter-dependence replaces dependence. The therapist inevitably disappoints the group since he is not the ideal parent and he cannot be relied upon. The trainee therapist may be seduced into this role and collude with the patients' infantile wishes by adopting a directive attitude, a most undesirable and anti-therapeutic norm. The experienced therapist however provides cues that he expects the group to assume responsibility for itself.

Counter-dependence shows itself as conflict and competitiveness. The patient has to find a way of securing his place in the group other than through dependency and he has competitors in his peers. This is a time of disappointment, frustration, and anger, the last directed at both therapists and fellow patients. Commonly the therapists will be criticized for 'not telling us what to do', for not leading the group. The occurrence of unpunctuality and absenteeism also reflects the patients' frustration and anger. Peer criticism manifests itself as sniping, aggressiveness, scapegoating, and impatience. Carl Rogers (1973) in discussing the comparable stage in the development of the typical encounter group suggests that the expression of negative feelings is the patient's best way to test the group's trustworthiness: 'can I really express myself, even negatively?' The expression of positive or tender feelings at this stage is much more difficult and dangerous because of possible rejection.

Top–bottom is a stressful stage, but has its positive side. Patients learn that they can express anger without disastrous results and this leads to greater confidence in taking risks. They need a leader who will help them to recognize the difficulties they are experiencing and the factors underlying them. George Bach (1954) has summarized the nature of this phase well in stating that: 'the group's low morale and disappointment in the early phases is the price it pays, the gate it has to pass, in order to develop the capacity to make use of the therapist as an expert, rather than as a fantasy figure or transference object only . . . It is a natural phenomenon, a step towards a healthy group therapy culture.'

3. *Near-far*

This is the stage of intimacy. With the evolution of a more realistic view of the therapist and with the disappointment in his lack of omnipotence worked through, the conflict between patients wanes. Successful passage through the tense top–bottom phase brings considerable relief. Patients 'pulling one another apart' is replaced by a 'pulling together'. Now the quest is for intimacy. Can I get closer (nearer) to others? In an effort to achieve this the group shows greater trust, sharing, and self-disclosure. Negative feelings may still be expressed but they are not of the same sort as in the previous phase. Now they occur within the context of a supportive framework built on understanding.

Problems arising during the development of the group
The passage between birth and transformation into a hardworking, mature group has taken months and called for skilled leadership.

Numerous threats to the group's welfare will have been encountered during that time, even by an experienced therapist. Dropping out is probably the most serious. Some loss of membership is inevitable no matter how rigorous the selection procedure. The morale of the group is undermined when a patient drops out and others may become ambivalent about continuing their own membership. Eight patients can stand the loss of one or two of their peers but greater attrition calls for replacements. Sometimes the addition of a pair of members simultaneously is less anxiety-provoking for the newcomers. A new patient should preferably not be introduced into a group which is in a state of crisis as there is a danger that he will be scapegoated. All newcomers require the same detailed preparation as the foundation members, and particular help in examining their expectations of entering an established group.

Absenteeism and lateness also undermine a group's successful growth. Regular, punctual attendance is essential and the therapists need to reinforce its importance repeatedly. A member unable to attend or knowing he will arrive late should automatically inform the therapist. Absenteeism or unpunctuality invariably represent important communications: resistance, anger, defiance, testing of the group (does it care about me?), and the like. For example, Jenny repeatedly arrived late to meetings and demanded a recapitulation of the events she had missed. The group soon showed resentment toward her but she seemed to thrive on their reaction insisting that it was not that important to come on time. Later it became clear that only by acting provocatively and inviting attack could Jenny relate to the group.

Drop-outs, missed meetings, and tardiness are matters of concern for the group and always need to be discussed when they occur.

The mature working group

Following the developmental sequence outlined above the group becomes a mature working unit. Hitherto a principal goal has been cohesiveness. With this achieved—although always threatened through regression, stagnation, conflict etc.—patients are engaged in a task of tackling their problems and those of their peers. Now the therapeutic factors should come into full operation, the most central being insight and learning from interpersonal action. The effectiveness of treatment is facilitated by a *here and now* focus, i.e. what actually transpires in the group, especially between patients, between patient and therapist, and between patient and group: change comes about as a consequence of patients recognizing and evaluating the ways they relate in the group. Apart from the present, there is also a future orientation. Before therapy the patient was asked to list the goals he wished to achieve as a result of treatment. These goals remain a prime focus throughout. Later, as the patient learns more about himself through his work in the group he is again encouraged to be future-minded: what options do I have? How will I choose between them? How will I translate my choice into action?

A *there and then* focus is discouraged. 'There' refers to events outside the group, most commonly crises. The danger exists that the group may become crisis-centred; thus the patient with the most pressing crisis uses the session and the group bounces from one patient's crisis to another. Crises are of course inevitable in a long-term group and they may be significant but emphasis on them jeopardizes the group's central purpose, that of individual change. When such events arise the therapist should bring them into a here and now context.

'Then' implies a historical enquiry, a search for antecedent causes of current behaviour. The danger here lies in an exclusive preoccupation with the sources of problems. Of course a patient's disclosure of his background—family and personal history—is helpful both in allowing the group to know him better and for his greater self-understanding. The danger for the group is in becoming bogged down in excessive archaeological exploration.

During the group's early life the therapist had the task of steering the patients into the here and now and explaining the importance of this focus. In the developed group the pattern is more automatic but the therapist is still periodically required to cut into there and then activity. There are infinite ways for therapist to maintain a here and now approach and the choice depends on the circumstances. Some illustrations follow:

— 'Who do you feel closest to/most intimidated by/most dominated by/etc. in the group?' (The patient has referred to intimacy, fear of others, or submissiveness.)
— 'Who in the group is most like you with respect to indecisiveness/passivity/aggressiveness etc.?' (Patient has indicated that he has one of these traits.)

— 'What has been the most difficult thing to share with the group today?'
(The patient has mentioned his difficulty in self-disclosure or
spontaneity.)
— 'Have you tried doing it in a group?' (Patient has referred to his inability
to commit himself to others, to express anger or tenderness etc.)

Furthermore, here and now comments may be focused on the
group as a whole:

— 'Each of you seems buried in private thoughts.' (Following an extended
silence.)
— 'How does each person see the meeting today?' (Half-way through
session.)
— 'How do you each feel about Peter's absence?' (Peter has not arrived
after 15 minutes and has not left any message.)

Another feature of the mature group is its ability to examine and
understand its own dynamics, i.e. the how and why of the group's
events, communications, interactions, and moods. Beyond the
session's events—what occurs overtly—the group operates at several
levels. Content is obviously necessary: things must happen, without
it the group would be dead—but this is not sufficient. The group
needs to examine carefully the events of all meetings in the context of
how and why.

Commenting on dynamics (the term interpretation is intentionally
avoided because it has so many different meanings) is mainly the
therapist's job. Patients are too immersed in the actual happenings
within the group to have a clear view of what lies behind them. This
task is undoubtedly the most demanding one for the therapist and
clinical experience helps. Even a whole chapter devoted to dynamics
would not suffice to cover the complexities. In any event, the
therapist will gain most of his knowledge via a clinical training to
which we turn later in this chapter.

Commonly made comments on group dynamics follow. They may
be addressed to the group as a whole, to a particular patient, or to a
sub-group of patients.

Group directed

— 'There is a tension in the room today as if we were all on tenterhooks
awaiting Jim's arrival.' (An absent member has not informed the group
that he would not attend.)

— 'The group is split, those supporting Claire and those critical of her.'
— 'It feels like we are unable to identify with Jack and his problem.' (Silence following Jack's disclosure about his homosexuality.)
— 'The group has moved completely away from Jane in the past few minutes as if her distress is too painful for us to bear.'

Patient directed

— 'You come across as extremely angry in talking about Paul's lateness.'
— 'You tell us things are O.K. but your body tells another story; you look shaky and tense.'
— 'I have the feeling that you're saying to the group "I want the group's attention on my terms or not at all!" '

Because the group roams over boundless territory there is obviously an infinite number of comments a therapist can make. Some general points apply to the process which serve as useful guidelines: the main object is to facilitate learning and not to display the therapist's observational skills, his wit, (there is, however, a place for humour in the group; see Bloch, Browning, and McGrath 1983 for an account of this interesting aspect of the therapentic process), or his cleverness. A patient can only benefit from the therapist's comments if he understands them and can integrate and make use of them. Thus the clearer the link between here and now content and the comment the better. Putting it another way, the more inferential and obscure the contribution the more difficult it is for the patient to follow and the less effective its impact on him. A direct statement is preferable to a question. The novice tends to act cautiously: 'Does the group think that perhaps . . .?' A better approach in the face of uncertainty is to preface a comment with: 'I have the feeling that . . .' or 'I could be off the mark but . . .'. 'Why' questions are particularly unhelpful and again should be replaced by a statement, e.g. 'James seems critical of you today' rather than 'why do you think James is critical of you today?'

Comments on non-verbal behaviour like seating arrangements, lateness, change in appearance, or silences are as important as those on verbal content.

The timing of any comment must be appropriate and generally is best related to here and now material while this is still fresh. Sometimes, however, it is better deferred, when the patient is too distressed or when the level of inference is still too high or when the therapist wishes to point out a repeated pattern of behaviour. For instance, it may be more effective to wait a couple of meetings before commenting: 'Chris has been relatively quiet for the last few meetings and is only involved when invited. His mind seems to be elsewhere.' There is also a risk of flooding the patient with comments to the extent that he becomes overloaded and confused.

Illustrative meeting

To illustrate aspects of the here and now, the therapist's comments on dynamics, and interpersonal learning, an account of a segment of an actual meeting is presented. Mary and David are the therapists and Rose, Doreen, Jack, Alan, and Carl the patients.

Carl has not arrived; there is obvious discomfort in the room as if every-body is waiting for him before beginning. Superficial chit-chat about an impending holiday weekend ensues (the group is obviously having difficulty settling into work). Jack comments in a matter of fact way that he expects a 'dramatic' weekend: his mother will be visiting him while his wife and kids are away on holiday. His mother, he says, is controlling and over-protective and treats him like an adolescent. Jack directs his comments to Mary alone who points this out but to little effect. She also suggests that he seems to be filling in time, presenting an important problem in a neutral, factual way; she wonders why the group has not responded at all to him (the group does indeed seem switched off while Jack has spoken).

Following the therapist's intervention, the group begins to discuss its non-responsiveness. Rose prefers not to respond as she does not want to take the role of mother and offer advice, something she has done frequently in the past with Jack and others. Alan, on the other hand, the rational scientist/engineer of the group, advises firmly: 'confront your mother and discuss the difficulties you have with her'. Doreen provides feedback to Jack by relating her own experience: her mentally ill sister has requested to visit for the weekend. Doreen has refused, indicating that she cannot cope with her at present. She has managed to work through her guilt and feels comfort-able at looking after her own needs first. David points out that Doreen seems to be telling Jack: 'assert yourself and let your mother know that you want your rights as a person recognized'.

All these comments have virtually no effect on Jack who sits passively, barely showing any emotional response. The group now begins to get bogged down as the members all try to advise him about what he might do about his mother's visit. However he remains non-receptive to whatever is said.

David now places a vacant chair opposite Jack and asks him to imagine his mother is sitting there. Talk to her directly, he suggests but Jack is unable to do so and shows much discomfort. He vacillates and then wriggles out of the task by describing in excessive detail the technical arrangements of how he and his mother contact one another by telephone. Jack's difficulty in expressing his feelings towards his mother is obvious to the whole group. Doreen exclaims that she is not surprised by Jack's behaviour today: she cannot empathize with him because of his matter-of-factness and she is frustrated as she wonders whether he is angry with his mother, guilty about his feelings towards her, or what? She also states that Jack's air of helplessness provokes her into acting, albeit reluctantly, maternally and over-protectively towards him. She wonders if Jack's relationship with his mother is not of a similar type. Both Rose and Mary express the same thoughts. A discussion follows on how much easier it is to relate to fellow patients when one can perceive how and what they are feeling. After a brief silence the group moves on to another topic.

The group's feedback, especially that from the women, clearly had some effect on Jack. Over the next several sessions he began to act more assertively and to assume more responsibility in tackling his problems. The group was able to relate to him on a more adult level and express their pleasure with the change.

Special methods

In the above account we note the exercise the therapist asked Jack to do. This is an example of a special method that can be incorporated into group therapy. There is no limit to the methods that can be adopted by the therapist, but a word of caution is called for before the eager student is seduced by them! They can be used to excess or inappropriately, and blind the therapist to his real tasks. Moreover we lack data on the efficacy of most methods. Space permits discussion of a few techniques only.

Videotape

Videotape can be used in several ways: the equipment is placed in the group room enabling immediate playback of segments selected by therapist or patient; segments chosen by the therapist as useful are viewed at the beginning of the next meeting; an extra session between regular meetings is held devoted to playback of the previous meeting's tape; part of a tape is shown to a particular patient in a specially arranged session.

All these possibilities have their advantages and drawbacks. Generally videotape has several advantages, e.g. patients obtain direct feedback on how they come across, a defensive patient who deflects everything that comes his way can be offered the chance to 'see for himself' what he is up to, or the group can be shown working productively or unproductively and the differences highlighted. Drawbacks include the obtrusiveness of the gear, its tendency to disrupt the group's rhythm, and the possibility of excessive control by the therapist. Whatever its ultimate place, videotape should be employed only as an aid and not as an exclusive therapeutic technique.

The marathon

Sessions traditionally last 90 minutes. The introduction of the marathon by Bach (1966) led to the practice of extending the meeting in a variety of ways. Bach's technique entails an extended session over about 36 hours during which patients sleep minimally or not at all. The resultant fatigue is intentional, the premise being that the patients' defences will evaporate and so allow an authentic encounter with the self and with other members. (The Greek runner who ran from Marathon to Athens promptly dropped dead after announcing the victory over the Persians; the Bach-style marathon is assumed not to lead to such grim consequences!) A less extreme application of the method is to extend the regular 90 minute meeting by an additional five hours or so or for the group to meet on a Saturday for about 6 to 8 hours. In my experience this mini-marathon has a markedly beneficial effect on the group, and especially contributes to its cohesiveness by increasing self-disclosure and the arousal of affect. There is evidence that an extended session should be held only after some months when the group has become reasonably established (Sklar, Yalom, Zimerberg, and Newell 1970).

Structured exercises

These stem from the traditions of psychodrama (Moreno 1971) and the T-group. Exercises can speed up the development of a group and permit the engineering of a specific pattern of behaviour, e.g. a patient with low self-regard is asked to brag about himself to each other group member in turn. There are however snags in the use of exercises: spontaneity may be undermined, the therapist may become overly directive, and they can be used ineptly, e.g. as a time-filler or when the group is stagnant. There is evidence from encounter group research that those groups with a high usage of structured exercises have a poorer outcome than low level groups (Lieberman, Yalom, and Miles 1973). Russell (1975) has prepared a catalogue of exercises which will give the trainee a clear idea of the vast range available to him.

The written summary

This is a simple technique which has been described fully elsewhere (Yalom, Brown, and Bloch 1975). In brief, the therapist prepares an account of each meeting which is typed up (one to one and a half pages) and mailed to the patients before the following one. The summary contains a narrative of the main events and associated editorial commentary. Although the technique has not been objectively tested, those therapists, including myself, who have prepared many such summaries are impressed by their usefulness. They serve several functions: they act as a bridge between sessions and so promote continuity, they offer a second chance to the therapist to press home a point he made in the meeting, the therapist can reinforce norms he wishes the group to adopt, and he can make a new observation that he did not think of during the meeting. Further, the summary fills gaps and allows an absent member to keep up with the group. The therapist also profits from the preparation of the summary: since it is a document for the group and his supervisor, he must make every effort to be accurate and clear.

Ending therapy

When a patient should end treatment is as much of a problem in group as it is in individual therapy. The whole concept of cure is raised. Should a patient stop treatment when he has achieved the goals he originally set with the therapists? Should he 'graduate' as does a student with a certain fund of knowledge and experience on the understanding that his education will continue thereafter.

The question of when to terminate tends to be different in a group than in individual treatment. The reason is obvious: the group can resort to a jury system to decide the question. Commonly, a patient raises the issue and asks the group for their reaction. If there is good consensus it is likely that termination is a reasonable step. The absence of consensus suggests that it is premature. The process should last some weeks enabling the graduate to share with the group what he has achieved, his hopes and expectations, and why he feels prepared to depart at this point. Both he and the group also need time to say farewell and to work through the impending separation.

Termination based on consensus is also a time for celebration. The patient has improved and feels confident enough to manage independently. The remaining members should be urged to note the change and to take encouragement from it; in this way they are reminded that they are also potential graduates and that the group is beneficial (the therapeutic factor of hope, discussed earlier in this chapter).

The above applies to an open group. In a closed group termination is usually predetermined and all members stop therapy at the same time. An open group may also agree to terminate as a group on a set date because of circumstantial factors such as the therapists moving on to other jobs. As the group must mourn the loss of any individual member who leaves so must it work through its own termination. Approaching the end of the group is akin to dying—a sad period for everyone and it needs to be discussed fully.

Training

Training in group therapy has several components: practical experience under supervision, observation of skilled therapists, participation in a T-group, and knowledge of the relevant literature on theory and technique.

A supervised practical experience is the most important of these. Commonly a pair of co-therapists meets with an experienced clinician at weekly intervals for an hour. Supervision should begin at the time of patient selection; as noted earlier the success of a group is heavily dependent on this and trainees require careful guidance. Supervisory sessions ideally take place as soon as possible after each group meeting while the events are still fresh in mind.

Two difficulties in supervision are the time taken for the trainees to report what occurred and their omission of material which may embarrass or threaten them (selective inattention obstructs supervision in all forms of psychotherapy). A simple method to reduce both problems is the use of the written summary described above (Bloch, Brown, Davis, and Dishotsky 1975). The summary sent to patients is also given to the supervisor, who can read the account before he meets the trainees. The therapists are less defensive as they have already exposed themselves in the summary and can thus provide a more honest account of their participation in the group. Supervision is best continued throughout the life of the group. After several months group supervision—two or three pairs of co-therapists meeting together—is a useful complement. Each therapist can compare with his peers his experience of leading a group.

Before and during their practical experience, the therapists need to acquire a knowledge of the salient aspects of theory and technique including pertinent research findings. Leading a group for the first time should not be like jumping into a pool and hoping to stay afloat. Without basic knowledge the likelihood of the therapist adopting poor techniques and lacking a coherent framework within which to work is high. Familiarity with various theoretical schools is necessary too. Inevitably a trainee tends to adopt the theoretical approach prevalent in the institution in which he is being trained. As we have only sparse knowledge on the relative effectiveness of different schools, a newcomer would probably find it advantageous to apply the model of group therapy described here which tends to the eclectic and non-doctrinaire. Later, attachment to a particular theoretical framework may arise and this can be incorporated by the therapist into his clinical work. The reader is referred to the Recommended Reading for suitable sources on various schools.

Trainees often become members of a T-group in order to learn at first-hand what it is like to participate in a group. They can acquire valuable information about group dynamics as well as recognize how they come across to their peers. The aim is two-fold: the T-group conveys to the therapist an idea of what patients experience in their group therapy and he uses the opportunity for self-exploration. It is debatable whether personal therapy is also a requisite for training and a thorough T-group experience is probably sufficient.

Viewing a skilled therapist either through a one-way mirror or on videotape has a place in training. The former is preferable as discussion with the therapist of his methods and of group events can immediately follow the session.

Other applications of the group process

Space does not permit a consideration of alternative theoretical models that have been applied to the out-patient group. These include, for example, the psychoanalytic, existential, gestalt, transactional analytic, and one derived from the observations of Bion. The reader is referred to the Recommended Reading list at the end of this chapter as well as to Bloch and Crouch (1985).

Although I have focused on the out-patient group in this chapter, it is obvious that the group process has been widely applied in the in- and day-patient settings, its particular mode of application depending mainly on whether the ward/day centre is run as a therapeutic community (Kennard 1983), or along more traditional psychiatric lines. In the latter case careful consideration has to be paid to the aims that can be realistically achieved. Thus, for example, in an acute admission ward where the average duration of a patient's stay is only a few weeks it would be fanciful to expect that his membership in a group could exert any radical change in personality. In this instance the need is for a specific model of treatment which enables appropriate goals to be realistically accomplished. One such model has been devised by Maxmen (1978) in which patients are members of a small, open group. Here they are taught to 'think clinically and respond effectively to the consequences of their illnesses'; that is, they learn to identify maladaptive patterns of behaviour and to avoid circumstances likely to precipitate recurrence of these patterns. Maxmen has set this objective on the premise that in short-term hospitalization the primary need is to modify as quickly as possible the patient's disturbed behaviour so that he can return to the community without delay. The therapeutic factors of instillation of hope, acceptance, universality, and altruism (see earlier in this chapter) are especially promoted.

In fact, these factors were found previously by Maxmen (1973) to be valued most highly by in-patients receiving short-term group therapy. Other factors such as self-understanding do not feature prominently in the model since it is assumed that patients are not in a position to profit from their use by virtue of their psychological state.

By contrast, the small group conducted in a therapeutic community—in which the average duration of a patient's stay (or daily attendance) is usually several months and there is a specific selection policy in the first instance—can operate more similarly to the long-term out-patient group discussed in this chapter, that is, have as a central goal not only symptomatic relief but also personality change. But even in these circumstances the approach will not necessarily be identical in the two settings. Clearly, detailed attention will have to be paid in the therapeutic community to the continuous and varied contact experienced by the community's members—either in other therapeutic group activities or in a host of informal ways.

A particular form of group meeting, the community group, may also be convened in either the traditional psychiatric ward or in the therapeutic community. Customarily, patients and staff assemble on one or more occasions during the week for periods ranging from 30 to 60 minutes. Despite their common application community meetings remain conceptually unsatisfactory (Kisch, Kroll, Gross, and Carey 1981). Both patients and staff are frequently unclear about their purpose. Moreover, as Whitely and Gordon (1979) note they are: 'usually seen by patients as a tense, threatening, punitive or confusing meeting and least orientated to treatment'. Should they be regarded as therapeutic forums, say the equivalent of the small group? Or should they be confined to administrative matters (for example to sort out the legendary washing-up rota!)? Or should they seek to identify and deal with tensions that exist between patients or between patients and staff that, if ignored, might jeopardize the overall therapeutic functioning of the community?

The most appropriate way to tackle this sort of question is to identify the objectives of the ward's therapeutic programme as a whole and then to ascertain the specific methods whereby the community group can contribute to that programme. A great deal of informed conceptual thinking is still needed before the community group can confidently gain its proper place. A most useful achievement in this context is Kreeger's (1975) edited volume, *The large group* (see the Recommended Reading list).

In the section on Special Methods, I mentioned the place for structured exercises and that these stem from the traditions of psychodrama. There is virtually no limit to the ways in which various forms of creative expression can be incorporated into group psychotherapeutic practice. Many of these are ideally suited to the group format—apart from psychodrama, dance, music, and art have been tried. The interested reader is referred to the volume by Kaplan and

Sadock (1983) for contributions on this aspect of group therapy.

A chapter on contemporary group therapy would not be complete without mention of the self-help or mutual-help group. Although the purist may demur from designating this application of the group process as a form of treatment, there is sufficient common ground shared by the self-help and conventional therapeutic group in terms of the people who are served by them, the theoretical assumptions underlying each of them, and the strategies applied. The self-help group however is distinctive in the sense that it is created and run by its members without professional leadership (although some organizations may consult professionals for advice). Alcoholics Anonymous is a good example: its membership is composed exclusively of alcoholics who meet regularly in groups in order to provide mutual help and support. Such a group activity is perfectly compatible with professionally-led group therapy. Indeed, there are good grounds to suggest that the two forms of group work are synergistic (Yalom, Bloch, Bond, Qualls, and Zimmerman 1978*b*).

In general, professional group therapists would do well to co-operate closely with the self-help movement since it is abundantly clear that the need for their expertise far exceeds the resources they can offer; the self-help group can contribute significantly to meet that need. Recent systematic research on self-help groups is one useful way of clarifying the role they can play in complementing the conventional group therapies (and psychotherapy in general) (see, for example Lieberman and Borman 1979).

Summary

Although group psychotherapy has a relatively short history it has become established as a common mode of psychiatric treatment. In this chapter we have examined the use of the long-term group, whose objective is personality change, as the optimal setting for training in group therapy methods. An eclectic model has been put forward; attachment to a particular school may follow after initial training and references to some of these schools are given at the end of the chapter.

We should remember that the group approach can be used in a wide variety of situations, from the community group in a psychiatric hospital to self-help groups like Alcoholics Anonymous. Space has permitted only brief mention of some of these 'group therapies'.

Again, the recommended reading list includes sources where the trainee may learn about these possible applications.

References

Bach, G. (1954). *Intensive group psychotherapy*. Ronald Press, New York.
—— (1966). The marathon group: intensive practice of intimate interaction, *Psychol. Rep.* **18**, 995–1002.
Bion, W. R. (1961). *Experiences in groups*. Tavistock, London.
Bloch, S. (1979). Assessment of patients for psychotherapy, *Br. J. Psychiat.* **135**, 193–208.
——, Bond, G., Qualls, B., Yalom, I., and Zimmerman, E. (1976).
—— Patients' expectations of therapeutic improvement and their outcomes, *Am. J. Psychiat.* **133**, 1457–60.
——, Brown, S., Davis, K., and Dishotsky, N. (1975). The use of a written summary in group psychotherapy supervision, *Am. J. Psychiat.* **132**, 1055–7.
——, Browning, S., and McGrath, G. (1983). Humour in group psychotherapy, *Br. J. med. Psychol.* **56**, 89–97.
—— and Crouch, E. (1985). *Therapeutic factors in group psychotherapy*. Oxford University Press, Oxford.
——, Crouch, E., and Reibstein, J. (1981). Therapeutic factors in group psychotherapy, *Archs gen. Psychiat.* **38**, 519–26.
——, Reibstein, J., Crouch, E., Holroyd, P., and Themen, J. (1979). A method for the study of therapeutic factors in group psychotherapy, *Br. J. Psychiat.* **134**, 257–63.
Bond, G. R. and Lieberman, M. A. (1978). Selection criteria for group therapy. In *Controversy in Psychiatry* (eds J. Brady and H. K. Brodie). Saunders, Philadelphia.
Burrow, T. (1974). In *Group psychotherapy and group function* (eds. M. Rosenbaum and M. Berger). Basic Books, New York.
Corsini, R. J. and Rosenberg, B. (1955). Mechanisms of group psychotherapy: processes and dynamics, *J. abnorm. soc. Psychol.* **51**, 406–11.
Foulkes, S. H. (1946). Group analysis in a military neurosis centre, *Lancet* **i**, 303–10.
Freud, S. (1955). *Group psychology and the analysis of the ego*. Hogarth Press, London.
Hoehn-Saric, R., Frank, J. D., Imber, S. D., Nash, E. H., Stone, A. R., and Battle, C. C. (1964). Systematic preparation of patients for psychotherapy: 1. Effects on therapy behaviour and outcome, *J. psychiat. Res.* **2**, 267–81.
Jung, C. (1974). In *Group psychotherapy and group function* (eds. M. Rosenbaum and M. Berger). Basic Books, New York.
Kennard, D. (1983). *An introduction to therapeutic communities*. Routledge and Kegan Paul, London.

110 *An introduction to the psychotherapies*

Kisch, J., Kroll, J., Gross, R., and Carey, K. (1981). In-patient community meetings: problems and purposes, *Br. J. med. Psychol.* **54**, 35-40.

Lazell, E. (1921). The group treatment of dementia praecox, *Psychoanal. Rev.* **8**, 168-79.

Lewin, K. (1951). *Field theory in social science*. Harper, New York.

Lieberman, M. A., Yalom, I. D., and Miles, M. B. (1973). *Encounter groups: first facts*. Basic Books, New York.

Marsh, L. C. (1974) In *Group psychotherapy and group function* (eds. M. Rosenbaum and M. Berger). Basic Books, New York.

Maxmen, J. (1973). Group therapy as viewed by hospitalized patients, *Archs gen. Psychiat.* **28**, 404-8.

—— (1978). An educative model for in-patient group therapy, *Int. J. Group Psychotherapy* **29**, 321-38.

Melnick, J. and Woods, M. (1976). Analysis of group composition research and theory for psychotherapeutic and group-oriented groups, *J. appl. beh. sci.* **12**, 493-522.

Moreno, J. L. (1971). In *Comprehensive group psychotherapy* (eds H. Kaplan and B. Sadock). Williams and Wilkins, Baltimore, Md.

Pratt, J. H. (1974). In *Group psychotherapy and group function* (eds M. Rosenbaum and M. Berger). Basic Books, New York.

Rogers, C. (1973). *On encounter groups*. Penguin, Harmondsworth.

Russell, J. (1975) In *The innovative psychological therapies: critical and creative contributions* (eds R. Suinn and R. Weigel). Harper and Row, New York.

Schilder, P. (1974). In *Group psychotherapy and group function* (eds M. Rosenbaum and M. Berger). Basic Books, New York.

Schutz, W. C. (1958). *Firo: a three-dimensional theory of interpersonal behaviour*. Rinehart, New York.

Sklar, A. D., Yalom, I. D., Zimerberg, S. M., and Newell, G. L. (1970). Time extended group therapy: a controlled study, *Comp. Group Stud.* 373-86.

Sloane, R. B., Cristol, A. H., Pepernik, M. C., and Staples, F. R. (1970). Role preparation and expectation of improvement in psychotherapy, *J. nerv. ment. Dis.* **150**, 18-26.

Sullivan, H. S. (1953). *The interpersonal theory of psychiatry*. Norton, New York.

Whitaker, D. and Lieberman, M. (1964). *Psychotherapy through the group process*. Atherton, New York.

Whiteley, J. S. and Gordon, J. (1979). *Group approaches in psychiatry*. Routledge and Kegan Paul, London.

Yalom. I. D. (1975). *The theory and practice of group psychotherapy*. Basic Books, New York.

——, Bloch, S., Bond, G., Qualls, B., and Zimmerman, E. (1978*a*). Alcoholics in interactional group therapy: an outcome study, *Archs gen. Psychiat.* **35**, 419-25.

——, Bond, G., Bloch, S., Zimmerman, E., and Friedman, L. (1978*b*). The effect of a weekend group experience on the course of individual psychotherapy, *Archs gen. Psychiat.* **34**, 399–415.

——, Brown, S., and Bloch, S. (1975) The written summary as a group psychotherapy technique. *Archs gen. Psychiat.* **32**, 605–13.

——, Houts, P. S., Newell, G., and Rand, K. H. (1967). Preparation of patients for group therapy. A controlled study, *Archs gen. Psychiat.* **17**, 416–27.

—— and Rand, K. H. (1966). Compatibility and cohesiveness in therapy groups, *Archs gen. Psychiat.* **13**, 267–76.

Recommended reading

General

Kaplan, H. I. and Sadock, B. J. (eds) (1983). *Comprehensive group psychotherapy*. Williams and Wilkins. Baltimore, Md. (Contains chapters dealing with therapy of special groups such as married couples, alcoholics, adolescents, and the elderly as well as chapters on different schools including psychodrama, psychoanalysis, and behaviour therapy.

Rosenbaum, M. and Berger, M. M. (eds) (1975). *Group psychotherapy and group function*. Basic Books, New York. (A general text containing over 60 chapters on all aspects of group therapy including several interesting contributions on its history.)

Whiteley, J. S. and Gordon, J. (1979). *Group approaches in psychiatry*. Rontledge and Kegan Paul, London. (Contains chapters on theory of group dynamics and different applications of the group therapeutic approach.)

Yalom, I. D. (1975) *The theory and practice of group psychotherapy*. Basic Books, New York. (An excellent account of the theory and practice of group therapy, with an important section on therapeutic factors.)

Schools of group therapy

Bion, W. R. (1961). *Experiences in groups*. Tavistock, London. (The 'Tavistock' approach in which the theoretical ideas of Melanie Klein are central).

Berne, E. (1966). *Principles of group treatment*. Oxford University Press, New York. (Transactional analysis as applied to groups).

Durkin, H. E. (1964). *The group in depth*. International Universities Press, New York. (Contains a good account of the existential approach to group therapy.)

Foulkes, S. H. and Anthony, E. J. (1973). *Group psychotherapy*. Penguin, Harmondsworth. (The approach of the London Institute of Group Analysis and influenced by psychoanalytic concepts and techniques.)

See also: Foulkes, S. H. (1975). *Group analytic psychotherapy: methods and principles.* Gordon and Breach, London. (Similar in content to *Group psychotherapy*.)

Yalom, I. D. (1975). *The theory and practice of group psychotherapy.* Basic Books, New York. (Covers the interactional model.)

Other uses of the group approach

Jones, M. (1968). *Social psychiatry in practice: the idea of the therapeutic community.* Penguin, Harmondsworth.

Kaplan, H. I. and Sadock, B. J. (1983). *Comprehensive group psychotherapy.* Williams and Wilkins, Baltimore, Md. (Broad-ranging volume which contains chapters on, for example art therapy in groups, psychodrama, dance therapy, group therapy with rape victims and battered women.)

Kennard, D. (1983). *An introduction to therapeutic communities.* Routledge and Kegan Paul, London.

Kreeger, L. (ed) (1975) *The large group: dynamics and therapy.* Constable, London.

Lieberman, M. A. and Borman, L. (1979). *Self-help groups for coping with crisis.* Jossey-Bass, London.

5

Crisis intervention
John Bancroft

Chapters 2 and 4 dealt with psychotherapies which are long-term and have as a main aim, personality change. In this chapter Bancroft focuses on a completely different form of therapy, which is short-term and designed to help persons who, overwhelmed by some stress, are in a state of crisis. In the first section he covers basic concepts relevant to crisis intervention; then follows a description of two main forms of therapeutic help—intensive care and crisis counselling, each with its own series of strategems. The emphasis throughout is on the practical steps to be taken by the therapist.

Crisis intervention as a concept has almost as many meanings as there are people writing about it. In spite of this it has served a useful purpose in drawing attention to an aspect of health care where there is overlap between the roles of psychiatrist, casualty doctor, general practitioner, social worker, probation officer, and lay counsellor. While each of these helpers can bring particular types of professional skill to the problem, there are non-specialist skills that most people in crisis need. It is this non-specialist role that will be considered in this chapter.

Caplan, one of the most influential workers in this field, defines a crisis as occurring 'when a person faces an obstacle to important life-goals that is, for a time, insurmountable through the utilization of customary methods of problem solving. A period of disorganization ensues, a period of upset, during which many abortive attempts at solution are made' (Caplan 1961). Whilst many other definitions have been suggested, this one suits our purpose and captures well the type of situation that calls for outside help.

Crisis intervention has as a minimum objective 'the psychological resolution of the immediate crisis and restoration to at least the level of functioning that existed prior to the crisis' (Aguilera and Messick 1974). It therefore involves immediate but short-term help.

Most of the theorizing and practical developments in crisis intervention have taken place within the United States and it is helpful to consider the social and political context in which this has happened. The pattern of health care in the United States, depending for the most part on expensive private practice or health insurance schemes, has inevitably led to a social and political reaction. Free 'walk-in' clinics emerged in many parts of the country, staffed by liberal minded, socially conscious professionals. This was followed by massive federal support for the development of community mental health centres staffed by professionals who were often keen to reject the health establishment on ideological grounds. As a consequence, this parallel pattern of health care developed, determined as much by the need to discard traditional medical values and methods as to any clearly formulated set of principles or objectives. It is not surprising that conceptual confusion has resulted and only recently has some order started to emerge. A need for an alternative to clearly medical care is difficult to refute, but because of our existing social structure, such care is often sought in medical settings as well as in the more clearly non-medical agencies such as social work departments or 'Samaritan' organizations. How to deal with individuals in crisis is therefore an important issue for medical as well as other helping professionals. For the doctor, there is the additional need to clarify the relationship between this type of help and medical treatment. And for the non-medical counsellor, there is the problem of knowing when to involve medical personnel.

The purpose of this chapter is to provide a practical framework for carrying out crisis intervention and to put it in context with medical treatment. The literature on the subject is voluminous but unfortunately it rarely provides the guidance that we can actually apply to practice. In any case it covers an exceedingly diverse range of approaches (for useful reviews, see Brandon 1970; Raphael 1971; Bartolucci and Drayer 1973; Aguilera and Messick 1974). Some common themes do emerge however. Raphael (1971) for example listed the following recurring factors: (a) helping the individual to gain cognitive mastery of the situation, (b) dealing with excessive use of the defence of denial, and (c) mobilizing and dealing with appropriate affect. Writers with psychoanalytic backgrounds have not provided clear practical direction for the would-be therapist, while behaviour therapists have not paid much attention to this area.

Cognitive therapy, which has its origins in behaviour therapy and other forms of directive psychotherapy, is becoming increasingly relevant. Problem solving, which features large in crisis intervention, is capturing the attention of behaviour therapists (Goldfried and Goldfried 1975) and cognitive therapists (Beck, Rush, Shaw, and Emery 1979). This chapter is written in an eclectic spirit but with a behavioural bias. Whilst it cannot deal with all clinical contingencies, it does aim to provide a practical framework that can be built upon and adapted. The approach to be described has developed in a particular clinical setting—the general hospital psychiatric service dealing predominantly with the patient who has attempted suicide; it has evolved however within a multidisciplinary team and has wider relevance than to this setting alone. Much of it involves the application of 'common sense' for which I make no apology. The field of crisis intervention has been hampered for too long by therapists needing to maintain special expertise for the sake of their professional identity. Before describing the approach, it is necessary to consider some basic concepts. Crisis can be usefully seen as a failure or insufficiency of coping. What do we mean by coping and what happens when it fails? What problems commonly over-extend coping resources? When is it appropriate to consider someone in crisis as 'ill' or in need of medical treatment? How far should we go in taking over responsibility for other people's problems?

Basic concepts

Coping and failure to cope

'Coping behaviour' is how we respond to a problem or threatening situation. This concept has been usefully developed by Lazarus (1966) and the comments that follow are mainly derived from his analysis. There are four principal types of coping behaviour:

(a) *Problem solving behaviour*

This is considered to be the basis of mature and adaptive coping and will be discussed in greater detail below. The other types of coping behaviour are less adaptive.

(b) *Regression*

The individual resorts to behaviour which he learned at an earlier stage of development and which in the past has enabled him to cope at least temporarily by transferring responsibility to others. Resort to alcohol or drug overdosage may be used in this way.

(c) *Denial*

The perception of reality is so distorted that the problem is no longer seen to exist. This may be effective if the problem resolves spontaneously but usually it only postpones and aggravates the problem.

(d) *Inertia*

A state of inaction based on the individual's conclusion that there is nothing effective or useful that he can do; while there are occasions when inertia is appropriate, it usually reflects the affect of hopelessness characteristic of depressive states.

There is a further aspect which fits less comfortably into Lazarus's model but which is relevant to crisis intervention, *the expression of affect*. The perception of a problem or threat usually generates affect. In some instances, for example when anger leads to aggressive behaviour, the expression of affect provides a direct and possibly adaptive way of coping with a problem or threat (e.g. the enemy retreats). The affective reaction is presumably a necessary and motivating force for coping behaviour, whether it be anger, fear or any other emotion. But frequently this affect becomes a problem in its own right, and has to be dealt with. Unless we can handle appropriately our feelings of anger, anxiety, grief, and the like, our ability to cope constructively becomes impaired. This can perhaps be regarded as 'second order' coping, i.e. coping with emotional reactions to problems or threats, and underlies the method for helping people to deal with grief that was first formulated by Lindemann (1944).

Normally we use combinations of these coping behaviours, but in certain situations they fail and the problems remain unresolved. Various factors can contribute to this: the problems may be too great, too numerous or too unfamiliar; the individual may use inappropriate or maladaptive methods of coping or generally be inept in this respect; his coping may be impaired by physical or mental ill-health; he may lack support from friends or family that would have otherwise enabled him to cope.

When coping is attempted and fails we can recognize what Caplan (1961) describes as the *four phases of crisis*: phase 1—arousal and attempts at problem-solving behaviour increase; phase 2—due to increased arousal or 'tension', some impairment of function occurs with resulting disorganization and distress. The arousal reaches a level which hinders rather than promotes coping behaviour: the person becomes too anxious or too angry, he is too aroused to sleep properly and so becomes fatigued, and so on; phase 3—emergency resources both internal and external are mobilized and novel methods of coping are tried; and phase 4—continuing failure to resolve the problems leads to a state of progressive deterioration, exhaustion, and 'decompensation'. Help can be offered in two very different ways during this sequence: at an early stage when the individual may himself mobilize help as part of his adaptive coping, and later in the decompensation phase when intervention by others becomes a matter of necessity to prevent further deterioration. The relationship with the helping agent is obviously different at these two stages, and this fundamental point is of central relevance to treatment. But before developing that theme, let us briefly consider the types of problems that commonly lead to the need for intervention.

The common problems tackled in crisis intervention

Jacobsen and his colleagues (Jacobsen, Strickler, and Morley 1968) have distinguished between 'generic' and 'individual' approaches to crisis intervention. The 'generic' approach focuses on the characteristic course of various kinds of crisis, whereas the 'individual' approach is more concerned with coping resources of a specific individual and the special meaning that a crisis holds for him. Whilst it seems unnecessary and undesirable to regard these approaches as distinct, it is nevertheless useful to identify the different types of problems commonly dealt with in treatment. The following categories are suggested.

(1) *Loss problems*

These may involve loss of a loved one by death or separation, loss of self-esteem, loss of body function (e.g. following amputation, when part of the body is also lost), and loss of resources, such as financial. The loss leads to a pattern of reaction characteristically seen in bereavement and which was so well described by Lindemann (1944), and since, by others (Parkes 1975). Initially the person is in a variable degree of shock; then follows denial of reality which gives way to the feeling of grief. When the grief is 'worked through', the person gradually attempts to restructure his life and fill the gap that has been created. Intervention, both at everyday and clinical levels, is concerned with helping the individual to experience, express, and hence 'work through' the affect of grief.

(2) *Change probelms*

Here the source of the problem is the arrival of a new condition that has to be contended with rather than the loss of a previous one. The principal types of change are: in role, such as work, marital status, and parenthood; and in identity, that accompanies that change of role (the transitional or maturational crises described by Erikson (1969) fall into this category). With these changes there is usually a positive aspect—the element of challenge in expectation of new and potentially rewarding developments. But they can nevertheless be very threatening. A particular form of role change which overlaps with the effects of loss, is entry into a 'sick' role in facing the threat or reality of the loss of health and function.

(3) *Interpersonal problems*

An enormous amount of stress can stem from troubled interpersonal relationships, especially between spouses or other close family members. This is almost certainly the commonest reason for non-fatal suicide attempts (Bancroft, Skrimshire, Casson, Harvard-Watts, and Reynolds 1977). The existence of a close but unsupportive relationship, as in an unhappy marriage, also increases the susceptibility of the individual to other stressful life events (Brown, Bhrolchain, and Harris 1975) and can therefore be a major factor influencing the outcome of loss and change problems. In these cases the helping agent needs to facilitate communication within the disturbed relationship with the goal of achieving satisfactory resolution of hostility.

(4) *Conflict problems*

The individual is faced with a difficult or seemingly impossible choice between two or more alternatives. Here the principles of problem solving, to be described later, are most directly relevant.

Whatever the type of problem, the therapist is faced with the distinction already mentioned, between offering help to someone who is mobilizing extra resources, that is, he is in phase 1 or 2 of crisis, or taking over responsibility for an individual temporarily because he is in a decompensated state, that is, he is in phase 3 or 4. The nature of the relationship between therapist and the person in crisis is in many ways the most fundamental aspect of treatment and yet usually the least considered. The next section deals with it.

The patient–therapist relationship

From time to time members of the helping profession debate the concept of illness. Usually the issue is the definition of illness for purposes such as classification or epidemiological and aetiological research, and for communication between professionals (Lewis 1953; Kendell 1975). It is much less often that they consider how, by describing a patient as ill, they affect not only their professional role and their relationship with the patient, but also the patient's concept of himself. Paradoxically, it has been left to people outside the medical and related professions to make comment. The concept of the 'sick role' was clearly formulated by Parsons (1951) who pointed out that in our society the 'ill' person is not held responsible for his incapacity and, even more important, is exempted from responsibility for his normal obligations on the understanding that he seeks appropriate medical help and places himself in a position of dependency on others. These ideas have stimulated useful research into the sick role (Mechanic 1977) and recently have been provocatively discussed by Illich (1975) who criticizes the medical profession for fostering dependency in the patient and for weakening his sense of sufficiency. More germane to crisis intervention is whether this dependency is a good or a bad thing. This issue will also be mentioned in the chapter on sex therapy (see Chapter 8), where it will be explained that for treatment to be helpful, the patient or couple need to accept responsibility for what has to be done and not regard themselves as sick.

Clearly there are many instances when it is entirely appropriate for a state of dependency and transfer of responsibility to be encouraged. The person who breaks a leg needs the sick role to allow healing to occur, as well as the expertise of the medical and nursing profession. After a time responsibility is gradually handed back to the patient who in the phase of recovery is no longer sick but expected to take on the onus for his active rehabilitation. This transfer of responsibility from the patient and back again is seldom made explicit, and in most cases is not even recognized by the patient or doctor. Consequently, it not infrequently 'goes wrong'; the sick role is accepted for too long by both doctor and patient, or the latter remains in the role when the doctor acts as if he had left it.

But when we return our attention to crisis intervention, we are faced with a further difficulty. Although, as already stated, the transfer of responsibility from the person is necessary and appropriate in some instances, do we, as a result, want to regard him as ill? If so, we imply that his state results from a morbid or pathological process, but in fact he may have been overcome by a 'natural disaster' (for example, an old age pensioner whose house has burnt down) or simply lack adequate coping resources and hence become overwhelmed by circumstances that would be met by most people. Do we in such cases want to encourage the sick role? On occasion the answer is a clear yes because the illness label serves to protect the individual's self-esteem or allows him to hand over responsibility when he would otherwise insist on retaining it. In other cases, the answer is no because it may discourage the individual from seeking out and learning new coping skills that would place him in better stead to handle similar stresses in the future.

This means that two decisions have to be taken at an early stage when confronted with someone in crisis. Is this person in or about to be in a decompensated state requiring urgent intervention and the take over of responsibility? And is it appropriate or therapeutically helpful to label him ill? These important decisions are based on clinical judgement. This is made all the more difficult by the fact that some individuals present themselves in a state of decompensation as a regressive method of coping; they have learnt to do this in the past and found that it worked, at least in the short-term. The therapist may have difficulty recognizing that this is happening unless he has knowledge of the individual's past history or evidence that he has reacted similarly on previous occasions. Obviously in such a case, it is in everyone's interest for the person to be encouraged to resume responsibility for his state with or without help.

Having considered these basic relationship issues, we can now turn to methods of intervention.

Methods of intervention

Initial assessment

Obviously the initial contact with someone presenting in crisis is used for assessment. This aims to establish as clearly as possible what recent events have affected the person and in particular those that have persuaded him to seek help. Much useful information can be obtained from a detailed inquiry of what has been happening in the previous 48 hours or so. This usually points to the chief current problems, though it may be some time before their precise nature or full extent become recognized. It is important to clarify what demands the person is facing at this time and what practical steps he is required to take. In the course of obtaining this account, attention should be paid to the person's mental state: the presence of suicidal ideas, the degree of anxiety, agitation, or distress, and in particular whether his condition will enable him to carry out any practical steps that are immediately called for. The therapist also assesses what sort of support the person can count on from family or friends and whether his home situation is helpful or not. The ultimate aim is to establish not only more about the background and development of · the current problems, but also to determine how the person has fared with problems in the past and the quality of his coping resources. This may have to wait until his mental state permits it or until another informant can be interviewed.

By the end of the initial assessment, the first clinical decision has to be taken: does responsibility for his affairs need to be temporarily taken over? If the answer is positive, a form of intervention appropriately called 'intensive care' is organized; care because the patient has to be temporarily looked after and intensive because he will require concentrated contact during that time. If such taking over is not appropriate, another form of help called 'crisis counselling' may be offered. In many cases the distinction between the two types of help is clear cut, in others it is less so as responsibility may be transferred only partially. What is important is that the therapist is clearly aware of what is happening in this respect. In any event, as for the man with the broken limb, intensive care is only a temporary phase following which responsibility is gradually handed back; the therapist–patient relationship changes from doctor–sick patient to adult–adult, with the therapist offering the patient the benefit of his experience and counsel.

Intensive care

The objective in intensive care is to reverse the patient's decompensation and restore him to his normal coping state as quickly as possible, so that he can resume responsibility. The following steps are taken.

(1) *Explicit transfer of responsibility*

The patient is told that for the time-being his normal responsibilities and obligations will be taken over by others and that he should allow himself to be taken care of. Whether this is justified to him on grounds of illness is decided at this time, after carefully considering the implications of doing so.

(2) *Organization of the takeover of immediate tasks*

The therapist must then ensure that the patient's current obligations are taken over by others. Children may need to be sent to relatives or taken into care, and employers contacted. Houses have to be locked, pets fed, and so on. The help of family and friends is mobilized as far as possible though social services and community agencies may need to be involved.

(3) *Removal of the patient from a stressful environment*

This is not always necessary and depends on how relevant the patient's home environment is in aggravating the problems and how supportive his immediate family is. A move to stay with friends or relatives may suffice. Admission to hospital or to a crisis unit is a further alternative which permits closer and continuing contact with the therapist and hence facilitates the objectives listed below.

(4) *Lowering arousal and distress*

Commonly the patient in need of intensive care is distressed, over-aroused, and often exhausted. As far as possible arousal should be lowered by psychological means: by spending time with and talking to the patient in a reassuring and concerned manner. Medication has a place, particularly if arousal is very high and unresponsive to psychological methods, and also to ensure adequate sleep.

(5) *Reinforcing appropriate communication*

Decompensation may present as the exhausted, distressed state described above, or less often as a state of 'shock', perhaps of sudden onset, in which the patient becomes almost mute and immobile. In either case, an important objective is to re-establish normal communication: to reinforce any normal and relevant conversation by paying more attention to it, and to discourage agitated, perseverative, or non-communicative forms of behaviour by ignoring them.

(6) *Showing concern and warmth and encouraging hope*

Underlying the two previous tactics is a need to convey to the patient that the therapist cares, to demonstrate empathy, and to instil hope for a positive resolution of the crisis. There are other ways whereby the therapist can help the patient during intensive care particularly after the initial state of over-arousal or shock have subsided, but these are also used in crisis counselling and are described below.

Crisis counselling

The key difference between crisis counselling and intensive care is that the patient receiving the former is not being treated as a sick or dependent person but as an adult with problems who is asking for help. Whether he has received intensive care previously or not, the nature of the patient–therapist relationship should be made explicit. Objectives of the counselling should be agreed, the extent of the therapist's involvement in terms of what he will undertake to do and how much time he will spend should be spelt out, and the need for the patient to accept responsibility for his outcome emphasized. In other words, a verbal contract is negotiated, though as counselling proceeds and circumstances change, this often needs to be modified, but always explicitly. For example, the initial objective may be simply to define the problems before any decision on what further steps might be taken. Having achieved that objective, a further contract involving problem solving might be made.

Patients who have difficulty in agreeing or conforming to contracts of this kind may be looking for a more dependent 'sick role' relationship with the therapist. In these cases it becomes a primary objective to help the patient to see the inevitable disadvantages of being passive and dependent and the constraint that this imposes on the therapist. Inability to alter this aspect of the patient may be an indication for more long-term psychotherapeutic help but it certainly precludes brief, goal-oriented crisis counselling.

Once an explicit contract has been reached, the therapist may make use of any of the following methods as appropriate; the choice will be determined to some extent by the nature of the particular crisis and by the characteristics and resources of the patient.

(1) *Facilitating the expression of affect*

As already mentioned, affect generated in crisis situations frequently becomes a major problem in its own right and impedes resolution of the crisis until appropriately dealt with. Good examples of this are grief, where cultural, family, or personality factors may inhibit its expression and hence prevent its satisfactory resolution (Lindemann 1944), and anger, where early acquired attitudes to it (e.g. 'it is wrong to show anger or lose your temper') or fear of its consequences may inhibit its expression. Unexpressed anger, lingering in the patient and often manifested by sulking, withdrawn, or generally negative behaviour, can have a devastatingly destructive effect on relationships. Expression of anger on the other hand, can dramatically improve the situation.

The therapist can facilitate expression of affect by listening for cues of it, encouraging the patient to talk about his feelings, and making it clear that he, the therapist, is prepared to accept their expression. He may similarly influence the expression of feelings between the patient and his spouse or relatives. Therapists are sometimes accused of encouraging the release of affect, particularly anger, for its own sake, the implication being that it is not necessarily helpful and may actually be harmful. Certainly one should not use this tactic indiscriminately. There are instances where affect may be a feature of a seriously disturbed mental state such as in agitated depression or morbid jealousy, and encouraging its expression is likely to aggravate the problem. But as a general rule, if feelings are perceived by the therapist as understandable reactions to the crisis and they have not been appropriately or sufficiently ventilated, then their expression is likely to be beneficial.

(2) *Facilitating communication*

Problems arise not only in the expression of feelings but also in communication of meaning. Once again this may be simply a reaction to crisis, but more often reflects basic difficulties in communication which render the patient and his family more vulnerable at times of stress. The patient's customary methods of communication can be observed in the context of the therapeutic relationship, or in a family or marital interview, or as described by him to the therapist. Feedback of these observations is helpful in demonstrating how communication fails and what effects it has on others. This can then lead to suggestions as to how communication can be improved. The presence of a therapist in family sessions often makes this otherwise sensitive topic easier to discuss.

(3) *Facilitating patient's understanding of both his problems and his feelings*

Much distress results from a patient failing to understand why he has got into his predicament and why he feels so upset. Helping him to appreciate these issues is therapeutic and distress-reducing in its own right and also serves the purpose of identifying the problems and their possible solution.

(4) *Showing concern and empathy and bolstering self-esteem*

The importance of concern and empathy have already been stressed in relation to intensive care but it is clearly important for any type of crisis intervention and there are occasions when it is all the therapist can usefully do. Bolstering self-esteem, whilst frequently difficult when the patient is surrounded by failure, is nevertheless an important task, all too often overlooked by therapists. Assessment of the patient's past life together with observation of his current behaviour provides the therapist with material to remind him of his strengths and assets. The therapist can also show the pleasure that he feels when progress is being made.

(5) *Facilitating problem-solving behaviour*

In many cases this is the essence of the therapist's work, though it is also here in particular that the adult–adult nature of the therapeutic relationship has to exist—problem solving and the resultant decision making are done by the patient, not the therapist. Common-sense steps of problem solving are:

identify and define the problem,
identify alternative methods of coping with that problem,
cognitively rehearse each alternative and become clear of its implications,
choose one alternative to follow,
define the behavioural steps required to carry out that alternative,
carry out the alternative step by step,
check the effects of this behaviour to ensure that the choice of alternative has been a suitable one.

As Goldfried and Goldfried (1975) have pointed out: 'there may exist many good problem solvers who do not utilise the exact seven step process, (but) the essential point is that poor problem solvers can be taught to increase the effectiveness of their decision making process by following this strategy'. A further point to stress is that the choice of alternatives does not necessarily follow logically from these steps. Choice may still be an intuitive process. But the ability to 'feel' the right choice is often enhanced by going through these preliminary stages.

The therapist can help with this process in the following ways:

(a) Explain the principles of problem solving to the patient; this is an educational procedure.

(b) Help the patient to define the problem appropriately (i.e. in terms that suggest possible methods of dealing with it) and realistically, e.g. by confronting the patient with facts or with feedback from other informants which have a bearing on the problem.

(c) Much problem solving depends on creative thinking, producing novel ideas (Davis 1973). Therapists can lend their own creative thinking to the patient as well as their specific skills in problem solving of certain kinds.

(d) Use assessment of the patient's previous coping resources to remind him where his strengths and weaknesses lie so that he will see more clearly which alternative is likely to succeed.

(e) Ensure that the patient has realistically considered the practical consequences and implications of each alternative (i.e. further reality confrontation).

(f) Encourage the patient to make a choice after due consideration and when the choice 'feels right'.

(g) Help the patient break down the chosen method of coping into small and manageable behavioural steps.

(h) Negotiate a behavioural contract with the patient, i.e. get his agreement and commitment to carry out the step in the behavioural sequence.

(i) Help him to check the effectiveness or otherwise of his coping behaviour.

In addition to these basically common-sense tactics of the therapist, there is also scope within this framework for the use of more psychotherapeutic skills. By setting behavioural goals in this way and by analysing in detail the difficulties that the patient has in carrying them out, the therapist can effectively and quickly identify key attitudes, resistances, and defence mechanisms that serve to obstruct the behaviour. Various types of psychotherapeutic strategy can be used to modify these attitudes and resistances; these will be discussed more fully in the chapter on sex therapy (see Chapter 8). There are two other methods that the therapist can use as part of crisis counselling: *giving expert advice* and *prescribing psychotropic drugs*. These have been left till the last partly because, in the case of medically trained therapists, they tend to be in the forefront of their minds whereas they should in fact be used sparingly and cautiously. There are obviously many situations where these treatment methods are appropriate, but they are seldom so in crisis counselling. Nevertheless, there are occasions when special guidance is useful either from the therapist or from another agency that the patient is referred to. Specifically medical, family planning, legal, or financial advice all come into this category. Agencies such as Citizens' Advice Bureaux are examples of community-based sources of advice. The patient may be advised to withhold temporarily from a course of action, e.g. to delay initiating divorce proceedings because of the possibility of change in the marital relationship. The therapist should be clearly aware that he is offering advice and satisfy himself that it is appropriate in the circumstances.

As far as psychotropic drugs are concerned it has already been mentioned that they may be indicated during intensive care. In that case it presents no particular problems as far as the patient–therapist relationship is concerned. On the other hand, when used during crisis counselling it is important to counteract the implication that 'prescription of drugs' equals 'illness' and hence the transfer of responsibility to the therapist. He needs to stress that drugs are being used only as an adjunct to other methods, as an aid to the patient's own problem solving efforts.

Indications for medication are briefly:

(a) To lower arousal in a patient where it is seriously impairing his ability to develop problem-solving behaviour or make decisions, and where psychological methods have failed. The aim of medication, usually a minor tranquillizer, is to reduce arousal so that effective coping behaviour can be resumed.

(b) To elevate mood in a patient whose depression is of such severity that he is unable to initiate or carry out any problem solving behaviour. The antidepressant is prescribed to improve mood sufficiently to allow the patient to participate actively in problem solving but is not intended to solve those problems

(c) To improve a patient's sleep—insomnia needs special attention because of its deleterious effect on his coping abilities. Care must be taken however to avoid the development of dependency on the hypnotic and such drugs should usually be taken only intermittently, for only two or three nights in succession.

Clinical illustration

The following case history illustrates the type of problem and objectives involved in both intensive care and crisis counselling.

Gerald, a 38-year-old accountant, and Elizabeth had been married for 12 years; they had two children aged 11 and 8. For the past three months, an old friend of theirs, Brian, whose marriage had broken up and who was having financial difficulties, had been staying with them. Twelve hours before Gerald was referred to the Crisis Unit, he had discovered Brian and Elizabeth having sexual intercourse. After an angry scene he had told them to get out, and they had both left in the middle of the night, driving off in Brian's car. A neighbour found Gerald the following morning in a distressed and agitated state. The two children were also distressed and frightened having heard the angry ejection of their mother.

When seen in the unit, Gerald was still agitated, expressing intense anger at his wife and Brian and alarm at the prospect of being left on his own to look after the children. He was making definite suicidal threats if his wife was not prepared to care for them. After initial assessment it was decided that Gerald's emotional reaction to the situation, involving anger, humiliation, and the threat of a single parent role, was sufficient to render him unsuitable to take care of the children or to be left on his own. Immediate intensive care was therefore indicated and the following plan was implemented:

(1) He was strongly advised to enter the unit for a period of 2–3 days, and to hand over responsibility for his children and work temporarily to the unit staff.

(2) Arrangements were made for the children to be looked after by a family friend.

(3) He was given an opportunity to ventilate his intense feelings of hurt and resentment with a staff member.

(4) He was given hypnotics to help him sleep at night.

After 36 hours he had largely regained his composure, and although still very angry he was judged capable of returning home to look after his children. At this stage the intensive care came to an end. It was then made explicit that he would have to resume responsibility for himself and his children, but if at any time he felt that he was once again incapable of doing so, he was to contact the unit immediately. He was also offered crisis counselling and an appointment was set to attend the next day. Over the next week, three such sessions were held during which the following problems were discussed:

(a) how to deal in the short term with his children—it was agreed that he would take time off work to be at home until his situation was clearer.

(b) What to do about his marriage—further ventilation of his feelings occurred and it was agreed that the therapist should contact his wife with a view to a joint session later.

After further sessions during the next three weeks, it became clear that the marriage was unlikely to resume and that Elizabeth had chosen to stay with Brian. She revealed long-standing discontent with the marriage. Gerald arranged for a part-time housekeeper so that he could return to work and started divorce proceedings.

This case illustrates the use of brief intensive care, leading on to crisis counselling of approximately one month's duration—there were six counselling sessions in all.

Practical aspects

The provision of intensive care requires special resources. Though these can often be provided by family or friends, there will be many situations where the professional looks for other more institutional settings. The use of traditional psychiatric facilities should be treated cautiously as these are often not designed to provide the type of support described here and may serve to prolong the stage of dependency. A number of special units have been developed to provide this type of intervention. Cooper (1979) recently visited a number of such units in Europe. Probably the Amsterdam Crisis Centre is closest to the setting advocated in this chapter. Cooper commented that in such units most clients did not fit the classical description of a person in crisis (Caplan 1961), i.e. the previously well-adjusted person needing help at the point of crisis, and showing its discrete phases before returning to his previous state. Presumably there are many such people but they are unlikely to seek help in such settings. Instead we find people with chronic personality problems, repeated crises, and generally poor coping resources. Nevertheless the rapid action, problem orientation, short-term planning, and emphasis on the 'here and now', which characterizes crisis intervention, is probably the most appropriate and cost-effective approach to such patients.

Training and conclusion

Clearly in carrying out crisis intervention there is much scope for skill and the benefits of experience. Some of this involves empathy and sensitivity, attributes with which some therapists are relatively well endowed from the start, but which all can improve by becoming sufficiently aware and analytic of their own performance. Clinical practice, ideally with a broad range of patients in crisis, under the supervision of an experienced therapist, is a vital aspect of training. Observation of the veteran practitioner by the use of videotape or one-way screen is also helpful. Knowledge of the literature, although it can lead to some confusion, is another facet of training, and to this end a recommended reading list is provided at the end of the chapter.

But for much of what we do we need to recognize not only the real alternatives open to us but also their limitations. Communicating a sense of competence combined with concern can be a major therapeutic achievement, particularly in the intensive care stage. Often inexperienced therapists feel unsure of themselves because they suspect that there are forms of help with which they are unfamiliar. Although the details are few and the complexity not fully apparent in this chapter, the range of possible types of crisis intervention is more or less covered. This is the 'menu' from which to choose. For the most part they rely on skilful use of commonsense rather than highly specialized professional skills. Recognition of these points will increase the would-be therapist's sense of competence as well as give him a framework within which to operate.

References

Aguilera, D. C. and Messick, J. M. (1974). *Crisis intervention: theory and methodology*. C. V. Mosby, St. Louis, Mo.

Bancroft, J., Skrimshire, A., Casson, J., Harvard-Watts. O. and Reynolds, F. (1977). People who deliberately poison or injure themselves: their problems and their contacts with helping agencies, *Psychol. Med.* 7, 289-303.

Bartolucci, G. and Drayer, C. S. (1973). An overview of crisis intervention in the emergency rooms of general hospitals, *Am. J. Psychiat.* 130, 953-60.

Beck, A. T., Rush, A. J., Shaw, B. F., and Emery, G. (1979). *Cognitive therapy of depression*. Guildford, New York.

Brandon, S. (1970). Crisis theory and possibilities of therapeutic intervention, *Br. J. Psychiat.* 117, 627-33.

Brown, G. W., Bhrolchain, M. N., and Harris, T. (1975). Social class and psychiatric disturbance among women in an urban population, *Sociology* 9, 225-54.

Caplan, G. (1961). *An approach to community mental health*. Tavistock, London.

Cooper, J. E. (1979). *Crisis admission units and emergency psychiatric services*. Public Health in Europe No. 11. WHO, Copenhagen.

Davis, G. A. (1973). *Psychology of problem-solving*. Basic Books, New York.

Erikson, E. H. (1969). *Childhood and society*. Penguin, Harmondsworth.

Goldfried, M. R. and Goldfried, A. P. (1975). Cognitive change methods. In *Helping people change* (eds F. H. Kanfer and A. P. Goldstein). Pergamon Press, New York.

Illich, I. (1975). *Medical nemesis*. Calder and Boyars, London.

Jacobsen, G., Strickler, M., and Morley, W. E. (1968). Generic and individual approaches to crisis intervention, *Am. J. publ. Hlth.* 58, 339-42.

Kendell, R. E. (1975). The concept of disease and its implication for psychiatry, *Br. J. Psychiat.* 127, 305-15.

Lazarus, R. S. (1966). *Psychological stress and the coping process*. McGraw-Hill, New York.

Lewis, A. (1953). Health as a social concept, *Br. J. Sociol.* 4, 109-24.

Lindemann, E. (1944). Symptomatology and management of acute grief, *Am. J. Psychiat.* 101, 101-48.

Mechanic, D. (1977). Illness behaviour, social adaptation and the management of illness, *J. nerv. ment. Dis.* 165, 79-87.

Parkes, C. M. (1975). *Bereavement: studies of grief in adult life*. Penguin, Harmondsworth.

Parsons, T. (1951). *The social system*. Free Press. Glencoe.

Raphael, B. (1971). Crisis intervention: theoretical and methodological considerations, *Aust. N.Z.J. Psychiat.* 51, 183-90.

Recommended reading

Aguilera, D. C. and Messick, J. M. (1974). *Crisis intervention: theory and methodology*. C. V. Mosby, St. Louis, Mo. (A concise and readable book; chapters 2, 3, and 5 are particularly useful.)

Caplan, G. (1974). *Support systems and community mental health.* Behavioral Publications, New York. (Chapter 1 contains a helpful account of the concept of support in relation to crisis.)

Davis, G. A. (1973). *Psychology of problem-solving.* Basic Books, New York.

Eisler, R. M. and Hersen, M. (1973). Behavioural techniques in family oriented crisis intervention, *Archs gen. Psychiat.* **28**, 111–16. (Contains useful practical ideas.)

Ewing, C. P. (1978). *Crisis intervention as psychotherapy.* Oxford University Press, New York. (A brief introduction to the theory and practice of crisis intervention.)

Goldfried, M. R. and Goldfried, A. P. (1975). Cognitive change methods. In *Helping people change* (eds F. H. Kanfer and A. P. Goldstein). Pergamon Press. New York. (Useful discussion of the principles of problem solving.)

Langsley, D. G., Machotka, P., and Flomenhaft, K. (1971). Avoiding mental hospital admission—a follow up study, *Am. J. Psychiat.* **127**, 1391–4. (Report on the results of crisis intervention with families.)

Raphael, B. (1977). Preventive intervention with the recently bereaved, *Archs gen. Psychiat.* **34**, 1450–4. (A research study on the effectiveness of crisis intervention in grief.)

6

Cognitive and behavioural therapies
Michael Gelder

Cognitive and behavioural therapies are brief treatments, directed to specific goals, and concerned with present rather than past circumstances. By themselves, these features do not distinguish cognitive and behavioural therapies from many other forms of brief psychotherapy. The features that distinguish cognitive-behavioural methods from other treatments are: they are concerned more with factors maintaining symptoms and abnormal behaviours than with original causes, they are based on psychological experimentation, and they have limited and rather specific indications. Most cognitive and behavioural treatments are also designed to encourage self-help. Each of these points will be elaborated in turn.

Cognitive and behavioural therapies are generally more concerned with factors maintaining a disorder than with factors that initiated the disorder. For example in treating phobic disorders, treatment is focused on the patient's tendency to avoid situations that provoke anxiety. This is done because avoidance prolongs symptoms that would otherwise diminish with the passage of time. Similarly, when treating anxiety disorders treatment is often focused on controlling 'fear of fear' (i.e. anxious thoughts about possible consequences of symptoms). This is done because fear of fear can prolong anxiety symptoms which would otherwise subside more rapidly. The reader will note that in the two examples just given, the first set of prolonging factors is behavioural, the second is cognitive.

Behavioural and cognitive methods are based on knowledge gained in psychological experimentation. In the early years of behaviour therapy most of this experimentation concerned animal behaviour, nowadays it is usually concerned directly with humans. Experimentation with animals is generally more exact than experimentation with humans but it is often remote from clinical problems. Experiments with humans usually take the form of studies of the short-time effects of behavioural or cognitive procedures on the feelings, thoughts, and minor neurotic symptoms of healthy people. Such experiments have proved to be a useful guide to treatment.

Most cognitive and behavioural treatments have limited and rather specific fields of application. This is partly because most have been designed to treat specific symptoms or behaviours such as phobias, general anxiety, obsessions, depression, eating disorders, and sexual dysfunction. Also, most techniques have been tested in clinical trials which have helped to define, within each diagnostic group, the patients who are most responsive. This specificity is an important difference between cognitive-behaviour therapies and other kinds of psychotherapy.

Many cognitive and behavioural treatments are designed to increase a patient's ability to help himself. For example in Beck's cognitive therapy, the patient takes an active part in identifying maladaptive cognitions and trying out ways of controlling them (Beck, Rush, Shaw, and Emery 1979). Similarly, modern treatments for phobic and obsessional disorders encourage the patient to take an active part in planning and executing appropriate behavioural tasks.

With these common features in mind, the reader will now be introduced to the historical development of cognitive and behavioural treatments.

The background to present-day treatments

Two lines of development have lead to cognitive and behavioural treatments. The first began with the observation, made by clinicians in the first part of this century, that neurotic patients can sometimes be helped by practice in facing fears. Janet (1925) used a method of this kind for agoraphobia, and he also described tasks intended to treat hysterical paralyses and tics. This approach continued to find some support throughout the 1920s and 1930s. However, it failed to achieve wide acceptance, possibly because it was based on clinical empiricism, and lacked the attractive theoretical justification of psychoanalysis which was becoming widely known at the time.

The second line of development starts with the attempts of

psychologists to apply to clinical problems some of the principles that were being worked out in the study of learning in animals. This work began in the 1920s with the demonstration that childrens' fears could sometimes be modified by conditioning methods. It continued in the 1930s and 1940s with aversion therapy for alcoholism which was used quite widely.

Progress in medicine depends on new ideas but they need to appear at the right time. The time for behaviour therapy came in the early 1950s when there was a growing opinion among clinical psychologists that their professional role, which at the time was largely concerned with mental testing, was unsatisfactory. They began to look for other ways of applying their knowledge of psychology to the care of patients, and when reports of the new work on behaviour therapy began to appear a receptive audience was waiting. The new work began in two places. In Britain a group of psychologists at the Maudsley Hospital began to apply learning principles systematically to the treatment of neurotic patients. They used psychological principles to devise a separate, tailor-made procedure for the problems of each patient. At about the same time a South African psychiatrist, Joseph Wolpe, developed a method which could be applied to a range of different problems (Wolpe 1958). For two decades Wolpe's technique of treatment, systematic desensitization, remained the most important single method of behaviour therapy for neurotic disorders. His success lay partly in providing a convincing theoretical rationale for his clinical approach, and partly in the clear and detailed descriptions which he gave of the procedures.

Wolpe's ideas and those of the British psychologists were made known to a wider audience by Eysenck. Unfortunately the latter's advocacy for behaviour therapy was coupled with an attack on psychoanalysis which alienated many psychiatrists who might otherwise have been interested in the new approach. Partly because of this, it was some time before it became generally realized that techniques of behaviour therapy are compatible with many forms of brief psychotherapy—certainly with those likely to be used by readers of this book—though not with psychoanalysis or comparable forms of highy specialized psychotherapy.

Before long the new ideas were taken up with enthusiasm by American clinical psychologists who soon incorporated information about operant conditioning. Also in the United States research developed concerned not with the treatment of psychiatric patients but with minor neurotic problems in otherwise healthy people. As already mentioned, these studies were useful in filling the wide gap between experiments on learning in laboratory animals and the problems of neurotic patients. As such they are a useful guide to the treatment; however they are not a substitute for clinical investigations with patients. It was in Britain that most clinical studies of behaviour therapy were carried out.

So far, we have considered the development of behavioural techniques. Cognitive therapy grew mainly from Beck's investigation of the cognitions of anxious and depressed patients (Beck, Lander, and Bohnert 1974). These studies showed that anxious and depressed patients are preoccupied with thoughts which exacerbate their mood disorder. Beck's findings led naturally to attempts to control these thoughts as a way of reducing the mood disorder. The time was ripe for this kind of approach because psychologists were becoming disillusioned with simple forms of behaviourism and increasingly interested in cognitive processes.

Indications and contra-indications

Methods of cognitive and behaviour therapy have been developed for use in a wide range of psychiatric disorders, including those encountered in children, the mentally handicapped, and schizophrenics. This account is limited to the treatment of neurotic disorders in adult life since this is broadly the scope of the other treatments considered in this book.

Although cognitive and behavioural treatments were developed from a psychological tradition which generally rejects the idea that it is useful to classify neuroses into syndromes, it turns out that the different neurotic syndromes require rather different kinds of treatment. Thus phobic disorders of all kinds usually respond to 'exposure' treatment (see p. 140). Many *obsessional neuroses* improve with 'response prevention' (see p. 141) especially when compulsive rituals are present. The symptoms of hysteria do not respond specifically to any kind of behaviour therapy though it is sometimes a convenient vehicle for treatment by suggestion. Some psychosomatic complaints are alleviated when relaxation training is combined with attention to stressful circumstances in the patient's everyday life. *Minor affective symptoms* of the kind met in general practice often improve with similar measures (Johnston 1978, unpublished observations), although the indications for behavioural measures on the one hand and social work intervention on the other have not been worked out fully. Cognitive behaviour therapy seems to shorten the course of *depressive disorders* of moderate severity. Because it is a lengthy treatment it is more appropriate for chronic or recurrent depressive disorders than for acute episodes.

Some *psychosexual problems* have been treated with behaviour therapy (see Bancroft 1983). The methods, which resemble those described in Chapter 8, will not be considered further here. Behavioural methods have also been devised for *marital problems* (Stuart 1969), and for *obesity, anorexia nervosa,* and *bulimia nervosa* (Fairburn 1983). Other methods have been devised to reduce smoking, to assist in the control of alcohol intake in patients with drinking problems, and to deal with certain disorders of motor behaviour such as tics (see Rimm and Masters 1974).

Attempts to relate the outcome of cognitive and behavioural therapy to measurements of personality or to ratings of symptoms made before treatment, have not succeeded. The most useful predictor is the effect of the first few sessions of treatment (Mathews, Johnston, Shaw, and Gelder 1974). It is good practice, therefore, to agree with the patient that the final decision about a course of treatment will not be taken until the therapist has observed the effects of the first few sessions.

What, in general, are the contra-indications for behaviour therapy? The most important is the presence of a psychiatric illness requiring separate treatment. The most serious mistake is to treat a behaviour problem while failing to observe the presence of a depressive disorder requiring physical treatment. This error is unlikely to be made if one of the steps in the assessment of patients for behaviour therapy is a thorough psychiatric history and examination of the mental state. Behavioural analysis by itself is not enough. Other diagnoses which may be missed when a patient presents with neurotic symptoms are in older patients the early stages of presenile dementia, and in younger ones schizophrenia. Care must be taken to assess fully any associated personality disorder. If a full psychiatric assessment is made in each case, behaviour therapy can be used safely in a wide variety of disorders (provided that care is taken to follow the procedural steps described later in this chapter).

Behaviour analysis

When the diagnosis has been made and the decisions taken about the need for treatment, the therapist carries out an analysis of the behaviour problems. Behavioural analysis differs from ordinary psychiatric history taking in three ways: it is almost wholly concerned with the present state of the patient's problems rather than their development; it requires a more detailed enquiry into the circumstances in which the problems occur; and whenever possible, abnormal behaviour is related to psychological processes. In the course of this analysis the therapist has two questions in mind. What behavioural techniques are likely to be helpful, and is the patient likely to carry them out? The example of a patient with agoraphobia should make these last two points clearer.

The first step in the behavioural analysis of the problem of an agoraphobic patient is to determine what physical symptoms (e.g. palpitations, muscle tension, hyperventilation) and psychological symptoms (e.g. fear of fainting) are experienced by the patient. Next, a detailed account is obtained of the situations in which these symptoms occur, listed in order of severity. For example, an agoraphobic patient might report anxiety when walking, travelling by bus or train, or entering a crowded shop. Each situation is then considered in more detail: the first of the three just mentioned will serve to illustrate the form of the enquiry. The therapist tries to discover the whole range of circumstances in which walking is accompanied by anxiety. He asks whether the symptoms begin after the patient had gone out, or whether the prospect of leaving home causes anxiety. He finds out how far the patient can walk before anxiety increases and what circumstances provoke the most severe anxiety. He then identifies situations between these extremes, that give rise to intermediate degrees of anxiety. This list of situations is called a hierarchy.

The analysis now turns to the patient's attempts to cope with anxiety. Avoidance is the most common of these—and the least adaptive since it helps to perpetuate the symptoms. Other coping strategies include distraction and attempts at relaxation, and these can be encouraged as adaptive responses. The analysis of anxious cognitions often takes a long time because at first many patients do not find it easy to identify these cognitions. The enquiry should cover all thoughts occurring during mood changes in the course of clinical interview as well as those experienced during variations of mood in everyday life. The latter changes can be identified more easily when the patient is asked to note down his thoughts and feelings as they occur.

The last stage of the analysis is concerned with motivation. Many patients who have learnt effective techniques of behaviour therapy fail to carry them out. There are several reasons for this failure. Firstly, after repeated experiences of fear many patients have given up many social activities outside the home. The therapist has to decide whether the patient really wants to revive these activities or is content to stay as he is. Some agoraphobic patients are solitary people who would be unlikely to socialize more even if they could leave home without fear. Secondly, repeated practice in going out is not immediately rewarding; the satisfactions appear only after substantial progress has been made. Until this has been achieved, the patient needs encouragement by other people, particularly the spouse. The therapist should find out whether these people are likely to encourage the patient. Finally, the therapist should assess whether behaviour therapy fits the patient's ideas about the sort of treatment that is likely to help him or whether he expects to benefit more from drugs or psychotherapy.

The steps outlined above apply to most neurotic disorders. Whatever the diagnosis, the situations which provoke symptoms are enquired into in detail. The patient's symptoms, fears, and motivation are considered, and his expectations about treatment are assessed. Two points deserve emphasis. Firstly the enquiry into motivation usually leads to a consideration of family interactions because other members of the family are often involved in the disorder (for example in obsessional rituals), and their collaboration is usually required in treatment. Secondly, the enquiries required are broadly similar to those undertaken by a psychiatrist, except that more emphasis is placed on finding out the exact circumstances in which the symptoms appear.

Preparing the patient for treatment

Many of the issues about preparing patients for treatment have been anticipated in the previous section. In cognitive and behaviour therapies it is usually possible to plan treatment in some detail from the start. It is desirable to discuss the plan with the patient so that he understands what he will be required to do. It also advisable to talk at length about the changes in his life that will have to be made if the effects of treatment are to persist. For example, an agoraphobic patient is unlikely to maintain the improvement made in treatment unless he makes efforts to go out regularly with friends, visit relatives, or engage in other activities outside the home.

When motivational problems were considered in the previous section, the role of the patient's spouse was emphasized. It is important to prepare the spouse for his part in treatment. If the spouse cannot or will not help, another relative or a friend may be able to assist. Otherwise it may be possible to treat the patient in a group of patients who are encouraged to help and motivate each other (e.g. Hand, Lamontagne, and Marks 1971).

Some therapists complete the preparation of the patient by drawing up a written contract which sets out what the patient will be required to do. Such a contract is sometimes useful because it can be discussed at home with the spouse, before being agreed at the next meeting. This procedure, although rather alien to everyday medical practice, can help to identify before treatment patients who are likely to drop out from the course of treatment which is being offered.

Some commonly used techniques

The many techniques of cognitive and behaviour therapy cannot all be reviewed in a short space. Even though this chapter is concerned mainly with methods used in the treatment of neurotic disorders, it is impossible to give more than a very general account. Further reading and supervised experience are essential before any of the methods is used. (Suggestions for further reading appear at the end of the chapter).

After the behavioural assessment the therapist may decide that it will be necessary to use more than one technique to treat the patient's problems. However, the therapist should avoid complexity for its own sake. The use of many technical procedures where one would do, usually signifies an incomplete understanding of the behavioural problem—just as the prescription of too many drugs generally indicates uncertainty about medical diagnosis. Moreover, just as it is better to use a few well tried drugs rather than employ each new preparation, so it is better to learn a few well established behavioural techniques rather than adopt each new variation as it appears.

Phobic disorders are usually treated with a combination of 'exposure' (a graded return to situations which have been avoided) and training in 'anxiety management' (Mathews, Gelder, and Johnston 1981). In the latter method, patients are taught to reduce symptoms of anxiety by relaxing and to tolerate them without becoming more afraid—for example a patient who fears that the rapid beating of his heart signals an impending heart attack, might be taught to control his fearful thoughts by repeating reassuring thoughts to himself. By themselves, these measures do not ensure a good result. It is important to add measures designed to increase compliance. Without this addition, many patients give up practising before lasting changes have been achieved. Compliance can be increased by providing written instruction about the reasons for treatment and the new behaviours that are to be practised. (Anxious patients easily forget verbal instruction.) Compliance can also be increased by enlisting the help of another person who is willing to assist the patient in planning activities and to show interest and satisfaction in his new achievments. This helper is usually the spouse but can be another relative or a friend.

This kind of exposure treatment can be used for agoraphobia, social phobia, or simple phobia. Among the simple phobias are some in which it is difficult to arrange planned encounters with the actual situations which provoke fear (for example, a phobia of storms). In these cases, the patient may be asked to imagine the situation vividly ('desensitization in imagination'). These cases are exceptions to the general rule that exposure to actual situations has greater therapeutic effects than exposure to imaginary ones.

Social inadequacy differs from social phobia in being general in its effects rather than focused on a limited range of social situation. Also, in social phobia the person possesses normal social skills (though he may be too anxious to use them appropriately), while in social inadequacy he either fails to acquire these skills or has lost them due to an illness such as schizophrenia. Training in social skills may help these people. This training has several stages. Firstly, the deficits in social skills are identified and shown to the patient (by means of a video-recording). Then more effective alternatives are demonstrated. Finally the patient is encouraged to practise these alternatives first at the hospital and later in his everyday life (see Argyle, Bryant, and Trower 1974).

Among patients with *obsessive-compulsive neuroses*, those with rituals are more likely to respond to behaviour therapy than those with ruminations. Also rituals can usually be treated more effectively when they are provoked by specific cues (Marks, Hodgson, and Rachman 1975). In the treatment of rituals it is usual to use a variant of the exposure method used for phobic disorders (Meyer, Levy, and Schnurer 1974). For example, if hand-washing rituals are provoked by contact with an object, the patient is encouraged to touch that object and at the same time helped to resist the ritual. Exposure to the provoking stimulus and prevention of the ritual only have a therapeutic effect when continued for a long time (up to several hours). Shorter periods may make symptoms worse. Some therapists begin by showing the patient what he has to do. This so-called modeling has been claimed to have therapeutic effects of its own but there is no convincing evidence that this is so (see Hodgson, Rachman, and Marks 1972). It is less certain whether there is an effective behavioural treatment for obsessional thoughts. In one procedure patients are taught to interrupt the thoughts, at first by a sudden external distraction such as snapping a rubber band over the wrist, and later by mental distraction, for example by thinking the word stop (Stern, Lipsedge and Marks 1973). This combination of procedures is sometimes helpful but has not been shown to be generally effective.

Anxiety neuroses are usually treated with a combination of relaxation, distraction from anxiety-provoking cues and cognitive procedures ('anxiety management training'). The cognitive procedures are distraction and the silent repetition of phrases chosen to neutralize the effects of anxious cognitions. For example a patient who thinks repeatedly that he is about to suffer a heart attack might be trained to say to himself that no amount of anxiety will damage his healthy heart.

Family and marital problems are often treated with joint interviews intended to improve understanding between family members. These methods are quite similar to those described in Chapter 7. There are also some specific behavioural techniques, usually known as contingency management (Stuart 1975). The essential idea is that each person should state what he most desires from each of the other family members, and what he is willing to give in return. In this way a form of bargain is struck between the family members. The procedure is less unfeeling than it might appear when described in this summary form. It can be effective in terminating self-defeating patterns of behaviour between family members and releasing the tender feelings towards others which the approach may at first appear to discount.

Sexual inadequacy can be treated with behavioural methods, but the treatment will not be discussed here as it is similar to that described in Chapter 8.

Depressive disorders can be treated with a special form of cognitive therapy devised by Beck (see Beck, Rush, Shaw, and Emery

1979). This treatment is directed at several kinds of abnormal thinking, notably 'automatic thoughts' and 'underlying assumptions', and 'logical errors', as well as to the lack of activity which characterizes many depressive disorders. Automatic thoughts are thoughts which appear repeatedly without conscious effort. In depressive disorders these thoughts have a negative content, being concerned with gloomy and self-defeating themes such as 'I am a failure' or 'I shall never get better'. Underlying assumptions are ways of thinking which distort the interpretation of experience, for example that people can only be happy when they are successful in their work. Beck has described four kinds of logical errors: arbitrary inference, selective abstraction, overgeneralization, and magnification or minimization. In this account there is space to give an example of only one of these (further information will be found in Beck *et al.* 1979). Arbitrary assumption refers to a conclusion reached on the basis of subjective impression without any considerations of alternatives. For example: when a friend drives past the patient and fails to greet him, the patient concludes that the friend no longer likes him; he does not consider that the friend may have failed to notice him because he was attending to the road ahead.

Cognitive therapy for depression is directed to identifying automatic thoughts as a means of finding out the nature of the patient's logical errors and underlying assumptions. The therapist attempts to alter these errors and assumptions, and he does so not by argument but by asking the patient to consider alternative explanations. Having underlined the errors and assumptions in this way, the therapist encourages the patient to test the old ways of thinking against new alternatives, and to act on the new ideas in his everyday life. This alternation between a questioning approach in the clinic and the performance of tasks designed to test new ideas in everyday life, is one of the characteristic features of this kind of treatment. It is partly for this reason that it is called cognitive-behaviour therapy.

This treatment for depression had been tested in two clinical trials which have shown that, at least in selected unipolar depressive disorders of moderate severity, it is as effective as tricyclic anti-depressant drug treatment (Rush, Beck, Kovacs and Hollon, 1977; Blackburn, Bishops, Whalley, and Christie, 1981).

The usual course of treatment in behaviour therapy

At first the patient is seen once or twice a week for about half to one hour on each occasion. In the intervals between treatment sessons, he is encouraged to practise what he has learnt, either by himself or with the spouse. Treatment usually runs an uneventful course. When it does not it is often because the original assessment was inadequate or because the procedures were not discussed thoroughly with the patient. For this reason adequate time should be set aside for discussion in the first few sessions. Treatment usually varies between four to six sessions and twenty sessions. Towards the end, sessions are usually spaced progressively so that there is no sharp break between treatment and follow up.

It used to be thought that cognitive and behaviour therapies would be followed by symptom substitution. This idea originated in the psychoanalytic dictum that symptoms are expressions of unconscious emotional conflict. In this view, cognitive and behaviour therapies merely suppress the symptoms, leaving the original conflict untreated. Thus the removal of one symptom would be expected to lead to the appearance of others provoked by the same emotional conflict. Unfortunately it is difficult to state this hypothesis in terms which allow it to be tested effectively. It cannot be maintained that every symptom which appears during treatment is the result of substitution, for the natural course of neurotic symptoms in untreated patients is to wax and wane without treatment. Also, as the therapist encourages the patient to enlarge his social contacts, symptoms sometimes come to attention which went unnoticed before. Clearly, symptoms arising for either of these reasons are not evidence for symptom substitution. When cases such as these are excluded, there is no satisfactory evidence that behaviour therapy leads to symptom substitution.

So far nothing has been said about the relationship between the therapist and the patient. In cognitive and behavioural treatment this relationship is not developed deliberately for direct therapeutic purposes as it is in other forms of psychotherapy. Nevertheless the relationship is not without importance for it forms part of the essential motivating forces which help the patient to carry out the therapeutic tasks. Thus, although effective behaviour therapy for minor neurotic symptoms can be carried out with tape-recorded instructions, the treatment of neurotic patients requires a therapist, though much of what he does is to persuade the patient to help himself.

Any therapeutic relationship can become one of dependency. Cognitive and behaviour therapies are no exception to the generalization though the risks of dependency are less than in most forms of psychological treatment. This is partly because the behaviour therapist encourages his patient to be self-reliant. However, although this procedure lessens the risk of dependency it does not remove it. Also, some techniques used in behaviour therapy add to the danger of dependency. These are: the use of relaxation and imagery as in desensitization, and the need to discuss intimate details of the patient's personal life. If the relationship should become unduly intense, there are the warning signs familiar to anyone who has carried out psychotherapy. It is important to heed these warnings.

The end of treatment

Problems at the end of psychological treatment often reflect lack of planning by the therapist in its early stages. Provided that dependency is not allowed to develop, there should be few difficulties in ending a course of cognitive or behaviour therapy. As we have noted, it is usual to space out the last treatment sessions at increasingly long intervals, and to go on to a few follow-up interviews over the ensuing months. Arranged in this way, the end of treatment need not be distressing. It the patient has not improved as much as expected, it may sometimes be appropriate to add a few more sessions of treatment. However, these sessions should be planned carefully and their number agreed in advance.

All cases should be followed carefully after treatment has ended for it is only in this way that the therapist can test his original predictions against the actual outcome and learn from this experience.

Training

It will be apparent to the reader that the therapist has three things to learn. He has to acquire a number of specific treatment techniques, learn how to plan treatment, and how to adapt general techniques to the special problems of individual patients. The treatment techniques can be learnt easily through apprenticeship with a skilled therapist, supplemented by reading. Also, audio- and videotape demonstrations are available for some of the more common methods.

The planning of treatment is less easy to learn. The important first step is to become competent in the analysis of behaviour problems. This requires ordinary interviewing skills coupled with a determination to obtain detailed descriptions of actual behaviour. These skills can be developed only by interviewing many patients, formulating their problems, and discussing the findings with an expert.

The therapist has to learn how to adapt general treatment techniques to the particular needs of individual patients. The acquisition of this skill requires supervised practice supplemented by discussion, for example in group supervision, of the cases of other trainees. Those who lack training in simple forms of psychotherapy or counselling will also need to learn the skills required to deal effectively with therapist–patient relationships.

Conclusion

The greater part of this chapter has been concerned with specific cognitive and behavioural procedures. We should end, as we began, with a reminder that in some cases it is appropriate to combine these procedures with other forms of psychological treatment. Counselling may be needed to help a patient to re-appraise his relationships with other people. It is often appropriate, with the patient's permission, to talk over problems with the patient's spouse, and occasionally formal marital therapy is required. Cognitive and behaviour therapies are part of the family of psychotherapies and they can be used most effectively by a therapist who has some understanding of other kinds of psychotherapy.

References

Argyle, M., Bryant, B., and Trower, P. (1974). Social skills training and psychotherapy: a comparative study, Psychol. Med. 4, 435–43.

Bancroft, J. (1983). Human sexuality and its problems. Churchill Livingstone, Edinburgh.

Beck, A. T., Lander, R., and Bohnert, M. (1974). Ideational components of anxiety neurosis, Archs. Gen. Psychiat. 39, 319–25.

——, Rush, A. J., Shaw, B. F., and Emery, G. (1979). Cognitive therapy for depression. Guilford, New York.

Blackburn, I. M., Bishops, Glen A. I. M., Whalley, L. J., and Christie, J. E. (1981). The efficacy of cognitive therapy on depression: a treatment trial using cognitive therapy and pharmacotherapy, each alone and in combination, *Br. J. Psychiat.* **139**, 181–9.

Fairburn, C. G. (1983). Eating disorders. In *Companion to psychiatric studies* (eds R. E. Kendell and A. K. Zealley). 3rd edn. Churchill Livingstone, Edinburgh.

Hand, I., Lamontagne, Y., and Marks, I. M. (1974) Group exposure (flooding) *in vivo* for agoraphobics, *Br. J. Psychiat.* **124**, 588–602.

Hodgson, R., Rachman, S., and Marks, I. M. (1972). The treatment of chronic obsessive compulsive neurosis: follow-up and further findings, *Behav. Res. Ther.* **10**, 181–9.

Janet, P. (1925). *Psychological healing.* Allen and Unwin, London.

Marks, I. M., Hodgson, R., and Rachman, S. (1975). Treatment of chronic obsessive-compulsive neurosis *in vivo* exposure: a two-year follow-up and issues in treatment, *Br. J. Psychiat.* **127**, 349–64.

Mathews, A. M., Gelder, M. G., and Johnston, D. (1981). *Agoraphobia: nature and treatment.* Guildford Press, New York.

——, Johnston, D. W., Shaw, P. M., and Gelder, M. G. (1974) Process variables and the prediction of outcome in behaviour therapy, *Br. J. Psychiat.* **125**, 256–64.

Meyer, V., Levy, T., and Schnurer, A. (1974). A behavioural treatment of obsessive compulsive disorders. In *Obsessional states* (ed H. R. Beech). Methuen, London.

Rimm, D. C. and Masters, J. C. (1974). *Behavior therapy: techniques and empirical findings.* Academic Press, New York.

Rush, A. J., Beck, A. T., Kovacs, M., and Hollon, S. (1977). Comparative efficacy of cognitive therapy and imipramine on the treatment of depresed out-patients, *Cognitive Ther. Res.* **1**, 17–31.

Stern, R. S., Lipsedge, M. S. and Marks, I. M. (1973). Thought stopping of neutral and obsessive thoughts: a controlled trial, *Behav. Res. Ther.* **11**, 659–62.

Stuart, R. B. (1969). Operant interpersonal treatment for marital discord, *J. consult. clin. Psychol.* **33**, 675–82.

—— (1975). Behavioral remedies for marital ills. In *Couples in conflict* (eds A. S. Gurman and D. G. Rice). Aronson, New York.

Wolpe, J. (1958). *Psychotherapy by reciprocal inhibition.* Stanford University Press, Stanford, Calif.

Recommended reading

Annual review of behavior therapy, theory and practice. Aldine, Chicago, Ill. (These volumes contain important papers published in the previous year.)

Bandura, A. (1969). *Principles of behavior modification.* Holt, Rhinehart and Winston, New York. (A thoughtful account of the theoretical basis of behaviour therapy; a little out of date now but still well worth reading.)

Garfield, S. L. and Bergin, A. E. (eds) (1978). *Handbook of psychotherapy and behavior change: an empirical analysis*. Wiley, New York. (Includes critical reviews of the main topics in behaviour therapy, extending more widely than its use in the neuroses; a good reference book.)

Hersen, M. and Ballaek, A. S. (eds) (1976). *Behavioural analysis: a practical handbook*. Pergamon Press, Oxford. (A detailed account of behavioural assessment with useful emphasis on the planning of treatment.)

Liberman, R. P. (1972). *A guide to behavioral analysis and therapy*. Pergamon Press, New York. (A short practical manual containing a clear account of the main treatment procedures; some readers may not like its programmed learning format.)

Rimm, D. C. and Masters, J. C. (1974). *Behavior therapy: techniques and empirical findings*. Academic Press, New York. (Gives practical advice about treatment methods; longer than Liberman and more complete.)

7

Marital therapy
Jack Dominian

Dominian introduces the chapter with a brief account of change in marriage as an institution. Following a section on theoretical aspects of marital therapy he presents a model for studying marital patho- logy: marriage has its own life cycle and the relationship has several different dimensions. The next section deals with marital therapy in practice and alternative approaches are discussed. The usual course of treatment and the problems that may arise are then dealt with. The chapter ends with brief comments on training.

Marriages have always had to face difficulties and conflicts which were resolved by the partners alone or with the help of external advice. Traditionally this advice was offered by those considered to be experienced and wise, and for a long time the clergyman, general practitioner, and lawyer were the triad from whom help was sought. They were not only considered to have the maturity and wisdom but also the authority which was binding on both parties.

There are two reasons for the gradual eclipse of this type of help and the advent of more professionally equipped expertise. Firstly the authority of these persons has gradually waned as society has become less authoritarian in structure. Secondly, the number of people seeking help for their marital problems has increased enormously. In the United States one in two of those married in 1970 are expected to divorce (Cherlin 1981), and it has been estimated that forty million American married couples need counselling (Kuhn 1973)! In Britain there has also been a steep rise in petitions for divorce which is illustrated in Table 1 by the figures for England and Wales (HMSO 1983).

After a sharp rise in the immediate post-World War II period a fall took place which came to an end in 1959–60. Subsequently there has

been a steady rise with a sudden jump in 1971, following the introduction of the 1969 Divorce Reform Act. Since this Act, which made
irretrievable breakdown the sole ground for a divorce petition,
numbers have continued to rise. Petition for divorce is the ultimate
step in a sequence of events involving marital difficulties for many
who do not reach the courts directly and seek help at different stages
with their difficulties. How many seek help is hard to determine but,
in one form or another, it must run into hundreds of thousands every
year.

Table 1.
*Petitions filed in England
and Wales*

Year	Number in thousands
1947	48·5
1950	29·7
1960	28·5
1965	42·9
1970	71·7
1971	110·9
1976	146·4
1981	170·2
1982	174·3

Couples or individuals today ask for assistance from general practitioners, marriage advisory councils, probation officers, social
workers, community nurses, health visitors, and other agencies. I
think it would be fair to say that the need for help has outstripped the
resources and, at a theoretical level, the scientific basis of the theory
and practice of marital therapy.

In passing, it is worth commenting on the reasons for the expansion of marital therapy (Dominian 1968). Over a period of some 40
years—since the end of the war—there have been large scale social
and psychological changes which have had a profound effect on the
expectations and behaviour of couples and families. Thus the greater
level of equality sought and obtained by women has had a major
impact on the man–woman relationship. The ascendency and
control over procreation has led not only to smaller size families but
also to more exact timing of the arrival of babies. This, coupled with
the advances in medicine making pregnancy and early childhood
much safer, has led to more time and energy being liberated for

women to use for other purposes, usually work. Finally, as material standards have risen, expectations have increased for fulfilment at the next layer of being, that is to say for emotional and instinctual fulfilment (Dominian 1972). Men and women now expect—consciously and unconsciously—far more from each other and are less prepared to tolerate lower standards of personal happiness. In the days prior to the Divorce Reform Act, when cruelty was still a basis for divorce, the grounds for such cruelty were extended to accommodate these greater expectations of spouses from each other. The courts gradually set higher standards for what was considered to be the minimum behaviour acceptable to a man or woman. Within the context of these changes, marital therapy has become increasingly important as couples consult therapists in order to acquire greater skills with which to relate to each other.

Factors contributing to marital dissatisfaction emanate from several sources. At the most elementary level the pressure of material needs and the presence of gross and cruel behaviour in one or both spouses are relevant whilst, at a more advanced level, more subtle emotional factors play a part. In a study of 600 couples seeking divorce with children under the age of 14, Levinger (1966) noted that in general, middle-class spouses were more concerned with emotional and psychological factors, whereas lower socio-economic class spouses were concerned with financial stability and the absence of physical aggression in their partners. There are marriages in which both factors operate. When the husband is the sole wage-earner, activity such as excessive gambling, drinking, or poor capacity to work may produce a situation in which a great deal of the money is diverted from family needs to the specific preoccupation of the husband and/or income is restricted by long periods of unemployment. But the inability of the husband to provide sufficiently for his family is a complaint which at times hides more complex co-existing emotional problems.

Theoretical background

The theoretical approach to the practice of marital therapy can range from the psychodynamic, based on, for example, Freud, Winnicott (1965) or Klein (1965), to the behavioural. I value an eclectic approach and use any theoretical concept that helps to facilitate improvement in a couple's relationship. With our current state of knowledge, there is little point in being dogmatic and sticking doggedly to one theoretical school in the attempt to understand and treat marital problems.

In practice, however, there are certain aspects of personality development which are invaluable for the understanding of marital problems. One important aspect is that we learn initially from our early family life what it means to participate in a dynamic, intimate relationship over an extended period. Marriage shares similar characteristics and for most people constitutes the second intimate relationship. In the course of childhood we experience a unique relationship usually with one but sometimes with more than one person of the same and opposite sex. Thus every girl learns first and foremost (or in technical terms, identifies with) from her mother and has a cross-identification with her father; the reverse applies to the boy. In marriage there is a tendency to relive these identifications and when the original ones have had disturbed elements, the possibility exists for the disturbance to repeat itself in the marriage.

Since no one emerges from childhood completely unscathed emotionally, it is surprising in an age when personal expectations are so high that more couples do not seek help. One probable factor is that many marriages contain their own healing element within the relationship. As we shall see in the course of this chapter, both partners bring to their relationship the accumulated 'wounds' of two or more decades. These wounds may spring from two sources: first, genetic and constitutional; and second, interaction with significant figures, usually father and/or mother. As far as the former is concerned, the partners may inherit propensities towards high levels of anxiety or to depressive swings; as a result of their relationships in their family of origin they may emerge with marked feelings of dependence, rejection, lack of self-esteem, hostility, and the like. By design or accident, a person with any of these features may marry someone who has the insight, maturity, and patience to provide the missing component of, for example, trust, acceptance, or affirmation; in this way a couple may complement (Winch 1958) one another and the marriage may provide the ingredients for life-long healing experiences. When a spouse cannot offer this healing capacity or, as is often the case, both partners are impaired in their personality so that they lack the resources to act as healing agents, a therapist is required to assume this role. It should be stressed however that in marital therapy the therapist aims to make himself redundant as soon as possible, hence protracted therapy, whilst essential in some instances, should be seen as the rare exception. On the contrary, the therapist aims to release or promote the natural healing ability of the couple in the quickest possible way.

An approach to marital pathology

The therapist will be better equipped to work with couples if he has some systematic approach to the issue of marital pathology. I have used a model over recent years which draws attention to two significant features: the marriage consists of several, different types of relationships any one of which can become disturbed, and marriage has its own life cycle and that some problems are more relevant to one phase than to another (Dominian 1972).

There are five main relationships between a couple: physical, emotional, social, intellectual, and spiritual. The therapist, instead of relying on his intuitive grasp of the 'marital problem', will find it useful to analyse the often complex range of material the couple offers him in terms of the five relationships by noting in which of them the most important difficulties occur. Thus, if a sexual (the physical relationship) problem is central, the therapist can readily determine whether this problem exists alone or whether it is a manifestation of, or co-exists with, disturbance in any of the other four relationships. Such a differentation not only saves unnecessary enquiry but also serves as a guide to treatment. Thus, for example, if the sexual relationship alone is disturbed the therapeutic approach is likely to be the type of sex therapy described in Chapter 8. If, on the other hand, the emotional relationship is also impaired and this seems the chief problem, the couple will be helped with this, before their sexual difficulties are tackled.

The therapist also takes cognisance of the fact that marriage has a life cycle of its own, divisible into three phases: the first phase comprising the first five years, which brings the couple to their late 20s or early 30s on average; the middle phase, covering the period during which the children are growing, and ending about the late 40s or early 50s when the youngest child has left home; and the third phase when the marital partners return to the state of being a couple and ending with the death of one of them. This division is helpful as certain problems are phase-specific or more likely to take place during one phase than another. Thus problems that occur during the third phase are unlikely to be present in the two preceding ones.

In assessing marital pathology, the therapist can place the couple in the appropriate phase and note which of the five relationships are disturbed. Let us now briefly consider the types of marital problems commonly found by combining the two features of our model.

First phase

Physical relationship

Very often in this stage of marriage sexual problems, if present, are relatively uncomplicated in that they do not result from emotional difficulties but spring directly from poor technique and respond well to sex therapy (see Chapter 8).

Emotional relationship

We can approach the problems in the emotional relationship of the early years by focusing on the readiness of one or both spouses to form a stable relationship, their ability to disengage themselves from their respective parents, and the projections through which they experience each other.

Some relationships seem to evaporate emotionally within the first marriage year. A close examination of the background of such a marriage shows that the husband or wife or both were not really ready to commit themselves to a permanent relationship with all that this implies; often there has been uncertainty about their own identity which has not been resolved by further growth but by negotiating a social event, namely a marriage. This has given them a status before society but has not resolved their confusion. As the weeks and months pass they continue to behave as if they were single people, unable to narrow their relationship to each other. They find each other increasingly distant and strange and have little in common, so much so that they gradually realize that they married for reasons such as the need to escape from home, loneliness, or status seeking.

Uncertainty of commitment to the relationship may result when one or both partners have trouble disengaging from their parents. This common problem may be reinforced by the inability of the parents to let go and a collusion is forged—the parents hold onto their child while the child is unable to act independently. When only one partner is unable to extricate himself from his parents, the personality of the spouse plays a vital role in what follows. If the spouse has the resources to adopt a transient parental role, the problem may be overcome, but when both partners are attached to their parents, the situation is more complicated and there is a greater need for therapist intervention. A particularly severe form of this problem is the situation where one or both spouses feel that by marrying they are repudiating and harming their parents. This is a powerful fantasy which parents can exploit: 'We have given everything to you . . . look what you are doing to us now . . .'. The fantasy of 'killing' parents through commitment to one's spouse can lead to enormous emotional upheaval between a couple, who may not realize its source. In therapy they are shown that parents can survive extremely well without frequent visits, telephone calls, and advice, and are encouraged to establish for the first time their own separate family system. The marriage, of course, may have taken place against the wishes of one or both sets of parents. In these circumstances not only is the support of the parents missing, but the couple also have to defuse the hostility directed towards them.

Another twist of the disengagement pattern involves the husband more than the wife. He comes from a home where his mother has been the dominant force. Enough emotional distance was negotiated by the son to marry but an attachment with his mother characterized by a mixture of dependency and hostility remains. A similar type of relationship develops with his new wife: his hostility may be acted out by returning late regularly from work, using offensive language, getting drunk, or having an affair. This behaviour is intended to demonstrate that no woman is going to rule his life.

Even when detachment from parents does occur, a danger still exists that one partner may treat the other as a parental substitute. In the case of both partners seeing the other as a parental figure, they tend to idolize each other and have difficulty coping with hostile or ambivalent feelings. The relationship is inevitably unstable and particularly vulnerable to the growth of one partner who no longer has a need to cling; equilibrium of mutual overdependence is thereby disrupted. Since the presence of a child threatens the couple, they avoid having children and seek the abortion of an accidental pregnancy.

In some marriages we see the opposite of dependence, namely a fierce independence, in which the husband, usually, is battling with his fears of being submerged, exploited, or lost in the world of women. This independence may be associated with excessive participation in manly pursuits, defiance and stubborness against any exhibition of dependence on women, and usually an aloofness from any overt display of tenderness and intimacy.

Emotional cheating

Sometimes men and women choose what appears to them to be a secure, powerful, extroverted, and dominant partner only to discover that beneath the policeman, pilot, explorer, nurse, teacher, is a dependent, gentle, and anxious person. Those who sought their security in the picture of strength and dominance feel cheated and become angry and antagonistic towards their partner on discovering the discrepancy between appearance and reality.

The sense of being cheated is seen in a variety of other situations. For example, a couple may meet when one partner is ill or recovering from an injury and receive support and encouragement from the other. On the basis of this affection marriage follows and only then does the previously ill person discover that the interest and tenderness is limited to situations when he is 'down' in some way. Another example is the case of the spouse who exhibits a marked degree of jealousy. Shortly following marriage he begins to press his partner for information about previous relationships and how they compare with the present one. The answers do not satisfy him: tempers begin to get short and violent scenes may ensue. Such a person is often also sensitive to criticism and envious of qualities that his partner has but which he lacks. Finally a form of cheating is sometimes experienced in the move from courtship to marriage and the time that the couple now have for each other. The husband may feel himself attacked for being excessively busy at work and depriving his wife of her expectation that the amount of time spent together would continue as premaritally.

Children

The arrival of a child obviously has a major effect on any marriage. For some couples the threat of a reduction in mutual attention or the challenge of the new responsibility is so great that pregnancy is delayed as long as possible or avoided altogether. Sometimes one partner insists on having a child while the other is reluctant. If the husband finds the pregnancy and threat of a new infant too anxiety-provoking, he may seek comfort by having an affair or be unable to visit his wife at the hospital or ignore the arrival of the child. The baby may consume all the wife's attention and lead temporarily to her losing interest in the outside world and in her husband. She may become depressed although in most cases this is short-lived.

Social relationship

In some spouses (husbands in particular) a combination of factors lead to excessive drinking, gambling, or passing a great deal of time away from home with resultant disturbance in the social relationship. This disturbance may also show itself when the husband cannot handle financial matters such as payment of bills through social immaturity and the wife in turn may be unable to cope with household management.

Intellectual and spiritual relationship

Sometimes a marriage is entered into hurriedly without the partners' awareness of each other's intellectual abilities and interests or value and moral system. After a short while when the couple realize that they have little in common in these spheres their relationship is threatened and may well peter out.

Second phase

All the problems of the first phase discussed above may occur in the middle years. There are however some features unique to the second phase, most associated with change.

Physical relationship

No particular sexual problems occur in this phase apart from the wife's loss of interest in sex following the birth of her children and increased dissatisfaction in either partner with sex that has never been satisfactory but it was hoped would improve with time. Rarely, impotence, premature ejaculation, and persistent dyspareunia or inorgasmia may be the subject of complaint.

Emotional relationship

With the passage of time—as the couple gradually acquire more self-confidence and feel more differentiated in terms of their identity—their relationship inevitably changes. If one partner of an interdependent pair becomes more resilient, the security of the other is threatened. When a previously dependent wife, for example, grows more self-confident she may begin to insist on conducting activities formerly carried out by her husband: using the car, having her own set of friends, collaborating on financial decisions, and the like. Couples usually change together but, if the wife's change is unilateral and the husband opposes it, she may increasingly feel hemmed in, her freedom and independence curtailed. Initially conflict is emotional; later, as it escalates, the wife may show her anger by withdrawing from sex and finally, if the husband is unco-operative she may seek an alternative relationship. Unilateral change can occur in a marriage in which one spouse has always accepted blame for whatever went wrong. The spouse comes to perceive that this is unreasonable and is now unwilling to act as scapegoat. Such 'rebellion' throws the partner who now has to accept responsibility for his own actions.

The occurrence of unilateral change leads commonly to growth and positive movement in one spouse and deterioration in the emotional state of the partner. When such a couple seeks help, the therapist may unwittingly accelerate the change process, encouraging the growth of one partner with resulting adverse effects on the other. Sometimes the complete breakdown of the relationship follows as one partner discovers his strengths and no longer wishes to continue the marriage. In particular this may happen if the partner was previously satisfied with minimal affection or sexual fulfilment but now is not prepared to remain deprived in this way.

In the latter part of the second phase, either partner may face the crisis of 'middle-age'. For example, the husband may find that although he has reached a certain peak in his career he has not achieved his own private goals; the wife on entering her menopause may perceive it as the end of her feminity and sexuality (Dominian 1977). This is also a time when the children, now usually late adolescents, contribute problems of their own—their need for independence for instance—which commonly have an effect on the parents' marriage. Marital therapy may need to be supplemented or replaced by a family approach.

Social, intellectual, and spiritual relationship

Occasionally couples marry to achieve security at a social, intellectual, or spiritual level; they desire the 'status' of marriage rather than its emotional and sexual aspects. After a short-lived desultory effort at both the latter they seek a brother–sister type of relationship. No problems follow if both partners have married for similar reasons; with discrepant goals in marrying, the relationship is bound to become disturbed. Sometimes the social relationship may change because one partner has moved into a different social milieu leaving his spouse behind in the original setting whence they both came; this leads to conflict and ultimately to possible marital rupture.

Third phase

Sexual relationship

A problem may arise if there is a decline of interest in sex in one or other partner. Until the work of Masters and Johnson (1970), there had been a widely-held misconception that sexual interest and performance waned after middle-age, particularly in women. This misconception still lingers and can lead to difficulties in the sexual relationship.

Emotional relationship

The process of change that began in the second phase may continue into the third. This sometimes underlies the painful experience of a middle-aged wife whose husband has an affair or leaves her for a younger woman. There may be several reasons for the husband's behaviour including his need to ward off middle-age sexual identity anxieties, or his attempt to enjoy the freedom and range of activity—appropriate to a man of his twenties—at a much later age when self-confidence and ego differentiation make it possible.

A not uncommon marital 'syndrome' involves the couple whose emotional relationship throughout their married life has been exclusively via their children; when the children depart the couple find that they experience each other as emotional strangers for, although they have lived and slept under the same roof, their main channel of communication has been with and through their children. There is an emptiness now that is difficult to fill.

Social, intellectual, and spiritual relationship

Change over the years may leave a couple distant from one another as they discover that their values, and social and intellectual interests have drifted off in different directions.

Marital therapy in practice

Ideally marital therapy is conducted with both partners together. This immediately raises a possible problem: one spouse may refuse to participate. Whatever the reasons, every effort should be made by letter or through the presenting spouse to persuade the missing partner to attend at least once and for them to be seen preferably together as a couple. One reason for non-attendance is the spouse's belief that the problem lies entirely in the partner's attitudes and with these changed, all will be well. The missing spouse can be attracted by the therapist stating in his letter that he has heard one side of the story and now wishes to hear the other. Such an invitation usually succeeds since the spouse is often convinced that no justice can be done to his case unless he can present his point of view. Another reason for not attending is the partner's fear that he will have to endure a judgemental ticking-off. The therapist must point out therefore in his letter that he is not concerned in taking sides or passing judgement; rather, he is there to hear what both partners have to say and to clarify the issues raised by them. Thus, if a letter is couched in a non-judgemental way and simply invites attendance in order to complete the picture, most respondents will co-operate.

Sometimes, however, the therapist is left with one partner alone. Is this a contra-indication to marital therapy? Usually not, at least initially, because it is possible to clarify even with one partner, some of the issues which may lead to change in him and ultimately in the marital relationship. With both spouses attending, should they always be seen together? Therapists are not unanimous about this question but in general it is preferable that the couple are seen together on all occasions. This continuity allows the couple to participate in a joint effort in which both partners have the chance to recognize their respective contributions to the original conflicts and to work towards the resolution of these conflicts. There are exceptions to this pattern. A member of a couple may have such extensive needs that only individual attention to them, initially, will prepare the way for both members to work together in therapy at a later stage. Another possible programme, following an initial joint interview, is alternative sessions together and then separately. This arrangement may allow revelations which are extremely hostile, damaging, or embarrassing to be communicated separately to the therapist; he can then judge carefully when sufficient goodwill has been established between the couple to be able to handle a particularly threatening encounter.

In addition to these differing arrangements, the question arises of how many therapists should be involved with a couple. There is no clear cut answer (as there is none in sex therapy, see Chapter 8) and the therapist's preference will be determined by learning what he finds most comfortable—working either on his own or with a co-therapist of the opposite sex. Only properly conducted outcome studies can resolve this issue. In the remainder of this chapter, I shall continue to refer to the therapist in the singular although it should be realized that all that is said about his role and activity is equally relevant to a pair of co-therapists.

What does the therapist do in using a conjoint approach? Basically he plays active roles as facilitator and teacher, and through his words and actions aims to change the couple so that they can perceive the nature of their marital difficulties and learn new modes of relating towards one another.

The initial phase of therapy is divisible into four stages.

First stage (listening)—during this stage the therapist aims to take a history; he asks the couple for basic information such as age, occupation, number of children and their ages and sex, and the length of the marriage. He then requests that they tell their story and he records which spouse says what. While this takes place he notes the feelings expressed and the link between them and particular aspects of marital behaviour. The story is elicited with minimal prompting. The childhood experience of the spouses in terms of their relationships with their parents is also looked at. If the couple have difficulty relating their story, the therapist may assist them by taking them through the five levels of relationship (see page 153).

Second stage (assimilation)—while listening the therapist assimilates the information. He can interrupt when he does not understand: 'I am not sure what you mean; you seem to be saying; can you tell me more please?'. The therapist's next task is to summarize what he has heard: 'It seems to be John that your wife is complaining that you work too hard /come home late/ do not show her affection/ do not talk to her . . . You, Jean, according to John, are always complaining—'whatever he does is never good enough.' Such a summary is meant to highlight the main feelings involved, and their association with the behaviours regarded as unacceptable by the spouses.

At this point the couple may agree with the therapist's summary or modify it. Sometimes the spouses' complaints need more detailed examination. A wife complains that her husband wants too much sex. What is too much sex? A husband complains that his wife is extravagant. What is extravagance? The therapist may have to establish not only these sorts of details but also the facts, and produce a new definition of the problem. On occasion a summary produces a violent outburst. 'I have been telling you this for years. You don't believe me. I told you a long time ago that you are selfish/lazy/hopeless, etc.' The spouse may retort: 'This is the trouble. If I admit to anything, I never hear the end of it. I can never win an argument.' The therapist's role is to go beyond the discharge of such feelings and to help the couple to face the nature of their respective complaints.

Third stage (diagnosis)—the therapist continues to summarize the situation until the couple agree with the definition of the main problems. The diagnostic process can then unfold. This defines faulty patterns of communication, needs which are not met, and what type of behaviour is felt to be unacceptable. After agreement on these points, the therapist may interpret the reasons for these problems. Childhood experience, personality, psychological disturbance may all be used in offering an interpretation. The couple may realize for the first time how factors in their childhood influence their current behaviour. For example, an insecure childhood makes them feel uncertain and often jealous and possessive because they fear losing their spouse. A deprived childhood leads a spouse to claim more attention which makes him or her appear attention-seeking and childish. A previous anxious-type personality makes a spouse easily agitated, impulsive, quick-tempered. The therapist's task is to show the emotional fit of the couple. If they are, for instance, both excessively insecure, anxious, or deprived, they try to get out of each other more than is available.

Fourth stage (selection of goals)—having reached a point where the couple have some understanding of their problems the therapist identifies some targets which the couple need to work on at home. These targets may include better communication, an improved show of affection, more time spent together, assuming greater responsibility, showing less criticism or more mutual affirmation.

The couple, in the course of treatment, should perceive the way they see each other (that is the projections they place on each other), the power structure in their relationship, their manner of communication—both verbal and non-verbal, and the areas in which the minimum needs of each is not being met by the other. All this can be accomplished by the therapist's interpretations and, more importantly, by the way he imitates, in an exaggerated way, the couple's pattern of relating particularly their methods of communication. For example, he can highlight to them the not uncommon pattern of what I have referred to as a dialogue between the deaf; when one talks the other—instead of listening—switches off and waits until it is his turn to resume; hour after hour is spent merely putting one's own point across without registering what the other person is saying, or perceiving that the partner may have hurt and angry feelings. By drawing attention to this dialogue between the deaf, communication can be established perhaps for the first time, sometimes dramatically expressed by the crying or other intense emotion of one or both partners. Having promoted the couple's ability to register, therapy can proceed without having to start repeatedly from scratch. The partners are now more in touch with each other. Attention should also be drawn to the type of non-verbal communication between them: an expression of anger, eyes raised to the ceiling, a vacant look, clenched fists, swinging of the legs, a sarcastic smile, nodding of the head; all these convey a wealth of feeling and significance of which the partners have hitherto been unaware.

Within the framework of a trusting, safe relationship with the therapist, channels of communication develop and these in turn facilitate the expression of a wide range of feelings, many of which have been suppressed for months or years. As the floodgates open, each partner becomes aware of painful feelings in the other, sometimes for the first time. The process also reveals the defences that the couple have used in relation to themselves and to one another and, when these are gradually lowered, more intimate awareness of each partner's vulnerability ensues. Couples now comment: 'Of course I ignored that remark . . . it was too painful . . . but I can see now how important it is . . . I feel I can cope . . . I can see why I could never let you finish . . . I could not stand what was coming . . .'.

Examining the pattern of power in the marriage is another common task for the therapist. In a relationship in which the sharing of power has failed, endless battles are waged over who is boss. In these circumstances, the wife in particular complains that her husband makes demands on her without respecting her wishes and treats her as if she were a servant.

Hearing the story from the wife alone conjures up an image of the husband as a bully of a man. On interviewing the couple, this image may be confirmed, but in some cases the husband is found to be a meek, hen-pecked man who in despair at his wife's excessive demands, has begun to counter-attack and make demands of his own. The therapist plays a useful role in clarifying with the couple the pattern of the conflict for power; his objectives are that they recognize the nature of the conflict and develop respect for each other's separatedness and autonomy.

In addition to modifying the patterns of communication and sorting out the issues of power between the couple, the therapist consciously uses himself as a model for learning. What is often missing in disturbed marriages is the expression of tenderness and affection. The couple, having expressed anger and discovered the reasons for it, reach a pivotal point in their exchange in which one or both reveal a sense of not being sufficiently loved. The therapist, through his modelling, now demonstrates a whole range of methods by which love and tenderness can be expressed. For example, he can show that genuine listening enhances the sense of being received and of being made to feel significant. The partners' appreciation of one another can be increased by encouraging them to affirm the value and importance of what each says or does, e.g. 'that's true . . . quite right . . . I never saw it before in your way . . . yes I agree . . .'. There are couples who, throughout their marriage, have never uttered a single word of tenderness or affection to one another; the therapist has a great opportunity to try to break through this block and to demonstrate how qualities like gratitude and appreciation can be expressed in the most simple of ways, often with electrifying changes. When the couple need to learn how to express tenderness in physical terms, the therapist can lay his own hand gently on one spouse to act as a model for the partner. This is particularly useful in a spouse who has marked anxieties of a sexual kind; the therapist can help by demonstrating how a stroke or a hug can 'reach' the partner more effectively than words could ever do. The couple note that, if the therapist can be outgoing in this way, then it is alright to imitate him. The learning that occurs is more than mere imitation; the couple's repertoire of behaviour in relating to each other expands and generalizes beyond the therapy sessions.

Finally, a word on transference in marital therapy. The phenomenon of transference in this type of treatment differs to that which occurs in individual therapy (see Chapter 2). Disturbed relationships between both spouses and their respective parents tend to be revealed in treatment partly or wholly, in the way feelings and attitudes, such as dominance, submissiveness, resentment, envy, dependency, and competitiveness are projected on to each other. Valuables clues about these disturbed relationships in marriage emerge as therapy progresses. The therapist may also be the target of transferences from both partners. In this case, he deflects the feelings expressed towards him, that is he minimizes these transferences by encouraging the couple to focus on *their* relationship rather than on the patient–therapist one, and by interpreting the projections they place on each other. This aspect of therapy is discussed in detail by Dicks (1967).

A behavioural model for marital therapy

The approach to the practice of marital therapy as described above is basically eclectic in nature, although it rests in part on psychoanalytic theory. An alternative model that has come into use in recent years is based on principles of behaviour therapy and employs techniques such as contingency reinforcement and operant conditioning (Stuart 1969; Liberman 1970; Crowe 1973).

Again, husband and wife are seen together. Particular attention is paid to the taking of a careful history of the presenting problems. In the process, the therapist assesses both areas of conflict and areas of satisfaction in the marriage in order to set up a hierarchy of the needs of each partner. The husband may, for example, want more sex or forgiveness and understanding for an extra-marital affair. The wife may want greater time spent together at home or more tenderness in lovemaking or more open communication. The principle underlying this approach is that both partners give to the other something they need or want and receive something in return. A case history illustrates the principle.

The wife was a medical practitioner, her husband a lawyer. Her main complaint on entering therapy was that, although the marriage could coast along well for long periods, when a crisis befell the family, severe marital strife would immediately follow. Just prior to treatment, their son had changed schools and was very unhappy at the new one. The mother, who had bitter memories of her own unhappy childhood in boarding schools, became agitated on receiving a letter from her son spelling out his misery. She began to press her husband to decide there and then what action should be taken. He replied characteristically that he wanted time to consider the problem and that he was not in a position to offer an instant decision. Dissatisfied with this reaction, she insisted all the more that he come up with a solution. The conflict between them continued into the early hours of the morning with the wife becoming more and more strident and the husband increasingly withdrawn. At a certain point however, he attacked her both verbally and physically. This episode was one of many which had occurred over the years and had led to an insecurity in the wife that her husband was no longer able to understand her and was no longer willing to help her at times when she felt anxious. Following these rows, the wife would invariably become cool sexually and a prolonged period would ensue before the sexual relationship was resumed.

The problem was clear-cut: the wife needed to share her anxiety with her husband over a problem like their son's unhappiness. The husband resented bitterly the long periods of sexual withdrawal by his wife and saw her action as extremely punitive. The therapist made no attempt to interpret the problems in dynamic terms. Instead, he arranged for the couple to negotiate a contract by which their needs would be respected by one another. Thus, the husband would make every effort to support his wife when she felt under pressure because of stressful circumstances. At the onset of such stress, the wife would inform her husband of her need for support; he in turn would not withdraw into silence but attempt to show his willingness to help. She agreed that she would not demand a specific solution to the problem at hand. She also promised not to use withdrawal from sex as a weapon against him. He in turn was encouraged to appreciate that he did not have to provide an immediate solution but simply to display a willingness to be involved in tackling the problem. Within a few weeks of the contract being set, the husband discovered that he could provide the support his wife wanted; she was satisfied with his new attitude, did not demand immediate solutions from him, and had no need to resort to sexual withdrawal. Their joint approach to problems led to a greater intimacy in their relationship in general.

The use of a behavioural approach, as illustrated above, enables the couple to bypass the dynamic factors underlying their problems and to plunge directly into dealing with these problems. The treatment also has the appeal of simplicity and is suited to couples in whom interpretation may mobilize more anxiety than they can cope with. For a detailed description of this form of marital therapy the reader is referred to the article by Stuart (1969).

Marital therapy in groups

Both the dynamic and behavioural methods can be applied to groups of three or four couples treated together (Gottlieb and Pattison 1966; Blinder and Kirschenbaum 1967). These groups can be composed of couples from the same or different phases of the marriage cycle. The group usually meets weekly for 90 minutes over

a period of some months to discuss the problems of all the participating couples. The approach enables each couple to recognize that
their problems are not unique to their marriage alone, and to learn
from the experience of their peers. Placing a couple in a non-couples
group or referring each partner to a separate group are alternatives,
but carry no special advantages and are therefore not favoured.
Liberman and his colleagues have studied couples' groups and in
comparing behavioural and dynamic approaches found the former
to be superior (Liberman, Levine, Wheeler, Sanders, and Wallace
1976). A limiting factor in the study, and in others similar to it, is the
lack of knowledge at present about patterns of marital pathology; in
comparing different marital therapy techniques we cannot be certain
that the *same* problems are being treated.

Usual course of treatment

Following the initial interview the therapist assesses how to proceed
with therapy. If only one spouse has come an attempt will be made,
as described earlier, to involve the other. Having got both partners
together, what practical steps follow? Ideally, the couple should be
seen together at intervals of between one and four weeks. The frequency is dictated by the following factors.

If the couple have manifold and complex problems which need to
be clarified and understood before any progress can be made,
intervals should be weekly or bi-weekly. Similar frequencies are indicated when anger and hostility are so marked that incessant rows
simply poison the therapeutic atmosphere, and in the case of spouses
who both have particular personal needs which require the
therapist's active intervention. Once the couple have sufficient
awareness of their problems or the hostility has abated or their individual needs have been met, intervals between sessions can be
increased. In effective marital therapy, the couple should achieve
some new insights and more effective coping mechanisms in each
session; they then need time to apply what they have learnt to the
marriage and discover *in vivo* what changes occur. After this is
accomplished, the frequency of sessions can be reduced to monthly
or six-weekly.

There are three common patterns of outcome. Firstly, one
(sometimes both) partner is adamant in not wanting reconciliation,
convinced that the marriage has ended. The reason he has come is to
have the therapist drive home the point to the reluctant partner or to

make the therapist responsible for her welfare and thus assuage his guilt for leaving her. The second pattern is the most rewarding to the therapist: through treatment the couple gain insight, develop a new effective mode of relating, and the marriage is happily reconstructed. In the third pattern of outcome, the marriage neither progresses nor deteriorates, but continues to go through ups and downs with the couple reluctant to stop therapy.

Each of these patterns is associated with a more or less predictable length of therapy. In the first pattern only three or four sessions are necessary to establish the irreconcilable nature of the marriage. The patient unwilling to separate may however experience a depressive reaction, comparable to mourning, and require counselling for several months. Occasionally the depression is sufficiently intense or prolonged to warrant hospital admission. In the second pattern, treatment lasts between three and twelve months. Usually, the partners are seen at the outset at one or two weekly intervals, later monthly, until it is clear to the therapist that insight and co-operation are well established. The third pattern poses difficulties. How long should treatment continue with a marriage that appears 'stuck' with no movement one way or another? In theory, the therapist could persevere indefinitely but generally, after several months of effort, involving between six and twelve sessions, he should point out the static nature of the situation and suggest that treatment stop and the couple return when they feel more prepared to work at their relationship.

Therapy terminates in a variety of ways: one spouse refuses to continue and the other sees no point in coming either; both partners are happy with the outcome and suggest termination—this is accepted by the therapist or he recommends additional interviews to confirm their sense of optimism; the therapist takes the initiative and indicates that no further therapy is required, or that there is little purpose in continuing at this stage. With the conclusion of therapy follow-up may take one of several forms. The therapist informs the couple that he will contact them by letter six months later to enquire about progress and to consider if further help is called for. In any event, he would like to hear from them at any time should they wish to communicate. Should the therapist have some concern at the conclusion of treatment, he may arrange to see the couple some weeks later.

Problems in the course of treatment

We have already discussed one problem encountered in marital therapy—the spouse who is unwilling even to participate; and suggested methods to overcome it. Once both partners are involved, perhaps the most important problem that the therapist has to contend with is the overt or subtle labelling of one of them by the other as 'the patient'. In fact, commonly in marital therapy, one spouse seeks professional help because he has reached an intolerable level of anxiety or depression. As in family therapy where the therapist has to ensure that no one member becomes the collective bearer of the family's difficulties—the scapegoat—so in treating a couple great care needs to be taken not to label one partner as sick and more in need of help than the other. The therapist emphasizes from the outset that the problem to be tackled is the relationship between the couple not either member of it. The therapist's task is made more complicated if one spouse has recently been treated in his own right as a patient or been psychiatrically hospitalized. Should he be receiving medication, this can be used as evidence by his partner that the problem lies with him alone. Indeed, the partner may go further by constantly reminding him that he is the 'patient', the 'mad' one and, if psychiatric admission has occurred, hold over his head the threat that another in-patient admission may be necessary unless he 'behaves' himself. For this reason the therapist should use medication judiciously in the context of marital treatment, and only when one or other partner presents evidence of, for example, a distinct depressive illness or anxiety state. In some cases of course one partner may be suffering from a psychiatric disorder unrelated to the marital problem. This patient should be helped first in his own right and marital therapy instituted thereafter, again bearing in mind the danger of the other partner's continuing to exploit the sick label.

Training

Marital therapy can be learnt in many ways. Professionals such as doctors, nurses, social workers, and psychologists can apply to one of the national marriage guidance councils for training or to certain specialist centres (in Britain the Tavistock Clinic and the Institute of Family Therapy are examples). Whatever training is obtained, its most important component is clinical experience under supervision. One-way screens and videotape are effective techniques which can enhance the supervisory process. Novices can also learn through observing or acting as co-therapist with experienced practitioners. Acquaintance with the relevant literature is useful preparation; the Recommended Reading list provided at the end of this chapter is a convenient starting-point.

Conclusion

Marital therapy is a relative newcomer to the field of psychotherapy. As there is little systematic research to guide the therapist at present, probably his best course is to adopt a flexible attitude and to apply techniques from any source which appear to be helpful. At the start of the chapter we discussed the impact of recent social changes on the institution of marriage and on the treatment directed to problems within it. Undoubtedly the institution of marriage will continue to change in all sorts of ways; marital therapy will have to keep pace and remain sufficiently malleable to accommodate these changes.

References

Blinder, M. G. and Kirschenbaum, M.(1967). The technique of married couple group therapy, *Archs gen. Psychiat.* **17**, 44–52.

Cherlin, A. J. (1981). *Marriage, divorce and remarriage.* Harvard University Press, Cambridge, Mass.

Crowe, M. J. (1973). Conjoint marital therapy: advice or interpretation, *J. psychosom. Res.* **17**, 309–15.

Dicks, H. V. (1967). *Marital tensions.* Routledge and Kegan Paul, London.

Dominian, J. (1968). *Marital breakdown.* Penguin, Harmondsworth.

—— (1972) Marital pathology, *Post-grad. med. J.* **48**, 517–25.

—— (1977). The role of psychiatry in the menopause, *Clinics Obstet. Gynaecol.* **4**, 241–58.

Gottlieb, A. and Pattison, E. M. (1966). Married couples group psychotherapy, *Archs gen. Psychiat.* **14**, 143–52.

HMSO (1983) *Population trends*, No. 33. London.

Klein, M. (1965). *Contributions to psychoanalysis.* Hogarth, London.

Kuhn, J. R. (1973). *Marriage counselling: fact or fallacy.* Newcastle, Los Angeles, Calif.

Levinger, G. (1966). Sources of marital dissatisfaction among applicants of divorce, *Am. J. Orthopsychiat.* **36**, 803–7.

Liberman, R. (1970). Behavioural approaches to family and couple therapy, *Am. J. Orthopsychiat.* **40**, 106–18.

——, Levine, J., Wheeler, E., Sanders, N., and Wallace, C. J. (1976). Marital therapy in groups. A comparative evaluation of behavioural and interactional formats. *Acta psychiat. scand.* Supp. 266.

Masters, W. H. and Johnson, V. E. (1970). *Human sexual inadequacy.* Churchill, London.

Stuart, R. B. (1969). Operant-interpersonal treatment for marital discord, *J. consult. clin. Psychol.* **33**, 675–82.

Winch, R. F. (1958). *Mate selection: a study of complementarity needs.* Harper, New York.

Winnicott, D. W. (1965). *The maturational processes and the facilitating environment.* Hogarth, London.

Recommended reading

Crowe, M. J. (1973). Conjoint marital therapy: advice or interpretation, *J. psychosom. Res.* **17**, 309–15. (Contains a clear description of the behavioural approach.)

Dicks, H. V. (1967). *Marital tensions.* Routledge and Kegan Paul, London. (Chapters 4–7 are especially valuable as an introduction to the psychoanalytic approach.)

Dominian, J. (1980). *Marital pathology.* Darton, Longman and Todd, London.

—— (1980). *Make or break: an introduction to marital counselling.* SPCK, London.

Gurman, A. S. and Kniskern, B. P. (1978). Research on marital and family therapy: progress, perspectives and prospect. In *Handbook of psychotherapy and behaviour change* (eds. Garfield, S. L. and Bergin, A. E.). Wiley, New York. (Includes a review of the effectiveness of marital therapy.)

Liberman, R. P., Levine, J., Wheeler, E., Sanders, N., and Wallace, C. J. (1976). Marital therapy in groups: a comparative evaluation of behavioural and interactional formats. *Acta psychiat. scand.* Supp. 266. (An important study comparing behavioural group and dynamic group approaches.)

Skynner, A. C. (1976). *One flesh, separate persons. Principles of family and marital psychotherapy.* Constable, London. (Comprehensive volume on the theory and application of family and marital therapy.)

8

Sex therapy

John Bancroft

In this chapter Bancroft concentrates on the treatment of the couple who present with sexual dysfunction. Following an account of the development of sex therapy he describes the treatment method—both its behavioural and psychotherapeutic components. The therapist's role in the latter is especially emphasized. Three clinical examples follow to illustrate various aspects of the therapy. The chapter ends with a section on some practical considerations.

The 1970s saw a remarkable increase both in the availability of treatment for sexual problems and in the demand for it. Masters and Johnson (1970) have pioneered this development, most of the current forms of 'new sex therapy' being derived from their approach. Their methods have been pragmatic, not based on any school or theoretical model of psychotherapy or behaviour change. Other workers in the field have also been refreshingly eclectic (e.g. Kaplan 1975) and this is one area of psychological treatment where collaboration and cross-fertilization of ideas between therapists from different theoretical backgrounds has occurred. The relatively circumscribed nature of the clinical problems—sexual dysfunction—and the ways in which they interact with a wide variety of other psychological and interpersonal processes, make contemporary sex therapy not only comparatively manageable, but also relevant to problems and therapies of a more general kind.

Much of the current emphasis is on the couple or the sexual relationship. This reflects a recent, widespread reaction against the traditional psychiatric concern with the individual patient, manifesting itself in the emergence of group, family, and marital therapy. Perhaps the pendulum is already swinging back: an interesting contrast between American and European sex therapy is the recent emergence of counselling, group processes, and self-help programmes for the enhancement of a woman's own sexuality. Often there is a specific goal of helping a non-orgasmic woman become orgasmic, but individually through masturbation. This trend appears to be part of a wider 'consciousness-raising' movement among American women which has not yet had the same impact in Europe.

This chapter will concentrate on treatment of the couple since this is still the most common form of help provided and because in many respects it is easier than individual therapy, for reasons which will become clear. Gaining experience with couple therapy is probably the best first step, before becoming involved with the individual patient. Some attention will be paid to individual therapy however, because a proportion of patients present for help without sexual partners. At the present time, at least in Britain, these are much more likely to be men than women, but this may well change with further shifts in sexual attitudes. Only the treatment of sexual dysfunction will be discussed in this chapter. Problems associated with sexual preference, gender identity, and deviant forms of sexual behaviour will not be considered. The reader is referred elsewhere for discussion of these areas (Bancroft 1974, 1983).

The category of sexual dysfunction traditionally covers such problems as erectile failure, premature or delayed ejaculation, and the inability of the woman to experience orgasm or to become sexually aroused. Whilst these 'target-organ responses' are a fundamental part of the problem, it is important to deal with them in the context of a sexual relationship, or, for the individual, the sexual self-image. As yet, a satisfactory classificatory system which incorporates both the physiological, and the psychological and interpersonal aspects has not been devised. But as will be seen, a large part of the sex therapy advocated here is aimed at interpersonal aspects.

The goals of sex therapy can be broadly defined as follows:

(a) Helping the individual to accept and feel comfortable with his or her own sexuality.
(b) Helping the couple to improve the quality of their sexual relationship.

Often problems under (a) have to be faced when dealing with (b). These goals are purposely broad and vague. Many sex therapists define much more specific goals such as 'becoming orgasmic' or 'delaying premature ejaculation'. I regard these treatment goals as collluding with the 'performance anxiety' and 'goal orientation' that often underlie the individual's or couple's problems, and prefer to direct them towards a more general improvement which is likely to result in specific changes eventually. This is a controversial issue as, for example, there are many who feel that a person is entitled to experience an orgasm, whether in or out of a relationship, and hence this is something worth striving for in its own right. These issues are inextricably caught up with the values that we personally attribute to sex and we must form our own opinion on these points.

The treatment method

Sex therapy is a good example of 'behavioural psychotherapy', the principles of which are as follows:

(1) Clearly defined and appropriate tasks are given and the patient asked to attempt them before the next session.

(2) Those attempts and any difficulties encountered are examined in detail.

(3) Attitudes, feelings, and resistances that make those behavioural tasks difficult are identified.

(4) Those attitudes, etc. are modified so that achievement of the behavioural tasks becomes possible.

(5) The next behavioural tasks are set, and so on.

A basic feature of this approach is that the patient or couple always has something *to do* between treatment sessions. Usually these tasks are small steps towards the final goals, though they may involve keeping records or otherwise monitoring behaviour as part of the analysis necessary for treatment. In sex therapy for couples, these behavioural steps are relatively standardized, at least in the early stages of treatment. I give the couple a set of notes, describing these tasks, to take home with them. (these notes are printed in full in Bancroft 1983).

There are other basic principles of this approach that need to be made explicit at the beginning of treatment.

(a) The responsibility for change lies with the patient or couple

This is not a curative process, where responsibility lies with the therapist as in the treatment of acute physical illness. The therapist provides expert help to the patient who has responsibility to make constructive use of that help. This is an 'adult–adult' type of relationship between patient and therapist, in which the latter can contribute nothing unless the patient is prepared to attempt the behavioural tasks recommended. This issue has been developed further in Chapter 5. It is necessary not only to make this point explicit at the outset but to return to it repeatedly, either because of the patient's previous expectations of medical help or because of his tendency to slip into a dependent and passive relationship with professional helpers. Failure to get the patient to accept this responsibility means failure of the treatment approach. Consistent with this form of therapeutic relationship is the need to agree on the frequency and timing of sessions, and the need for the patient or couple to have sufficient time to carry out home assignments, free from major distractions such as moving house, changing job, or having mother-in-law to stay. Sometimes it is appropriate to delay the start of treatment until a reasonable period, free from such distractions, lies ahead.

(b) The approach includes a basic educational component

The objective of sex therapy is for the patient or couple to learn certain principles 'of interacting that not only will improve the current situation but can be made use of in the future when similar-type problems may be encountered. It is not sufficient therefore for behavioural improvement alone to occur. The patient should have an understanding of how that improvement has occurred. In this respect it is often useful for a couple to experience a set-back before treatment is concluded so that they have the opportunity to reapply the principles that were learned earlier. In this way, they can gain confidence that if such set-backs were to occur again, they would be able to cope with them without having to seek professional help.

It is nevertheless important to realize that there is more to sex therapy than education. It is true that in a proportion of cases, the therapist need only set appropriate behavioural goals, instruct the couple in basic principles of communication, and provide information on anatomical and physiological aspects of sex—here the educational approach is at its simplest. Most often, however difficulties are encountered in carrying out the behavioural tasks, and helping the patient to overcome these difficulties requires particular therapeutic skills; these will be considered later in the chapter.

The treatment approach will therefore be presented under two headings; the Behavioural Component and the Psychotherapeutic Component. I will first describe in detail the behavioural steps involved in a typical case of sex therapy with couples, and then discuss common behavioural approaches in individual sex therapy. The psychotherapeutic component is similar whether one works with a couple or an individual.

The behavioural component with the couple

The behavioural component of sex therapy with a couple can commence almost immediately without waiting until a detailed history is taken. Limited physical contact for example can be suggested whatever the nature of the couple's problems allowing the therapist and hence the couple to learn from the difficulties that are encountered in tackling these initial stages. There is no quicker way of finding out the relevant issues in a relationship than giving the couple a joint collaborative task, particularly of this kind.

If, on the other hand, these early stages are carried out without difficulty, nothing is lost and the couple can progress quickly on to the next stage. Treatment of this kind is therefore always a parallel process of behavioural change and discovery. It is essential to emphasize this special effect of combining limited but carefully chosen behavioural goals with careful analysis of the difficulties encountered in carrying them out. Some behaviourally-oriented therapists regard these difficulties as irritants, obstructing progress. They are misled, because the recognition and resolution of these difficulties is an essential ingredient of the therapeutic process.

The fact that in therapy with the couple we can use a standard behavioural programme, at least in the early stages, makes this form of treatment much easier for the inexperienced therapist than a method which has to be individually tailored. It is nevertheless important to remember that resistances to behavioural change that are likely to occur will be varied and idiosyncratic and it is this aspect of treatment which presents a challenge to the therapist. Having a clearly defined behavioural framework however gives him confidence and a secure base from which to operate. Let us now look at this behavioural programme in more detail; it can be divided into six stages, regardless of the nature of the sexual dysfunction.

Stage 1

Each partner is asked to practise 'self-asserting' and 'self-protecting', that is, making quite clear what 'I' like, prefer, or find unpleasant or threatening. Beginning a statement with 'I would like . . .' or 'I feel hurt because . . .' instead of the more usual 'shall we . . .?' or 'why don't you . . .? is often difficult. The customary method of communication, regarded as unselfish, is to think or guess what your partner would like rather than putting your wishes first. This frequently goes wrong, and because of reluctance to hurt the partner, misunderstandings remain concealed and usually persist. Providing both partners are able to state their own wishes, there is no cause for resentment, no misunderstanding, and differences of opinion can be resolved by open negotiation. The therapist should advise the couple to try this style of communication in relatively trivial, non-sexual situations before using it during the sexual tasks (e.g. 'I would like a cup of tea, would you?'). The emphasis is on the word 'I'. This fundamental principle is incorporated throughout the rest of the treatment programme.

The specially sexual goal in Stage 1 consists of *'touching your partner without genital contact and for your own pleasure'*. An explicit agreement is made to ban all attempts at intercourse as well as genital or breast contact during this stage. This ban is important for reducing performance anxiety, and allowing both partners to feel safe. It is an effective way of testing trust in the relationship, often of crucial importance. Breaking the ban, or reluctance to keep it, can provide valuable information for the therapist as will be illustrated later. The couple are asked to have no more than three sessions of lovemaking before next seeing the therapist; this is to avoid too much happening, as only a limited amount can be properly discussed at the next appointment. When those sessions occur depends entirely on the couple, and obviously the more spontaneous the better. But they are asked to alternate in who suggests a session and to agree as to who will be the first to initiate. On these occasions, the person who has 'invited' starts by touching the partner's body, other than the out-of-bounds areas, in whatever way is found pleasurable; the objective is for the toucher to enjoy the touching. The partner being touched has only to 'self-protect'—to say stop if anything unpleasant is experienced. After a while roles are reversed and the person who has been touched now does the touching in the same way. They should not expect to get strongly aroused by this, though they sometimes do. The goal is simply to enjoy the process in a relaxed way. This stage is often difficult for couples to grasp as they are so conditioned to think of touching as a way of giving pleasure rather than receiving it. This can lead to their recognition of deeply held attitudes, such as 'you should only enjoy sex if you are giving pleasure to someone else'—which may be of central importance in the overall problem.

The therapist ensures, by careful inquiry, that these behavioural steps have been carried out with both partners feeling relaxed and secure before proceeding to Stage 2.

Stage 2

'Touching your partner without genital contact, for your own, AND your partner's pleasure.' Sessions continue as before with the initiator alternating, and touching done by one person at a time. Now, however, the person being touched gives feedback of what is enjoyable as well as what is unpleasant. The toucher can use this information to give as well as to receive pleasure. There is still a ban on genital contact.

Sometimes a partner expresses concern that the ban on intercourse will lead to unresolved sexual arousal and frustration. Reassurance is given that usually unpleasant frustration of this kind only arises if one is not clear what to expect, i.e. if the possibility of going on to intercourse or genital stimulation remains. Clear and explicit acceptance of limits on these activities generally avoids this. However, if after a session either partner is left feeling aroused and in need of orgasm, then it is acceptable for them to masturbate individually but not as a pair.

At an appropriate point during the first two or three sessions, the therapist should describe in a straightforward didactic way, the main points about the anatomy and physiology of sexual response in both sexes, emphasizing those aspects which are commonly misunderstood and often underlie sexual dysfunction. This short 'lecture' should be given however sophisticated the couple may be; it is rare for a couple to be aware of all the points the therapist will cover. This is also an opportunity to establish a suitable vocabulary that can be used for discussion and reporting back during the genital stage of the programme.

Stage 3

Touching with genital contact. The same principles of alternating in touching apply, but the genital areas and breasts can now be included. The position adopted by the couple for this purpose should be discussed with them; they should be encouraged to explore and decide on positions that suit them best. Careful questions about their reactions to different positions may reveal important feelings and attitudes.

Communicating to one's partner what is enjoyable about the touching often presents difficulties at this stage. It is necessary for the therapist to emphasize that pleasure varies from occasion to occasion and that it is therefore important for the couple always to keep open the channels of communication between them. Their only goal is to relax and enjoy the experience. The partner being caressed may or may not become sexually aroused; the occurrence of ejaculation or orgasm does not matter and need not signify an end to the session, but orgasm should not be the goal.

From the start of treatment, the couple have been told about the 'spectator role'—becoming a detached observer of what is happening to oneself or to one's partner rather than a participant. Detachment is likely to generate performance anxiety and interfere with normal sexual response; it can only be effectively avoided by actively pursuing some other mental activity. One useful method is to concentrate on the local sensations experienced whilst touching or being touched, i.e. 'lend oneself to the sensations'; if this is insufficient, the person carries out a simple relaxation procedure, and if that fails, informs the partner that the problem has arisen and suggests a temporary halt to the session. After a short period of conversation or other activity the session can be resumed.

When premature ejaculation is a problem, the couple are also introduced to the 'stop-start' (Kaplan 1975) or 'squeeze' techniques at this stage (Masters and Johnson 1970) and asked to incorporate either of them into the genital touching sessions. (The reader is directed to the two references for details of these techniques.) In the case of vaginismus, gradual vaginal dilatation with finger or graded dilators is used. The timing of these aspects of the programme and whether they should be carried out on an individual or conjoint basis remains variable (Kaplan 1975), though Masters and Johnson (1970) adhere to a fairly fixed procedure. This point will be discussed further in relation to individual therapy.

Stage 4

Simultaneous touching with genital contact. Touching is done by both partners simultaneously. It is important not to move on to this stage until both partners are comfortable with the preceding stages; often important problems, particularly those related to the ability for taking the initiative or of being assertive, are only clarified when touching is done by each partner in turn.

Stage 5

Vaginal containment. Once genital and general body touching is progressing well and the male is achieving reasonably firm erections (or has started to gain control over ejaculation during manual stimulation), the couple can move on to the next stage of vaginal containment. Although initially there was a ban on intercourse, the couple should have been discouraged from regarding their love-making as divided into foreplay and intercourse; until now they have experienced a wide range of physical contact over which they were able to set and accept limits. Now, during the course of a touching session, the woman introduces the penis into her vagina, having first adopted the female superior position. This not only makes it easier for her to guide the penis in but also means that the man remains in a 'non-demand position' with the woman in control and able to stop or withdraw whenever she wants. At first the couple are instructed to try short periods of this vaginal containment without any other movement or pelvic thrusting, simply concentrating on the sensations of the 'penis being contained' or the 'vagina being filled'. The length of time can be gradually prolonged. This stage then merges into *Stage 6* when movement and pelvic thrusting are allowed although initially for only short periods. Again, one is trying to break down the 'big divide' between foreplay and intercourse which, if present, provokes anxiety whenever the step from one to the other is anticipated. Instead a continuum of behavioural steps is involved merging into intercourse.

The couple are encouraged to practise stopping at any point in the sequence at the request of one or other partner. This is to counter the common notion that once loveplay has begun it must continue until its physiological conclusion, with no escape for either partner *en route.* The feeling of confidence that at any stage during lovemaking either one can say 'stop' without incurring anger or hurt in the partner is a fundamental feature of a good, secure sexual relationship. Once the confidence is there, the need to say stop will seldom arise. In addition the couple are encouraged to experiment with different positions and methods of touching one another to discover what is most satisfying to them and to provide some variety.

The behavioural component in individual therapy

I have already expressed a definite preference for working with couples whenever possible. But the assumption that this is superior remains to be properly demonstrated and we should consider the cases in which individual therapy may be indicated. The most obvious category is those people without current sexual partners. There are also those who have sexual partners but where the partners are not willing to participate in couple therapy; this presents a problem, as the partner's refusal implies a negative quality to the relationship. In my view, individual treatment is only appropriate if there is a clear-cut and appropriate goal which does not depend on the co-operation or even involvement of a partner for its attainment. The person with inhibited attitudes about sex, who feels uncomfortable with his or her body and sexual responses comes into this category. Other examples include vaginismus, when the woman is unable to allow anything into her vagina, such as tampons, her own or the doctor's examining finger; and inability to experience orgasm during masturbation in either men or women. Sometimes when erectile difficulties or premature ejaculation are marked even during masturbation individual therapy may be worthwhile.

But should we ever work with such an individual when the partner is prepared to co-operate in couple therapy? This is again a point on which we should keep an open mind. With vaginismus, there may be women, especially those with marked phobic features or personality problems, in whom individual therapy may precede or even obviate the need for couple therapy. A current view among some female sex therapists in America who work with anorgasmic women, either individually or in groups, is that the experience of self-induced orgasm through non-couple oriented sex therapy has such an enhancing effect on self-esteem and sexual self-image that improvement in their sexual relationship readily follows (Barbach 1976). The mutually supportive function of a group of like-minded women treated together may play an important part in this respect.

It is also worth considering that there is a long tradition of treating non-consummation due to vaginismus by working with the woman alone. This has been established in the British Family Planning Association under the initial guidance of Michael Balint (Tunnadine 1970). The main emphasis of treatment is on the vaginal examination and the woman's emotional reactions to it. Only female doctors are involved and a major theme is the 'giving of permission' by an older or authoritative figure.

Having decided to work with the individual rather than the couple, the behavioural programme is likely to be more varied and less standardized. However, in a large proportion of cases, the goals of treatment are related to 'increasing comfort with one's body' and a self-touching and exploration approach directly comparable to Stages 1, 2 and 3 of couple therapy can be employed. The use of sexual aids such as vibrators may be useful, particularly in helping women to experience orgasm for the first time. Their place in couple therapy remains less certain. (For a description of this sort of programmes, see Heiman, Lopiccolo, and Lopiccolo 1976.)

More varied in their needs and more taxing of the therapist are patients whose principal problem lies in the area of 'socio-sexual approach behaviour'—difficulty in initiating and maintaining the early stages of a sexual or potentially sexual relationship. In these cases, the therapist obviously lacks the advantage of seeing the patient interact with a partner that is provided during couple therapy. He needs to conduct a careful and time-consuming 'behavioural analysis' of recent attempts at dating or courting in order to identify the most likely reason for failure. Once again it is advantageous to have the patient actively involved at the earliest opportunity. Even though several sessions of careful history taking may be necessary in some cases before an appropriate behavioural programme is devised, it is often possible to start the work of therapy without delay with 'self-touching programmes' or by giving the patient the task of carefully monitoring his own behaviour between sessions. Eventually a programme of approach behaviours can be decided upon. Thus he may be asked to decide which particular woman he is going to approach during the next week, and what the nature of that approach will be, e.g. invitation to join him for lunch in the work canteen, or to go out for a drink. There is again a need to set limits to the behaviour that is attempted; since the agreement of the as yet uninvolved partner is not obtainable, various strategies that will enable the patient to set limits without loss of face may need to be worked out and rehearsed.

As a general principle it is valuable to emphasize that only a pro-portion of potential partners will be suitable for such an approach, that selection is necessary, and some misjudgement inevitable. Also it is almost always helpful for the patient to be able to share his sexual anxieties with a partner at an appropriate time and certainly before engaging in overt sexual behaviour. With suitable selection, there is a reasonable chance that the chosen partner also has similar anxieties and being able to share these is virtually half the battle won. The therapist has an important educational task, informing the patient what he can expect and, as important, what will be expected of him, and how his behaviour may be interpreted by the partner. There are obvious advantages in having either the same-sex therapist—who can provide a model of the experienced male or female—or an opposite-sex therapist who can offer insight into what will be expected of the patient. When therapists of either sex are available, the main needs of the particular patient should be con-sidered in making the choice. The presence of phobic anxiety about the opposite sex or the likelihood that the opposite-sex parent played an important role in reinforcing negative sexual attitudes, would be indications for using an opposite-sex therapist.

The psychotherapeutic component

The setting up of behavioural tasks is the relatively easy part of sex therapy, especially when working with couples. Helping the patient overcome obstacles to carrying out the behaviour is really the essence of the therapeutic process. By planning specific tasks with the patient, the therapist is 'giving him permission' and perhaps implicitly countering any negative attitudes or fears he may have. In some couples the setting of agreed limits and the provision of basic information by a third person may so reduce performance anxiety that normal sexual responses occur. In these cases, which respond with gratifying speed, it is especially important to ensure that the couple have learned how they overcame the problem and do not remain dependent on the involvement of an authoritative outsider. Otherwise, relapse is likely to occur sooner or later. It is in many respects reassuring to encounter difficulties during therapy as this probably indicates that relevant tasks are being directly tackled.

A discerning therapist may recognize a wide variety of individual and interpersonal problems in the course of treatment. One advantage of sex therapy is that attention can be focused on those problems, and on fears or attitudes, which are obstructing achievement of therapeutic goals. In this way the therapist avoids being side-tracked into other less relevant areas. Although the problems that hinder progress are varied, certain themes occur commonly and can be categorized under four headings: misunderstanding about the treatment and its aims; ignorance or incorrect expectations about sex; negative or inhibiting sexual attitudes; and problems in the relationship, especially unresolved resentment and conflicts.

(a) *Misunderstanding about the treatment*

Before a therapist can expect a couple to apply specific behavioural recommendations, it is reasonable to ensure that the couple understand why they are being given these assignments and accept the reasoning behind them. The rationale has to be explained, therefore, in terms suitable for the particular couple. The patient has a right to understand: this approach has no place for the mystique which surrounds so many forms of psychotherapy. Difficulty in achieving understanding and acceptance may stem from the therapist's failure to explain adequately or from a negative therapist–patient relationship. In some cases the style of the treatment conflicts with personal values about sex. Commonly a couple complain that they dislike the lack of spontaneity involved in the therapy: the feeling that the therapist is not only instructing them what to do but looking over their shoulder at what should be a private, intimate affair. This is an understandable objection but it should be gently and firmly pointed out that they are in this position because they have a problem, that the intervention by the therapist is intended as a temporary bridge between the present unsatisfactory state of affairs and a new mutually rewarding and spontaneous sexual relationship. It is worth adding that although the therapist does take a fairly authoritative role initially in setting limits and suggesting behavioural steps, this control will be transferred progressively to the couple as treatment proceeds. The therapist also needs to remind himself repeatedly of this fundamental point.

Apparent difficulty in accepting the treatment approach can reflect a reluctance in one or both partners for the treatment to succeed. At an unconscious level they seek failure to justify either ending the relationship, accepting a non-sexual one or engaging in extra-marital affairs.

Problems in accepting limits, especially the ban on genital touching and intercourse, are common and discussion of them often fruitful for the couple. Although simple failure to understand the purpose of these limits may account for the difficulty, more often other factors are involved; an example of this is given in the clinical illustrations later in the chapter. The agreed limits may be rejected by one or other partner (more often the woman) as an act of sabotage because sexual progress is too rapid and the prospect of 'cure' looms up before basic underlying problems have been exposed and dealt with. Typically, this sabotage reflects the woman's resentment at being sexually used by her husband. This 'bartering' aspect of sex is relevant all too commonly.

(b) *Ignorance or incorrect expectations about sex*

Patients' misunderstandings about sex are numerous and just a few will be mentioned here. A commonly held notion is that an erection indicates advanced sexual arousal and the need for intercourse, at a time when the woman may only be starting to respond. Erection is obvious to both partners whereas internal vaginal lubrication, the equivalent physiological response in the female, may pass unnoticed. Both occur, however, with similar speed and often as the first response to sexual stimulation. The belief that if an erection goes away it cannot return, needs to be corrected. It is often assumed that 'normal sex' involves simultaneous orgasm, this leading to considerable performance anxiety. Another common belief is that a woman experiences orgasm from vaginal intercourse alone, and that failure to do so or reliance on clitoral stimulation in addition indicates abnormality. The therapist needs to emphasize that only a minority of women on a minority of occasions achieve orgasm without clitoral stimulation, either by themselves or by their partner.

(c) *Negative sexual attitudes*

These are usually acquired during childhood or adolescence and precede the current relationship. Common examples are: 'it is wrong for nice women to take the initiative or to be active during love-making'; 'it is only acceptable to experience sexual pleasure when you are giving it to your loved one'; 'sex is unpleasantly messy because of vaginal fluid and semen'—often felt by people who are generally fastidious about their bodies and cleanliness; 'one should never lose control of oneself'—either because it is wrong to do so or frightening. Many more similar examples could be given.

(d) Problems in the relationship

The distinction between this category and the preceding one is not
entirely clear-cut as sexual attitudes are often reflected in the choice
of partner. However, there are common, unresolved problems that
stem from the couple's difficulty in adapting to one another. By far
the most important is the presence of veiled resentment, related to
the bartering aspect of sex in a relationship which was mentioned
earlier. This may give rise to the syndrome of 'post-marital decline'
in which sex, formerly exciting and enjoyable for both, gradually
loses its interest for the woman and to a lesser extent the man. A
similar decline is commonly seen after childbirth when the contri-
butory factors are likely to be complex.

What does the therapist do?

Having mentioned some problems that frequently cause difficulty in
carrying out the behavioural programme, let us now consider how
the therapist goes about resolving them and examine his psychotherapeutic role. This aspect of treatment has been seriously
neglected in the past. Recent developments in cognitive therapy
however are beginning to provide us with a framework (e.g. Beck
1976). The therapist's objectives can be considered under two main
headings:

    (1) helping the patient to understand the specific difficulties
        encountered during the behavioural programme;
    (2) taking active steps to help the patient resolve those dif-
        ficulties.

(1) Facilitating understanding

Reaching an understanding of why one has difficulty carrying out a
particular task is often followed by a reduction in that difficulty. In
psychotherapy the most likely explanation for this improvement is
that the understanding leads to a reappraisal through adult eyes of
the problem and the beliefs and values associated with it. Female
patients often report difficulty or reluctance in taking their turn to
initiate lovemaking during the course of treatment. Usually this is
because they feel that for a woman to initiate is to show a somewhat
improper degree of enthusiasm, making her especially vulnerable to
refusals by the partner which are then taken as further evidence of

the unacceptability of the behaviour (men are conditioned differently; for them to have their advances rejected is much less threatening to their self-esteem).

By reconsidering these assumptions, acknowledging that certainly in an established relationship it is normal and appropriate for the woman to take the initiative, and accepting one of the basic principles of this therapy, that both partners should be able to say no at any time, 'cognitive restructuring' occurs, allowing the previously difficult behaviour to occur without difficulty. Such a process may continue covertly and between treatment sessions, but what can the therapist do to facilitate it?

(a) Setting further appropriate behavioural tasks may help to focus on the specific problem. Identifying the difference between one's reaction to two subtly different tasks may be particularly helpful. Why, for example, is it easy to show your partner what you find unpleasant, but difficult to indicate what is pleasant, how or where you like to be touched?

(b) Encourage examination and appropriate labelling of the feelings experienced at the time of the behavioural difficulty (e.g. is it fear, guilt, disgust or anger?)

(c) Encourage the patient to find an explanation for this difficulty. The therapist should be producing his own list of likely explanations and evidence for and against each one, but it is probably more effective if the patient can be helped to provide the best explanation or interpretation rather than have it offered by the therapist, who may be overkeen to demonstrate his own skills.

This is unlikely to happen until the patient has experienced a 'need to understand' a particular difficulty, and this often does not happen when the difficulty is first encountered. The therapist can facilitate this by exposing the patient to the same difficulties by repeating homework assignments.

If the patient does not produce the explanation then 'Socratic questioning' may help. Here the therapist, with a particular explanation in mind, asks questions in a way that encourages the patient to look at the situation in a particular way. If this fails, then the therapist as a 'last resort' can offer explanations, preferably more than one, so that the patient can still choose.

The 'cognitive restructing' that accompanies such a process may be sufficient to remove the obstacles to behavioural change. But if not, what else can the therapist do?

(2) Direct steps to resolve the difficulty

The therapist's tactics can be considered under four headings.
(a) *Making explicit the patient's commitment to specific changes.*
At the outset, as already mentioned, goals of treatment are
purposely vague. But as specific obstacles are encountered it
becomes necessary to establish explicitly whether or not the patient
wants to overcome each identified obstacle, e.g. does the woman
want to be able to initiate? Does the man who finds his partner's
genitàlia slightly repellent want to overcome that feeling? In other
words is the obstacle a 'resistance' regarded by the patient as a
nuisance, i.e. ego-alien, or is it consistent with his or her value
system, i.e. ego-syntonic and therefore something that is not right to
change? Obtaining an explicit commitment of this kind is the next
appropriate step in therapy.
(b) *Set further appropriate behavioural steps specifically designed
to overcome the difficulty.* Often problems stem from fear of a
'phobic' kind. A graded or hierarchical approach can then be used.
A woman who fears anything entering her vagina should be asked to
insert her own finger for a short distance and for a short time. This
approach uses small steps which do not overwhelm the patient with
anxiety, and give encouragement to 'stay with' the anxious feelings,
rather than avoid them, until they start to decline.
(c) *Reality-confrontation.* Anxiety can be challenged at a cognitive
level. When it is ego-syntonic, or the patient has no obvious wish to
overcome a particular resistance, then the therapist has to consider
how incompatible this is with the aims of treatment. Thus the suggestion that masturbation may help to achieve orgasm or overcome
inhibition may be rejected by the patient on the grounds that masturbation is an unacceptable form of behaviour. If the patient is seeking
help for the sexual relationship with the partner then some
alternative approach should be suggested. If, on the other hand, a
patient objects to touching his or her partner's genitals then the
incompatibility of such an attitude with the aims of treatment should
be emphasized.

Patients may need to be confronted with other inconsistencies
between belief and actions, or between their understanding and the
facts of the matter. Thus the view that 'normal' women experience
orgasm from vaginal intercourse also has to be challenged. Per-
mission-giving by the therapist, often an essentially important role,
often involves pointing out the inconsistences between the patient's

values and the therapist's.

(d) *Facilitating the expression and communication of affect.*
Negative emotions play an important part in establishing or maintaining sexual dysfunction. The first step in coping with such
emotions is to label them correctly. Resentment within the relationship is a very common factor in sexual problems. More often
than not, appropriate expression of this resentment is required
before it resolves. The therapist can aid this process in three ways: to
educate the couple in the various ways that unexpressed emotions
adversely affect them and the benefits of appropriate expression; to
help the couple to recognize specific instances where such difficulties
arise, that is, to provide feedback; and to help the couple to work out
satisfactory ways of expressing and communicating their feelings.

It is helpful to remember that one of the most important reasons
for reluctance in carrying out a behavioural assignment is a lack of
understanding of its purpose or a lack of confidence in the therapist
in the approach he is using. These difficulties are particularly
important in the early stages of treatment, before a sound therapeutic alliance has been established. The therapist should assume
that the rationale of therapy needs to be given more than once. It is
often better understood after the first attempts at the behavioural
assigments. The couple should be told that what they are being asked
to do is based on common sense and not magic. It is therefore
the therapist's responsibility to explain why an assignment is
appropriate and the patients should be encouraged to ask if it is not
clear to them. This not only allows the patient to express doubts
about the therapy, but also emphasizes the educational as opposed
to the 'curative' function of therapy.

When working with couples in the above ways it is important to
maintain a balance when dealing with the two partners, particularly
when only one therapist is involved.

There are other non-specific therapeutic activities which are also
important. These include reassurance, promoting hope, showing
warmth and empathy, reinforcing specific patient-behaviour by
reacting with pleasure or praise, and inoculating against failure by
preparing the patient for possible setbacks so that when they arise,
he will not be overly discouraged, but rather make constructive use
of them.

Most of these strategies have no special mystique. Obviously there
is considerable scope for expertise, and therapists will vary not only
in their initial aptitude for the tasks of sex therapy but also in their

capacity to learn from clinical experience. It is important to emphasize however that the above account covers the principal repertoire of therapist activities.

Clinical illustrations

Some clinical examples follow to bring the above concepts to life and to show their application.

Case 1: Jane and Bob

Jane and Bob, married for three years and both 25 years old, had stopped all sexual activity following a brief period when Jane was unable to touch Bob's penis. When asked what happened when she considered doing so, she described a strong feeling of disgust—but could explain it no further. The therapist asked what she thought disgust meant and eventually offered the explanation that disgust was a mixture of attraction and repulsion—an interesting idea that may apply in some patients but in any event does have therapeutic value. Jane was then requested to define the difference between touching Bob's penis and other parts of his body, which she was prepared to do. After unconvincing attempts to explain the difference in terms of texture and shape, she was asked what it meant to be disgusted by something that Bob obviously found pleasurable. She then expressed her fear that he would lose control if she touched his penis and made him aroused. Bob, asked how that made him feel, expressed surprise at Jane's apparent lack of trust.

Following this session Jane began to touch his penis, though initially she felt transient nausea whilst doing so. During the next two weeks she began to enjoy her genitals being touched, a new experience for her, and described being aroused. She was still reluctant to touch Bob's penis for more than a brief period. Jane was asked why she was now able to enjoy being touched herself but was reluctant to give Bob his pleasure. She returned to the loss of control theme, indicating that she felt confident she would not lose control herself, but expected Bob to do so when he approached orgasm. What did this loss of control mean to her, what consequences did she fear? She described the break in communication that occurs when partners are approaching and experiencing orgasm. The break was a threat to her and she needed to feel that she remained in contact. She was asked to describe other situations where a similar break in communication might occur—such as Bob falling asleep. This did not concern Jane because she knew she could wake him if necessary. She was then asked how the time scale of Bob going to sleep compared with his reaching orgasm. After some consideration, she acknowledged with surprise that the orgasmic 'time out' was of very short duration, and appeared to be reassured.

Case 2: Mary and Peter

Mary and Peter were an unmarried couple who had been living together for four years. Mary presented complaining of orgasmic dysfunction—she experienced orgasm during her own particular form of masturbation but not during intercourse. Peter expressed considerable doubts at the outset that he would be able to accept the ban on genital touching and intercourse. The rationale was explained to him and he was asked if he understood it—he expressed partial understanding but explained that during a session he might become sexually aroused and could not be held responsible for what happened. Once aroused he would expect to have intercourse. He was asked why he would be unable to control himself and he attributed this to his 'normal maleness': men when sexually aroused were not responsible for their actions. He was asked whether this would apply in any situation, i.e. if he became aroused, would he be in danger of raping his partner; Peter admitted that this was unlikely. He was asked what had happened during his early courting days with Mary, before they started having intercourse and he acknowledged that he had been able to accept limits then.

Asked if she would lose control were she to become aroused, Mary replied negatively. Both were confronted with the common stereotype of the controlled woman and the uncontrolled animal-like man and were asked if there was any evidence to support this. They were then presented with a reasoned argument that this stereotype was to a large extent imposed by society rather than being biologically determined. Peter was asked if he preferred to see himself as an 'uncontrolled sexual animal' and did it make him more masculine to be so. Mary was asked what the issue of control meant to her and she described how it made her feel insecure during lovemaking and unable to let herself go because she needed to retain control. Peter was asked if this could be relevant to her orgasmic difficulty and he felt that it probably was. The importance of feeling safe in a sexual relationship was stressed and Peter agreed to accept the limits of Stage 1.

Case 3: Richard and Susan

Richard and Susan had been married for two years. Both 23, they had had a courtship since 17 and begun having intercourse early on. Initially sex was enjoyable for both, although Richard, coming from a strictly religious family, had felt some guilt. About a year before Richard and Susan married, his parents had expressed shock and dismay on discovering that they were living together. Richard then decided that they would stop having intercourse until their marriage. Susan hoped he would eventually change his mind but he persisted. Whey they resumed intercourse after marriage Susan was no longer responsive.

During Stages 1, 2 and 3 of treatment Susan repeatedly described how she resented touching Richard because he enjoyed it and became aroused while she did not. She at the same time presented herself as a failure who was reluctant to initiate sessions because she would fail yet again. This couple had obvious problems in dealing with their resentment. Susan was able to show anger about certain issues but not about others whereas Richard rarely showed any anger at all. He feared that if he became angry with Susan she would remain upset for a long time and it was therefore easier to conceal his feelings. The therapist concluded that Susan's unresolved resentment was a result of Richard's pre-marital rejection of her sexuality, and encouraged her to express this but she persistently denied that she felt any anger; in fact, the experience had made her feel inadequate rather than angry. At the same time, she continued to make provocative comments about resenting Richard's pleasure. Richard was asked how he felt about Susan's comments; he denied being hurt or upset, but was rather puzzled.

Eventually, the therapist decided, because of the couple's block in expressing anger and the resultant impasse in treatment, to introduce some of his own reactions. He described his sense of feeling exasperated by Susan's mixed message of the denial of any angry feelings together with her provocative remarks, and her opting out of efforts at new behaviour on the grounds that she would only fail. The session became tense with Susan visibly, though not verbally, angry. The therapist stated that he would feel angry if he were in Richard's position.

At the next appointment, Susan stated that she had not wanted to practise any of the behaviours since the previous session. She had found the last occasion humiliating and therefore had stopped thinking about treatment. Richard was more expressive than he had been before, indicating his concern that the therapist had been rather hard on Susan. The therapist then explained that contrary to Susan's conclusion, he did not regard her as a failure but rather felt angry and frustrated by her attitude. He had felt the need to express his feelings but had worried after the session that he may have acted too harshly; he was pleased and relieved that she had returned. He now suggested that there was a similarity between Susan's reaction to the last session—feeling angy, regarding herself as a failure and opting out of the behavioural programme (i.e. the relationship), and her reaction to Richard's withdrawal from the pre-marital sexual relationship. By the end of the session the tension was much reduced. The therapist pointed out that though there had been a risk of a break in the therapeutic relationship everyone had weathered the crisis and now felt more relaxed and secure. At the next session, Susan reported pleasurable involvement in Stage 3 and was able to describe in more detail how hurt she had felt before the marriage.

In this case the therapist not only provided a model of affect expression by sharing his own feelings but also revealed himself as a 'genuine' and 'feeling' person with concern for the couple; an obviously important therapist characteristic. As this case shows, the timing and handling of such an intervention can prove difficult, however, and there is always a danger of a patient dropping out from therapy.

Some practical considerations

Couple therapy varies in duration but on average requires about 12 sessions spread over four or five months. This is in contrast with the concentrated daily sessions of the two-week programme advocated by Masters and Johnson (1970). Criteria for choosing between the two regimes remain to be established, but in any case the more intensive format is impracticable within a non-private setting where usually once-a-week sessions are the most frequent that can be practically arranged. The other unresolved question is whether, with the less intensive approach, sessions should be less often than once a week.

So far research evidence has not indicated any clear advantage of giving particular frequency of treatment session (Bancroft 1983) and the therapist is therefore entitled to be flexible, adjusting to the needs of the particular case. It is appropriate to start treatment on a weekly basis and to extend the interval between sessions when it becomes clear that major issues such as unexpressed resentment or communication problems or undue passivity have been effectively dealt with. It is certainly desirable to space out the last two or three sessions over a few months so that the couple have an opportunity to consolidate their progress and cope with any relapse before finally terminating.

With some couples progress is slow or non-existent and the therapist is uncertain about how long to continue treatment. As a rough guide, it is fair to say that if substantial progress has not been achieved by about session 18, it is unlikely to occur with further treatment of this kind. In any event, it is generally advisable to avoid open-ended contracts. A specified number of sessions should be agreed on at the outset with a proviso that when they are completed progress will be assessed and decisions taken on whether to continue and for how long. In cases with reasonable prospects, an initial contract of 10 sessions with scope for agreeing on a further two, three, or four is sensible.

One advantage of this treatment approach is that in most cases, signs of progress and the couple's ability to make use of therapy will be evident within the first four sessions. In cases where the therapist is uncertain of the prospects at the outset, e.g. when one partner seems ambivalent about the relationship continuing, or where there is considerable overt hostility making constructive collaboration unlikely, a limited contract of three or four sessions is advisable. The couple are told at the first contact that further treatment will depend on evidence of at least slight progress during those first few sessions. It is also relevant that people who drop out of therapy usually do so around the third or fourth session (Bancroft and Coles 1976).

The time required for each treatment session also varies. When progress is satisfactory and no major obstacles are encountered, 30 minutes is usually sufficient; frequently however, longer is needed. When appointments have to be time limited, it is preferable to allow one hour, though if pressed, 45 minutes may suffice.

Another practical issue is whether there should be one or two therapists. Masters and Johnson (1970) are strong advocates of the dual-therapist team. Economically, this obviously requires substantial justification. As yet no one has demonstrated superior results when using two therapists rather than one (Bancroft 1983). The advantages are obvious: both male and female points of view can be represented and apparent collusion of therapist and one partner in the couple more easily avoided. In addition, it is possible for one therapist to remain more objective and aware of what is happening while the other is directly involved. Against this, it is important to realize that the co-therapist relationship is not necessarily an easy one and the choice of colleague may be crucial. Also, to make proper use of the arrangement, time is required outside the treatment session for adequate discussion and communication between therapists. Co-therapy can be a valuable training model, provided that the more experienced therapist takes care not to unduly dominate the therapy sessions. Further research is necessary to identify couples for whom the use of a dual-therapist approach could be important. In the meantime it is perfectly reasonable to do sex therapy with one therapist or two as opportunities present themselves or as preferences dictate.

In the case of individual therapy, it is more difficult to lay down guide lines on these various practical issues because of the much greater variability in objectives and therapist involvement. However, the same underlying principles should still be applicable.

Training

Sexual dysfunction, because of its psychosomatic nature, will have aetiological factors of a medical kind in a proportion of cases. For this reason, it is important that sex therapy is provided in a setting where there is ready access to medical skills. Once medical aspects have been dealt with, however, the characteristics of a suitable therapist are determined more by personality and appropriate experience than by any particular professional background. Doctors, clinical psychologists, social workers, nurses, and marriage guidance counsellors have all been effectively trained in this approach.

At the present time there are a few formal training programmes for this type of therapy in the UK. What is required is help from an experienced therapist either in the ongoing supervision of therapy or in cotherapy. The Association of Sexual and Marital Therapists has recently produced criteria for a training programme of this kind.

Conclusion

This kind of sex therapy can cope with problems with a wide range of complexity. At one extreme, a simple behavioural programme with minimal therapist intervention will suffice, at the other, considerable psychotherapeutic skill may be required. Most cases fall between these two extremes. In all cases, however, the same basic framework is employed and this is an advantage for the inexperienced therapist.

References

Bancroft, J. (1974). *Deviant sexual behaviour: modification and assessment.* Oxford University Press, London.
—— (1983). *Human Sexuality and its Problems.* Churchill Livingstone, Edinburgh.
—— and Coles, L. (1976). Three years experience in a sexual problems clinic *Br. Med. J.* i, 1575-7.
Barbach, L. G. (1976). *For yourself: the fulfilment of female sexuality.* Anchor Books, New York.
Beck, A. T. (1976). *Cognitive therapy and the emotional disorders.* International Universities Press, New York.
Heiman, J., Lopiccolo, L., and Lopiccolo, J. (1976). *Becoming orgasmic. A sexual growth programme for women.* Prentice Hall, New York.
Kaplan, H. S. (1975). *The new sex therapy.* Bailliere, Tindall, London.
Masters, W. H. and Johnson V. E. (1970). *Human sexual inadequacy.* Churchill, London.
Tunnadine, L. P. D. (1970). *Contraception and sexual life: a therapeutic approach.* Tavistock, London.

Recommended reading

Bancroft, J. (1983). *Human Sexuality and its Problems.* Churchill Livingstone, Edinburgh. (A comprehensive text covering all aspects of sexual behaviour, problems, and treatment).
Belliveau, F. and Richter, L. (1971). *Understanding human sexual inadequacy.* Hodder and Stoughton, London. (This is a readable and concise account of Masters and Johnson's approach.)
Fairbairn, C. G., Dickerson, M. G. and Greenwood, J. (1983). *Sexual problems and their management.* Churchill Livingstone, Edinburgh. (A brief clinically-oriented text.)
Kaplan, H. S. (1975). *The new sex therapy.* Bailliere, Tindall, London. (This is the most comprehensive text on sex therapy to date and provides a refreshingly balanced and eclectic account: particularly

recommended are Chapters 7-10 on psychological causes and Chapters 11-14 on basic principles of treatment.)

—— (1979). *Disorders of sexual desire*. Brunner/Mazel, New York. (Overlaps considerably with the 1975 book but covers some aspects more fully.)

Lopiccolo, J. (1977). Couple therapy. In *Handbook of sexology* (eds J. Money and H. Musaph). Excerpta Medica, Amsterdam. (Gives a slightly different approach to Masters and Johnson and Kaplan, and contains some useful ideas.)

Masters , W. H. and Johnson, V. E. (1970). *Human sexual inadequacy*. Churchill, London. (Describes the classic 'Masters and Johnson' approach to sexual dysfunction.)

9

Family therapy when the child is the referred patient

Arnon Bentovim

Family therapy has expanded enormously over the past two decades. In this chapter Bentovim describes the form of family therapy used when the child is the referred patient. Following a brief historical perspective he highlights the importance of assessment and suggests useful frameworks within which it can be done. Attention is also paid to indications and contra-indication for family therapy, various theoretical models, and problems that arise in the course of treatment. A case report is presented to illustrate aspects of both assessment and therapy. The final section deals with research findings on family therapy effectiveness and with training.

This chapter provides an account of the form of family therapy practised when a child or adolescent is the referred patient. The treatment may be given in a variety of settings including the child guidance clinic, social service department, general hospital child psychiatry department and the private office of child psychiatrists, clinical psychologists, or psychiatric social workers.

Since the 1970s the target of psychotherapy in these settings has gradually shifted from the child as patient to the group with whom he has intimate contact, namely his family and other important figures around him. Here we will focus on the child and his immediate family, but it is important to realize that his wider social network— school, other relatives, friends, neighbours—needs to be carefully considered in assessing the nature and origin of the presenting problems and in planning a course of treatment.

Historical perspective

Freud (1977) was one of the first to include a parent in the psycho-therapy of the child. He worked indirectly with 'Little Hans's' phobic problems by communicating with the boy's father and also saw them together. The subsequent development of psychoanalytic treatment with children followed the model with adults—intensive psychotherapy on an individual basis (Hug-Hellmuth 1921); a later innovation was the use of play materials to enhance communication between therapist and child patient and Melanie Klein's (1948) contribution in this regard was particularly important. Classically, the child was seen four or five times a week and the main emphasis in therapy was on his intra-psychic life.

A new pattern of treatment emerged with the expansion of the child guidance clinic in the 1920s and 30s—weekly sessions with the child as well as regular casework with one or other parent. This constituted the standard approach until the 1950s when an interest in treatment of the family as a group was stimulated by studies of communication patterns in families containing a schizophrenic member (Bateson, Jackson, Haley, and Weakland 1956; Lidz 1973). Several research groups began to examine the role of family factors in the genesis of schizophrenia and of various psychiatric disorders of childhood. The therapeutic implications of their findings soon followed, culminating in the publication in 1958 of Ackerman's *The psychodynamics of family life*. His work, the first systematic description of psychotherapy of the family as a group, was based on psychoanalytic concepts. Over the next decade other approaches to family therapy evolved, some remaining in the analytic tradition and others offering new theoretical models. Important examples of the latter were the work of Haley (1971) and Minuchin (1974) to which we will return later in the chapter.

Professionals working with children were slow to shift to these new treatment methods. To many the child-guidance clinic model of individual child therapy and casework with the parent seemed satisfactory although it had never (and still has not) been subjected to proper research scrutiny. Only in the 1970s did therapists' reluctance begin to wane so that today there is a much greater acceptance of the family as a legitimate focus of treatment when a child is the referred patient. In part this has been due to the development of theoretical models about family life and psychopathology which have in turn led to specific methods of intervention. As a result therapists have begun to explore this new 'territory' with a greater sense of confidence.

Models of family therapy

As there is no uniform theory of family development and dysfunction it is not surprising that several models of family therapy have been elaborated in recent years. Useful summaries of current approaches are provided by Madanes and Haley (1978) and Bentovim (1979). Only brief mention can be made of the more important ones in this chapter. The interested reader is referred to the Recommended Reading List.

(1) Psychodynamic and related models

Many of the early family therapists were psychoanalysts who transferred their traditional analytical concepts from the treatment of individuals to the family group (Ackerman 1966). Dicks (1967) was a pioneer in this transfer of analytic ideas to marital therapy. In the psychodynamic model the task of the therapist is mainly interpretive, and through the relationship with himself he has to bring the family members' unconscious ideas and experiences into current awareness and especially to help them appreciate associations between past and present behaviour. The ultimate goal is insight, integration, and a change to healthy functioning. Because the therapist assumes that dysfunction stems from early childhood experiences, treatment is orientated to the past. A family's current behaviour may, for example, be related to a continuing conflict in which a shared experience of a dead person such as a grandparent is significant; when families repress this aspect of their past, they must be helped to see the connection in order to change (Lieberman 1980; Byng-Hall 1973, 1982). Attention is paid both to family members as individuals each with their own pattern of repression and to the family with its characteristic mode of functioning (Zinner and Shapiro 1974).

(2) Communication, systems, and strategic

Unlike the psychodynamic model this approach was not a modification of a previous form of psychotherapy but evolved out of research on family patterns of communication (Jackson and

Weakland 1961; Watzlawick, Beavin, and Jackson 1969). The premise on which therapy is conducted is that relationships between family members are dependent on the communication of messages or rules between them; relationships become disturbed when this communication is faulty. The aim of therapy is therefore to promote a different pattern of communication. This might amount at the most basic level to the therapist arranging for members to talk to one another—something they may not previously have managed to do at all.

Under the rubric of the communication school, various aspects of communication are emphasized by different therapists. Minuchin (1974) for example is concerned with family structure (hence the **structural approach**) and hierarchy. Families consist of a number of sub-systems—parental and sibling are the obvious ones—with the parental sub-system assumed to be in a position of leadership. Family pathology occurs when no differences exist between sub-systems and all family members are enmeshed together or when conversely, each member constitutes his own sub-system and the family is entirely fragmented. Treatment aims to modify the structure so that independent sub-systems can develop but which work in harmony with one another (Minuchin and Fishman 1981). This is accomplished by engineering changes in communication. Parents for example are taught to talk to one another without interruption from their children or a mother is encouraged to set aside a regular time to communicate with her adolescent daughter. Sub-systems are discussed again in the context of family assessment.

Another variant of the communication approach referred to as strategic therapy (Haley 1963, 1971, 1977) emphasizes the clear setting of goals which are closely related to the presenting problem, and the planning of strategies to achieve their goals. Therapy proceeds in stages according to the goals and strategies decided upon. It is assumed that the presenting problem represents the disturbed way that family members communicate with one another and that the target of treatment must therefore be on their pattern of communication. The therapist is particularly active in issuing directives to change the way in which members relate to one another. These directives include paradoxical ones—given with the aim that they will be defied, change results by the family breaking the rules instead of following them (see also Watzlawick, Weakland, and Fish 1974). Treatment is exclusively bound to the present and does not rely on the members' self-understanding of the problems.

(3) Behavioural

This approach is based on principles of learning theory and is also applied in the therapy of couples (see Chapter 7). The aim is to change directly specific aspects of behaviour as desired by the family themselves. Parents and children specify the behavioural changes they want to see in each other; a 'contract' is negotiated in which they commit themselves to do something the other wants, e.g. the wife may call for a 'social chat each evening after dinner' in exchange for the 'more regular sexual intercourse' requested by the husband (Liberman 1970). Children agree to stop soiling or having temper tantrums in exchange for specific rewards.

(4) Other approaches and techniques

There are a large number of other approaches and techniques to family treatment which can only be listed here:

extended family school—relatives of the nuclear family, friends, and neighbours are involved in therapy on the premise that all of them are part of the family's system and its dysfunction (Speck and Attneave 1971);

multiple family group therapy—several families meet together with one or more therapists (Curry 1965);

family sculpting and role play—the family portrays a scene or incident by arranging themselves physically into a group pose and their reactions to the 'sculpture' are then discussed (Simon 1972);

videotape—this technique is used in several ways and allows the family to observe for themselves the way in which their communications, particularly non-verbal, are disturbed (Alger and Hogan 1969).

Selection

Indications and contra-indications

In the brief history of family therapy it has not been possible as yet to establish clear indications and contra-indications for treatment (Walrond-Skinner 1978; Skynner 1969). In general the family approach is used when the referred patient—a child in the context of this chapter—presents with problems which are so closely bound up with faulty family functioning that individual treatment is not appropriate. Common disturbances of family function include marital disharmony, conflict between parents and one or more children, e.g. an adolescent battling for his independence, problems in the child like conduct disorder, sibling rivalry, school refusal, and psychosomatic conditions such as asthma and eczema where family factors appear to contribute to their precipitation or maintenance. Other problems in the child that are regarded as indications include anorexia nervosa and anti-social behaviour.

In the case of a family seeking help as a group, rather than through one of its members, the circumstances are usually a family crisis such as a death, divorce, or a move to a new town. Family therapy can be a suitable mode of treatment in these situations.

The treatment could be contra-indicated in the case of a child who presents with a severe problem which, although having an effect on the rest of the family, appears to be unrelated to them and needs help in its own right. Infantile autism is an example of such a problem as is a maladaptive response to a traumatic experience like hospitalization in early childhood. In some cases the therapist may only discover in the course of family therapy that the child originally referred is not deriving benefit and that an individual approach may be more helpful. Family therapy can, if necessary, be resumed at a later point. Some therapists use family and individual methods in combination but the indications for this approach are not clear.

Family therapy cannot obviously succeed if a key member, particularly a parent, refuses to participate or does so reluctantly, constantly resisting the therapist's efforts. The chance of it being effective is also reduced if one member, again particularly a parent, suffers from a disturbance such as a paranoid personality which prevents him from achieving any insight into his own problems or those of the family.

Framework for the assessment of the family

In assessing whether a family is suitable for treatment, the therapist will find it useful to consider the following three frameworks: the family life cycle, the three-generational model of family life, and family function in the here and now.

(1) *The family life-cycle (Rapoport 1963)*

The family has a typical life cycle of its own and passes through a more or less predictable series of stages. These are:

(a) Pre-parenthood—two people select one another as partners and progress through courtship, engagement, marriage and pregnancy.

(b) Early parenthood—the family consists of an infant or toddler, and later, perhaps a second infant.

(c) The oldest child is between two and a half years and school age and may be attending a play-group or nursery school.

(d) The oldest child has begun school and later proceeds to early secondary school but is still pre-adolescent.

(e) The oldest child has entered adolescence but not yet left home.

(f) The phase between the oldest child's departure from home until that of the youngest.

(g) All children have now left home and one or both parents are still working.

(h) The phase between the parent/s retirement and their deaths.

At each stage of this cycle demands and challenges confront one or more family members: for instance, the wife becomes pregnant, the husband becomes a father, the toddler has his first experience of a new sibling or of relating to persons other than his parents, the child has his first school experience with demands for learning and relating to peers, the child enters adolescence and faces his own sexuality and need for independence, the older adolescent tries to form relationships with the opposite sex, the parents have to relate to each other in a new way following the departure of their children from home, and must now deal with them as young adults. At the same time as individual members face these various challenges the family as a whole must change and grow in order to negotiate successfully each stage of the cycle. There is an obvious interplay between development of the family and that of each of its members; for example, parents cannot obviously have the same attitude to their adolescent child as they had to him as a toddler.

(2) *The three-generational model of family life*

A second useful framework concerns the families of origin of the two parents. Knowledge of their families can throw light on many of the current family's problems. For instance, the very choice of spouse and the nature of the marital relationship may have been determined by either or both partner's attempts to resolve a conflict which could not be satisfactorily dealt with in their own families.

Experiences of the two parents in their families of origin, such as a domineering or rejecting father or an over-protective mother, may lead to a particular 'script' of child rearing in the current family. Thus parents who were unduly protected as children may replicate this pattern or adopt an entirely opposite approach so as to avoid giving their own children an experience they themselves found undesirable.

In some families a 'myth' is handed down from generation to generation from which no member can escape (Byng-Hall 1973). Two issues are interrelated here: the myth—e.g. 'ill-luck has always dogged the Browns' or 'the Smiths have been an argumentative lot for generations'—is shared by the family as if they were one ego mass (Bowen 1966), a single psychic entity (Zinner and Shapiro 1974). The family members are not perceived by one another as separate persons with their own unique qualities but as mere elements within the mass. In this way the current family automatically stamps on itself a specific seal inherited through the myth, which contributes in large measure to their problems and to the manner in which they perceive these problems.

(3) *Family function in the here and now*

The third framework pertinent to assessment is the style in which the family typically functions in the here and now to meet each member's needs for survival and growth. In a successfully functioning family the following should be provided: a setting for each member to fulfil his potential, a model for socialization that can be transferred to the outside world, parental models for sexual identification, and boundaries demarcating parents and children so that the latter respect the leadership role of the parents with all its implications. This last provision of boundaries suggests that a family is made up of various sub-systems each of which are bound by a set of rules. The parental sub-system for example involves the responsibility of making certain types of decisions for the child sub-system. Other systems, apart from the obvious generational one, occur in terms of sex, age, values, and interests. We shall return to this topic later.

Family function (and its associated problems) can be conveniently considered under six headings (Loader, Burck, Kinston, and Bentovin 1981).

(a) *Communication and exchange of information*—the family

communicate with one another both verbally and non-verbally, the latter often having the greater impact on the recipient. Communication can vary considerably in terms of whether it actually occurs at all, how clear it is, how open and direct it is, how responsive family members are to one another, and so on. Often an incongruity between what is stated and what is expressed non-verbally is an obvious indicator of family pathology.

(b) *Affective state*—the expression of a wide variety of feelings is a salient facet of family functioning. Some families may be highly restricted in their range or a single emotion such as anger may predominate. In others there is a virtual absence of emotional expression with a resultant sense of deadness or blankness. Feelings may be expressed by particular members but fail to elicit an appropriate response in the rest of the family.

(c) *Atmosphere*—the expression of affect contributes with other factors to the family climate. Every family has a distinctive atmosphere: chaotic, panicky, over-excited, apathetic, critical, aggressive, lively, humorous, gay, ironic—the list of qualities is infinite. Of course all those listed may occur in any one family at different times but commonly a particular constellation tends to predominate.

(d) *Cohesiveness*—a family has its own unique sense of solidarity, belongingness and loyalty—a sense of all members working together to ensure their continuing life and to enhance their welfare as a group. This cohesiveness is threatened when alliances form which exclude some members, when discord develops between two or more members, when a child or parent is scapegoated for a problem that the whole family should share, and when members behave vainly and ignore the well-being of the rest of the group.

(e) *Boundaries*—as mentioned earlier the family consists of various sub-systems each with their own boundaries. In an effectively functioning family these are permeable enough to facilitate easy communication between sub-systems but yet sufficiently intact to allow their autonomy. The family is also respectful of the rules that govern both relationships between sub-systems and the internal process of each of them. In some families these boundaries do not exist and all members are completely enmeshed together. For example, an adolescent child facing an exciting challenge which should be his alone may be robbed of the experience by parents who failed to maintain adequate distance between themselves and the boy. In other families the boundaries are so rigid that members act as totally separate persons who merely happen to be sharing the same household.

(f) *Family operations*—the family faces many tasks in managing its day to day affairs: for example, to resolve conflict, to make decisions, to solve problems, and to deal with the changes inherent in the family life cycle. Families vary considerably in the way they handle these tasks. For instance the family may deal with a conflict effectively, avoid it, make do with inadequate solutions, or allow a child to play an unduly prominent role.

Assessment of the child and his family

With the three frameworks in mind we can now turn to the task of assessment. The therapist's aims in assessing a child who is the referred patient, and his family are: to understand the problem in terms of the child presenting it; to understand the origins of this problem and the role that the family has played in its genesis and maintenance; to determine the changes required in child and family for the relief of the problem and for the improvement of family life; to motivate the family to accept the need for change and to negotiate a therapy contract.

Unlike the individual patient who usually seeks out help members of families are commonly requested by the therapist to attend for treatment. They may well express surprise at the invitation when 'it is clear that only Janet has the problem' and show reluctance to come. Thus the therapist's first objective in assessment is to encourage the whole family to be seen. Referring agencies such as teachers and general practitioners need to learn how to broach the subject with the family. In some cases the family require a home visit to explain carefully what they can expect in treatment and to deal with any resistance (therapists serving specific catchment areas have long practised interviewing families in their homes). Such an interview can provide a tremendous amount of information about factors like cohesiveness and atmosphere mentioned earlier.

When a therapist writes to a family inviting them to his office he should stress his (or the clinic's) policy for the family to be seen together as a group and its importance. He should also offer an appointment time that is likely to be convenient. Families are usually much more willing to attend after school hours and if possible after work hours. The content and style of the therapist's letter are important matters and require careful consideration. The reader is referred to Skynner (1976) where model letters are reproduced.

The first session with the family

The room in which the family is seen should be comfortable and completely private with chairs placed in a circle and ample play material available for any young children. Sufficient time should be set aside on this first occasion, usually about two hours. This is made up of an initial hour with the family followed by some 30 minutes for consultation between co-therapists (we turn to the subject of co-therapy later) or with a colleague, and then a final period again with the family in order to provide feedback and to set therapy in motion (provided of course that a family approach is deemed appropriate).

As the parents tend to dominate the first session an important task for the therapist is to encourage the participation of all family members, particularly the children who usually feel overawed, inhibited, and anxious. Asking them neutral questions at first like their age and school paves the way for a more emotionally-loaded enquiry. Another method to promote participation is by having the parents explain to their children the reason for the consultation if this has not been previously done. The therapist then checks whether the children have understood the explanation and how they react to it.

Parents often express concern about talking openly in the presence of their children lest they should criticize or humiliate them. The parents' own sense of shame and embarrassment may prevent them from disclosing feelings they have about the problems facing the family. From the outset the therapist needs to encourage the family to communicate freely and to share feelings; he can reassure them that they probably are already familiar with one another's views. In most cases, by the end of the first session channels of communication have opened up. At the first meeting and until family therapy is firmly instituted, the therapist plays a much more active role than is customary in other psychotherapies. His chief goal at this point is to engage the whole family in the therapeutic process. Several techniques have been described which he can use to this end. Let us consider those discussed by Minuchin (1974): joining and accommodation, mimesis, and tracking.

(a) *Joining and accommodation*

The therapist forms links between himself and the family as a group and with each of its members by clearly showing that he understands their unique positions and experiences. For example, in a family where Peter has three older sisters the therapist may comment to him that it must be rather good being the only son and yet difficult to be the youngest with so many older sisters. He can remark to the girls that it must be awkward at times having a younger brother and yet good that both sexes are represented in the family. To the parents he may note that it must have been confusing to accustom themselves to a son following three daughters despite the pleasures involved. To accomplish this 'joining' process the therapist accommodates himself or adjusts to the family's particular atmosphere and pattern of communication and modifies his style to facilitate their acceptance of him; this brings us to mimesis.

(b) *Mimesis*

This term refers to the process whereby the therapist adopts a style of behaviour which matches that of the family. Thus he may take on their way of speaking, for example, imitating their pace and volume. He may take off his coat when the father does so or share a cigarette with him. He may use some of the family's terms. Like a chameleon he allows himself to change in order to get closer to the family. Mimetic responses are usually unconscious—the experienced therapist spontaneously blends in with the family. As part of this technique the therapist may also share aspects of his own family experience particularly when they have something in common with the family he is trying to join.

(c) *Tracking*

This technique concerns the content of family communication and the therapist's response to it. He keeps track of what occurs in the session by asking the family to clarify or elaborate particular points. Rather than challenge the members he leads them on by expressing interest at what he has heard, by echoing their statements and by encouraging them to amplify. He may initiate communication but his object is to follow the family and at the same time attempt to involve all members.

Exploration of the presenting problems

It is important for the therapist to encourage the family to describe presenting problems in detail, not only to make a diagnosis and understand their origin but also to demonstrate to the family that they are being listened to. He needs to ask when the problem began, who first noticed it, what effect it has had on various family members, who has benefited most from the focus on the person with the problem, who has been the most distressed, who has done what to try to change the problem, and what has been the result.

Furthermore, whilst the problems are described the therapist notes the behaviour of each family member: who becomes angry or sad in response to the other? who smiles or makes eye contact? who repudiates whose statements? He also observes the presence of sub-grouping—what sort of alliances exist and who comprises them?

The therapist in making his observations tries to place the presenting problems in the context of the overall functioning of the family. Pauline, for example, a 12-year-old girl presenting with school refusal, sat in the assessment session on a couch close to mother with father situated at the other end of the room. The therapist might have assumed from this seating pattern that Pauline and mother had formed a collusive bond which excluded father. The therapist noted however that instead of looking to mother for reassurance when her problems were under discussion Pauline constantly made eye contact with father indicating a distinct affiliation with him. When this was probed it emerged that father and daughter had an intense, overly close relationship which played an important part in her school refusal.

Exploring family life cycle and inter-generational issues

To understand why a family is troubled at a particular time an idea of their past history and development is usually helpful. In exploring the family life cycle the therapist pursues a number of issues: what originally attracted the parents to each other and made them marry; how did they feel about the birth and development of each child; how have they responded to crises and significant family events during the life cycle? The children in turn add their comments to the picture provided by the parents.

As discussed earlier in the chapter the therapist explores the parents' experiences as children in their own families. Their preparation of a family tree is often most illuminating and provides a link between assessment and actual therapy.

Family therapy in practice

Planning therapy

Before the therapist can devise a specific treatment plan he has to set up a *hypothesis*, based on all the information available to him, to explain the origin of the presenting problems and of those which he has observed in the course of assessment. Further, he will find it helpful to formulate goals by which he can evaluate the outcome of therapy. In so doing it is helpful to try to see how the presenting problem fits in with patterns of family interaction in the here and now, and with the family's handling of stress in the past (Kinston and Bentovim 1980).

A wide variety of hypotheses are needed to fit the tremendous range of family dysfunction seen. For instance a child's disturbance may reflect his anxiety about the parents' fragile marital relationship; parents may be overwhelmed by the challenge of their adolescent daughter's development because they themselves experienced difficulties when passing through this period; the family may share difficulties in coping with a major loss or other life crisis. A family map illustrating boundaries and relationship patterns can guide the therapist in helping to set treatment goals. These goals may need to be step-wise, that is, attempting to solve one aspect of the family's dysfunction at a time. He may focus first on the anxiety of the children in the face of a poor parental relationship. His next step might be to deal directly with the parents' difficulties. Another distinctive focus may be the parents separately if they each have problems that require help in their own right.

There is no consensus about specific *time intervals* between sessions or about the *duration of treatment* with families. Some therapists prefer to meet with families every two to four weeks, each session lasting one hour or more. Clinical experience with families given treatment when the child was the referred patient showed that when the dysfunction was long-standing six months were necessary for any substantial change (Kinston and Bentovim 1978). In families where problems are more severe, sessions might be held more frequently. When weekly sessions are appropriate, their frequency and duration should be firmly adhered to.

The family therapist has a choice of working on his own or with a *co-therapist*, ideally of the opposite sex. Co-therapy has certain advantages: it provides all family members with a model of their own sex, the two therapists in their joint work can demonstrate effective ways of relating to each other which family members can imitate, and in treating a group of people with so much happening at any one time, 'two pairs of eyes are better than one'. Some therapists, however, prefer to work on their own and feel constricted in the presence of another. Others feel that a co-therapist is best placed behind a one-way screen where he can observe the session, but not be pulled into the family system as may be the therapist. The observer then acts as consultant to the therapist (sitting in a corner of the room must do in the absence of a screen).

Clinical illustration

A case history is now presented to illustrate the therapists' (there were two co-therapists) approach to a family in terms of assessment and treatment.

Margaret, aged 10, was referred to a child psychiatric clinic with a six-year history of tics (Bentovim and Kinston 1978). These consisted of sniffing, coughing, snorting, teeth clenching, flapping her elbows, slapping her chest or thighs, and sudden stamping on the floor. Her parents were both schoolteachers and she had two sisters, Alice aged 13 and June aged 15. Assessment of the family showed the following main features:

(a) Depression was a common response in all members to situations of loss or change which the family had experienced during its life cycle. For example, the several moves made by them over the years had invariably been followed by periods of unhappiness.

(b) A dominant characteristic shared by parents and children was conscientiousness; they set themselves and the rest of the family excessively high standards.

(c) The children had always been treated as though much younger than their years; Alice and June in particular were not granted the freedom and responsibility that conventionally accompanies early adolescence.

(d) There was little verbal or non-verbal expression of feeling, and communication generally was minimal. Feelings such as anger and depression in any one family member were avoided by the others.

(e) The family seemed to denigrate itself as a group and only minimal appreciation of members for one another was expressed. Because they could not acknowledge their achievements an atmosphere of flatness prevailed.

The therapist hypothesized that the family had a marked tradition of control over all spontaneous, emotional expression in order to avoid feelings of anger and depression. Margaret's tics enabled her to express feelings which were otherwise forbidden. The family, it was felt, had learned to control unpleasant affect because of experiences that the parents had had in their own families. The therapists also concluded that the high standards expected of Margaret combined with lack of support and appreciation by the family had led to a sense of low self-esteem and depression in her.

Based on this hypothesis they set the following goals: the family should become less inhibited in its pattern of communication, their feelings should be expressed more freely, and they should show more mutual appreciation and support.

The family co-operated actively during the assessment session, accepted the need for a family approach and agreed to the therapists' suggestion to attend on 10 occasions at three weekly intervals. The next couple of sessions confirmed the therapists' initial impression about the family's dysfunction. Particularly striking was the behaviour of June who prevented any communication between family members by completely dominating her parents and competing vigorously with both Alice and Margaret in whom she showed absolutely no interest. The entire family seemed to collude in granting June her power to rule and divide. The therapists pointed out June's role to the parents, demonstrating how she stopped them from relating to each other or responding to the other children. This role was soon challenged by the therapists who rearranged the seating so that the parents sat together and June at a distance from them; the parents were instructed to talk specifically to Alice and Margaret. With these changes it became abundantly clear how overprotective mother was towards all three daughters and how incapable she was of allowing them any measure of independence. It emerged that mother's dependency needs had not been met originally after her own mother had developed severe arthritis. Father appeared as the family scapegoat and his efforts to meet the family's and his own expectations were experienced as frustrating by all members.

At a separate interview with the parents it was revealed that June had been conceived earlier than desired. Father had then become worried about the family's financial situation while mother had become depressed. This set a dysfunctional pattern in which parents (and later the sibs) were monopolized by June.

In the course of treatment the therapist repeatedly encouraged the family to show greater expression of feeling and appreciation of one another's achievements. At follow up the family had shown some improvement in that the parents enjoyed a closer relationship with each other and a more realistic one with all three daughters, and Margaret's tics had diminished considerably. There were however some residual problems such as in the parents' sexual relationship.

Some problems in the course of treatment

A wide range of problems can disrupt the progress of therapy; only a few can be discussed here. Not all families improve even with well planned intervention. Since the marriage is the axis around which the family revolves, a critical view of the parental relationship must be taken by the therapist when treatment seems to be 'stuck'. In some cases one or other parent has a severe psychiatric problem in his own right and either individual treatment or more intensive family therapy is indicated. When family dysfunction has been present for several years and is particularly marked, it is not surprising that treatment does not lead to rapid change.

The issue of missed appointments should always be raised with the family through a telephone call or letter. The therapist can arrange a home visit if he feels particularly concerned but should first write to the family of his wish to do so. They must be given the chance of opting out of a treatment which they perhaps find too threatening. The therapist may not perceive how frightening the treatment is for a family and they in turn may not reveal their distress at discussing certain sensitive areas. He therefore needs to check their reactions to particular sessions and be constantly alert to any cues of distress that they emit. The absence of any one member automatically requires family discussion as does his eventual return to therapy. Should a member not be able to make a session the rest of the family should be assigned the task of informing him about what transpired. The problem of premature dropping-out is discussed below.

Poor progress in treatment may be attributed to the therapist. Thus his vague, diffuse approach to treatment may provoke the family to wonder what benefit they gain from attending. Therapy tends to drift and the outcome is inevitably poor. This drift can be minimized if the therapist has a clear idea of his objectives and works actively towards them. Treatment can also be interfered with by the therapist unwittingly entering into a continuing alliance with any one member or part of the family. As the coalition often reflects feelings in the therapist which stem from his own family experience, he needs to ask himself regularly if his responses are objectively determined or not. Is the son with whom he feels sympathy in the same position as he himself was in his family? Is the husband on whose behalf he feels anger towards the wife in some way paralleling his own marital experience or that of his parents? A therapist who feels blocked with a family may learn that they are up against a similar problem to that which he experienced in his own family and which was never satisfactorily dealt with. A female therapist finding it difficult to divert a mother from constantly scapegoating her son may learn that she, the therapist, had unwittingly colluded with her own mother in attacking an elder brother.

Problems in treatment can arise when a member undermines the rule of openness by offering the therapist information but at the same time instructing him to withhold it from the rest of the family. The therapist may be tempted to accept this communication but should desist vigorously. He should make it clear that all information needs to be divulged to the whole family and that 'secrets' hinder treatment. A possible exception to this is the issue of sexual problems in the parents which are best discussed with them alone. The children are then told that a separate meeting between parents and therapist has been planned to discuss matters of no concern to them. It is surprising, however, to what extent the parents' relationship can be openly talked about in the family as a whole and how reassuring this can be to the children.

Dependency on the therapist is less of a problem when working with a family than it is in individual therapy. The transference relationship of members to the therapist is not emphasized but rather the relationships between the members themselves. None the less, some families, particularly those seen on an intensive, weekly basis over an extended period, do become overly attached to their therapist and have considerable difficulty in terminating treatment. Regarding him as a sort of parental figure they feel bereft during a vacation break and might express this by becoming frustrated and angry. Recurrence of problems in the referred patient or in the family generally may occur as the end of treatment approaches. In such situations the problem of dependency has to be worked through as part of the therapy. If treatment is intended to be intensive from the outset when the therapist negotiates a contract, he should emphasize that he expects the family to assume a large measure of responsibility for themselves and to carry on the work of treatment between sessions. In this respect assigning the family homework tasks can be most useful.

Termination

If the therapist negotiates a specific number of sessions with the family at the outset of treatment, termination poses less of a problem. He will, however, need to remind them periodically about the number of sessions still to go. Towards the end of the agreed programme a review by therapist and family of progress made is helpful. Should problems still remain the therapist can negotiate a new contract for another series of sessions; indeed it is possible to arrange two or three separate phases of therapy each with its own set of goals.

Termination is usually smoother when the therapist has a clear idea of the aims of his intervention—this involves the delineation of problems, the setting of goals, and the formulation of criteria for achieving them. A regular review of these goals can then guide the therapist in planning the final phase of the treatment programme. Apart from the relief of specific presenting problems his overall aim is to improve family functioning as seen in freer communication, a more harmonious atmosphere, a situation in which all members can grow and develop, and a greater ability to deal with problems on their own. Some families with more limited goals may terminate early, either when the referred patient's symptoms have diminished or when they realize that the process of change will confront them with painful, long-avoided issues. The therapist may have to accept the family's decision or confront them with their resistance; this decision calls for keen clinical judgment. We discussed earlier the opposite problem with termination—families who become dependent on their therapist and have difficulty in separating from him.

Research in family therapy

There is a rapidly expanding literature on family therapy. Until recently the contributions were chiefly anecdotal, consisting of therapists' descriptions of their own approaches to treatment. Many reports on systematic studies of process and outcome are now being published.

Two comprehensive reviews of the results of family therapy show that various forms of treatment are effective—an average 73 per cent of treated families improved (Gurman and Kniskern 1978, 1981). These therapies are at least as effective as, and probably more so, than other common modes of psychotherapy e.g. individual therapy for problems that clearly involve marital and/or family conflict.

Family treatment has been shown to be effective when the referred patient presents with psychosomatic symptoms, e.g. Lask (1979) found that children with severe asthma benefited in terms of their physical status when family therapy was a part of their management; improvement of a range of psychosomatic conditions has been claimed by Minuchin and his colleagues (Minuchin, Baker, Rosman, Liebman, Milman, and Todd 1975) but their work did not include controlled groups. Our own research (Bentovim and Kinston 1978), which applied predetermined criteria in the evaluation of outcome found improvement in a variety of childhood problems with time-limited family treatment. The family as a group however changed much less than the referred child.

For the moment we can state that family therapy is a valuable therapeutic approach but at the same time we must recognize that many aspects of it await further systematic investigation. Particularly in need of study is whether different forms of family treatment exert differential effects, i.e. the question of comparative efficacy.

Training

The most difficult task for the novice is to make sense of the mass of information presented to him as he begins to work with a family. He not only has to pay attention to the child with the presenting problem but also to each of the other members and to the family as a dynamic group. To familiarize himself with the ways in which families respond to therapy he needs to observe them being treated by experienced practitioners through a one-way screen or on videotape or film. His own therapeutic efforts should be closely supervised. Here again the one-way screen and videotape are valuable teaching aids. The supervisor observes the trainee's work with a family and offers appropriate feedback while the trainee himself has an opportunity to note his own performance on tape. If he is a member of a supervision group, he can also benefit from the comments of fellow trainees after they have viewed his performance. There is a particular advantage in immediate feedback while issues are still fresh.

A therapist also gains from the experience of participating in a group with fellow students in which, through techniques such as role play and sculpting, they can study different patterns of normal and disturbed family functioning. Another profitable method in the study of families is for the trainee to think back to his own family experience. Constructing his family tree is useful in this regard and he may even consult with family members in doing this. In this way family 'secrets' which were buried for years may be brought to light, exploded, and their significance assessed.

As we noted earlier there are many different models of family therapy. The trainee needs to experience and evaluate several of them in order to select the one which best suits him. Observation of different therapists, his own attempts to practise various approaches, and a close reading of the literature will aid the trainee in his choice. The reading list at the end of this chapter points to sources which provide detailed information on the main contemporary schools. References are also provided on important aspects of family functioning.

Conclusion

Family therapy has expanded rapidly since the 1950s. Today therapists are faced with an exciting but bewildering field: many differing theoretical models compete for their attention and a wide range of questions remains to be studied systematically. A newcomer will have to familiarize himself with these various models and choose the one which he can use most comfortably. But whatever his selection he should not allow himself to be restricted by rigid theoretical boundaries. As important as the model is the careful setting of goals and formulation of a treatment plan for each family with which he works.

References

Ackerman, N. W. (1958). *The psychodynamics of family life*. Basic Books, New York.

—— (1966). *Treating the troubled family*. Basic Books, New York.

Alger, I. and Hogan, P. (1969). Enduring effects of video-tape playback experience in family and marital relationships, *Am. J. Orthopsychiat*. **39**, 86-98.

Bateson, G., Jackson, D., Haley, J., and Weakland, J. (1956). Towards a theory of schizophrenia, *Behav. Sci.* **1**, 251-64.

Bentovim, A. (1979) Theories of family interaction and techniques of intervention, *J. Fam. Therapy* **1**, 321-45.

—— and Kinston, W. (1978). Brief focal family therapy when the child is the referred patient—I Clinical, *J. child Psychol. Psychiat*. **19**, 1-12.

Bowen, M. (1966). The use of family theory in clinical practice, *Compreh. Psychiat*. **7**, 345-73.

Byng-Hall, J. (1973). Family myths used as defence in conjoint family therapy, *Br. J. med. Psychol.* **46**, 239-50.

—— (1982). Dysfunctions of feeling. Experiential life of the family. In *Family therapy: Complementary frameworks of theory and practice* (eds A. Bentovim, G. Gorell Barnes and A. Cooklin). Academic Press, New York.

Curry, A. (1965). Therapeutic management of a multiple family group, *Int. J. Grp Psychother*. **15**, 90-6.

Dicks, H. V. (1967). *Marital tensions*. Routledge and Kegan Paul, London.

Freud, S. (1977) In *Case histories* (ed A. Richards) Vol. 1. Penguin, Harmondsworth.

Gurman, A. S. and Kniskern, D. P. (1978). Research on marital and family therapy—progress, perspective and prospects. In *Handbook of psychotherapy and behaviour change: An empirical analysis* (eds S. L. Garfield and A. E. Bergin). Wiley, New York.

—— and Kniskern, D. P. (1981). Family therapy outcome: Research, knowns and unknowns. In *Handbook of family therapy* (eds A. S. Gurman and D. P. Kniskern). Brunner/Mazel, New York.

Haley, J. (1963). *Strategies of psychotherapy*. Grune and Stratton, New York.

—— (1971). *Changing families: a family therapy reader*. Grune and Stratton, New York.

Haley, J. (1977). *Problem solving therapy*. Bassey-Joss, San Francisco.

Hug-Hellmuth, H. (1921). On the technique of child analysis, *Int. J. Psychoanal*. **2**, 287-305.

Jackson, D. and Weakland, J. (1961). Conjoint family: some considerations on theory, technique and results, *Psychiatry* **24**, 30-45.

Kinston, W. and Bentovim, A. (1978). Brief focal family therapy when the child is the referred patient—II. Methodology and results, *J. child Psychol. Psychiat*. **19**, 119-43.

—— and Bentovim, A. (1981). Creating a focus for brief marital or family therapy. In *Forms of brief therapy* (ed S. H. Budman). Guildford Press, London.

Klein, M. (1948). The development of the child. In *Contributions to psychoanalysis 1921–1945*. Hogarth, London.

Lask, B. (1979). A controlled trial of family therapy in the treatment of severe asthma in children, *Archs Dis. Childh.* **54**, 116–19.

Liberman, R. L. (1970). Behavioural approaches to family and couple therapy, *Am. J. Orthopsychiat.* **40**, 106–18.

Lidz, T. (1973). *The origin and treatment of schizophrenic disorders*. Basic Books, New York.

Lieberman, S. (1980). *Intergenerational family therapy*. Croom Helm, London.

Loader, P., Burck, C., Kinston, W., and Bentovim, A. (1981). A method for organising the clinical description of family interaction—the family interaction summary format, *Aust. J. Fam. Therapy* **2**, 131–41.

Madanes, C. and Haley, J. (1978). Dimensions of family therapy, *J. nerv. ment. Dis.* **165**, 88–98.

Minuchin, S. (1974). *Families and family therapy*. Tavistock, London.

—— and Fishman, H. C. (1981). *Family therapy techniques*. Harvard University Press, Cambridge, Mass.

—— Baker, L., Rosman, B. L., Liebman, R., Milman, L., and Todd, T. C. (1975). A conceptual model of psychosomatic illness in children. Family organisation and family therapy, *Archs gen. Psychiat.* **32**, 1031–8.

Rapoport, R. (1963). Normal crises, family structure and mental health, *Fam. Process* **2**, 68–80.

Simon, R. (1972). Sculpting the family, *Fam. Process* **11**, 49–58.

Skynner, A. C. R. (1969). Indications and contraindications for conjoint family therapy, *Int. J. soc. Psychiat.* **15**, 245–9.

—— (1976). *One flesh, separate persons. Principles of family and marital psychotherapy*, pp. 388–90. Constable, London.

Speck, R. V. and Attneave, C. (1971). Network therapy. In *Changing families* (ed J. Haley). Grune and Stratton, New York.

Waldrond-Skinner, S. (1978). Indications and contraindications for the use of family therapy. *J. child Psychol. Psychiat.* **19**, 57–62.

Watzlawick, P., Beavin, J. H., and Jackson, D. D. (1969). *Pragmatics of Human Communication*. Norton, New York.

—— Weakland, J., and Fish, R. (1974). *Change: principles of problem formation and problem resolution*. Norton, New York.

Zinner, J. and Shapiro, R. (1974). The family group as a single psychic entity, implications for acting out in adolescence. *Int. Rev. Psychoanal.* **1**, 179–86.

Recommended reading

Bloch, D. A. (ed) (1973). *Techniques of family therapy: a primer.* Grune and Stratton, New York. (An American text with useful contributions on home visits, action techniques, and a literature survey.)

Bentovim, A., Gorell Barnes, G., and Cooklin, A., (eds) (1982). *Family therapy: complementary frameworks of theory and practice.* Vols. 1 and 2. Academic Press, New York. (A broad-based view of family therapy, covering different approaches to theory and practice.)

Glick, I. D., and Kessler, D. R. (1981). *Marital and family therapy.* Grune and Stratton, New York. (Probably the best introductory text in the American literature.)

Guerin, P. J. (ed) (1976). *Family therapy.* Gardiner, New York. (A lively collection of American contributions on ways of working with families.)

Hoffman, L. (1983). *Foundations of family therapy.* Basic Books, New York. (Excellent account of different theoretical models, in an historical perspective.)

Minuchin, S. and Fishman, H. C. (1981). *Family therapy techniques.* Harvard University Press, Cambridge, Mass. (An excellent text of the structural approach.)

Satir, V. M. (1964) *Conjoint family therapy.* Science and Behaviour, Palo Alto, Calif. (A pioneer account of family therapy.)

Skynner, A. C. R. (1976). *One flesh, separate persons. Principles of family and marital psychotherapy.* Constable, London. (An excellent British account which attempts to integrate different therapeutic approaches and contains a useful guide to the literature.)

Waldrond-Skinner, S. (1976) *Family therapy–the treatment of natural systems.* Routledge and Kegan Paul, London. (The best British introductory text.)

10

Child psychotherapy

Sula Wolff

In this chapter Wolff focuses on dynamic and non-directive psycho-therapy which involves the child as patient in his own right. This chapter is best read in conjunction with Chapter 9 on Family Therapy. In the first section she provides an account of the development of child psychotherapy and gives special attention to the contributions of Anna Freud, Melanie Klein, Virginia Axline, and Donald Winnicott. The main section of the chapter then follows—a description of practical aspects of therapy and the various therapeutic tasks involved; these include the role of the therapist, his relationship with the child's parents, the first interview, and termination. The indications and contra-indications for this type of treatment are also covered in this section. Detailed consideration is then given to research findings on outcome, and the chapter ends with an account of the various constituents of training.

When children are referred for psychiatric treatment, the approach must be a dual one: to view the child in his own right and as a member of his family, perhaps also of his school and wider community. Whatever the problem and therapeutic intervention, the clinician is responsible to the parents and at times, especially if a teacher first identified the difficulty, to the school as well. But it is the clinician's task also to see the child as a developing person in his own right and, whatever his current life circumstances, to accept that he has an independent responsibility for his future. This may mean that, to ensure his best possible personal development, real changes must be fostered in the child's home or school environment. To this extent, the clinician becomes the child's ally and advocate, quite apart from his role as psychotherapist.

Whenever a child is the referred patient and whatever the main treatment given (whether this is behaviour modification, remedial education, family therapy, group or individual psychotherapy, or medication), the communications with the child should be such that (a) he can understand what is said to him and (b) he benefits in the sense of actually feeling better and making developmental gains. Such therapeutic communications with children are based on the general principles of child psychotherapy which clearly have something to offer to all professionals looking after disturbed children, whether they be doctors, nurses, social workers, teachers, psychologists, or occupational therapists.

In the last 30 years, a striking feature of the practice of child psychiatry has been the development of multiple treatment methods. In the early years of the child guidance movement therapeutic efforts were largely limited to once-weekly individual psychotherapy for the child using methods derived from psychoanalysis and from client-centred (Rogerian) non-directive therapy, together with social casework for parents. Analytic, non-directive, and activity-based methods of group psychotherapy for children (e.g. Foulkes and Anthony 1957), and at times for parents, were an occasional later addition. Behaviour modification techniques began to play an increasing part from the 1950s onwards and the family therapies, originating at around the same time, had a sudden flowering in the 1970s.

Much effort has always been invested in the treatment of parents often with the expectation that the children will benefit indirectly. 'Consultation work' with other professionals, an increasing commitment of most clinicians in child psychiatry, is also based on the idea that other people caring for children (e.g. teachers, nurses, and child care staff) can with help increase their understanding of disturbed children and their parents, and improve their own treatment skills for children in their care.

While analytic and non-directive child psychotherapies take note, explicitly or implicitly, of the child's emotional and cognitive developmental level and of the underlying causes and psychological explanations for his disorder, this is not so for behavioural approaches. The principles underlying these treatments are precisely the same for children as for adults. In practice, behaviour therapy for children is often, and to excellent effect, undertaken by parents or teachers. The techniques for helping these to become their children's behaviour therapists will not here be discussed. The reader is referred to McAuley and McAuley (1977) and to Patterson (1974).

Family approaches, including those using behavioural methods, are described in Chapter 9. It is important to be aware that, as Heincke and Strassmann (1975) have pointed out, behaviour therapy constitutes a profound change in a child's environment. Family therapy techniques too can be looked at from the viewpoint of their impact on the individual child.

The present chapter will focus on dynamic and non-directive psychotherapies which involve the child as patient by himself. Despite a common misperception, they do not conflict with either behavioural or family approaches. On the contrary, these different treatment methods can often helpfully be combined either sequentially or concurrently, although different therapists may need to be involved. Despite the multiplicity of current psychological treatments for children and the diversity of theories to back these up, there is remarkable uniformity in the process of child therapy as practised in different centres (Group for the Advancement of Child Psychiatry 1982).

Different models of child psychotherapy

Most psychotherapy offered to children in the British National Health Service is weekly and short-term (three to six months). This is not only because of limited staff resources. Brief interventions are often helpful especially when patients are prepared for this in advance (Frank 1974; Holmes and Urie 1975), and most families cannot commit themselves to a more intensive and more open-ended contract.

Although, especially in the practice of family therapy, it is currently fashionable to dismiss the contribution of psychoanalysis to the theory and practice of psychotherapy, the hypotheses set up to understand family systems, the strategies devised, and the apparent 'common sense' applied are successful, so it seems to me, because the really skilled practitioners have developed their new methods on the basis of a thorough grounding in psychodynamically-oriented psychotherapy.

Newcomers to the field are at a disadvantage unless they bring to their understanding of maladaptive behaviour and of neurotic symptoms in childhood a clear grasp of the sources of anxiety at different stages of early life (Wolff 1981); of psychological defence mechanisms (A. Freud 1946a); of the structure of the self; of transference phenomena; and, most of all, of both cognitive and psychoanalytic theories of child development (Piaget and Inhelder 1969; Erikson 1968; A. Freud 1965).

Although these topics lie outside the range of this chapter, it must be stressed that psychotherapy with children repeatedly provides powerful and poignant experiences for the therapist of the validity of psychoanalytic and cognitive developmental theories. In particular, children often reveal quite openly psychological defence mechanisms which, in adults, are totally outside conscious awareness; and the animistic, pre-rational world of the under-sevens lies exposed.

Background and theory

1. The founders of child psychoanalysis: Melanie Klein and Anna Freud

Following Sigmund Freud's analysis of little Hans, with the child's father as therapist and only a single encounter with the phobic 6-year-old in his father's presence (S. Freud 1959), Anna Freud in Vienna, and later in London, and Melanie Klein in London developed theories and techniques for the direct psychoanalysis of children. Both believed that many child psychiatric disorders develop on the basis of unconscious neurotic conflicts and that they improve as a consequence of self-observation, self-awareness, and insight, aided by the verbalizations of the therapist which facilitate maturation of the child's ego. Both held that insight does not occur without a process of 'working through'. Both also believed that in interaction with the therapist, in play or words, the child repeatedly displays his basic conflicts and that interpretation of his feelings, thoughts, and motives, fosters mastery of conflicts and maturation.

Melanie Klein (1963, 1961) was the first to equip a play room with small, non-mechanical toys, representing people, animals, cars and trains etc. drawing and cutting-out materials, and water and sand. She took everything the child did in his sessions as a significant transference communication and saw the analyst's prime tasks as understanding and interpreting the symbolic content of the child's play on the basis of a coherent framework of theory (both of child development and of the genesis of symptoms). At the same time, she held that the analyst must be aware of the unique life situations and idiosyncratic experiences of each individual patient while alert to recurrent dominant anxieties, emotions, and object relations which find symbolic expression in his play. The repeated re-enacting of his most anxiety-laden life experiences and the therapist's repeated commentary on their underlying meaning is the helpful 'work' of analysis.

Anna Freud (1946*b*) took issue with Klein's view of the transference in child analysis. She saw the therapist not only as a recipient of projections but also as a real person and even educator for the child. Non-transference relationship factors are especially important for children with 'ego-deficits' (e.g. borderline and other constitutionally-impaired children). For these the therapist must act as an auxiliary ego. For all children the therapist is, quite apart from his interpretative functions, a model for identification and a provider of real gratifications, as well as a mediator between child and parent. Fatherless children, for example, are best helped by a male therapist. She thought the role of toys in therapy was overrated and stressed that:

'Analysis is neither abreaction, which would be associated with lay therapy nor "corrective emotional experience" . . . It is rather the changing of the inner balance or focus to bring about that widening of consciousness which is insight into motivation. These are three different concepts of the therapeutic process. Insight does not occur without a working through process' (Sandler, Kennedy, and Tyson 1980, p. 70).

She did not regard the psychoanalytic process as unique: ordinary, good methods of upbringing also foster the child's self-observation and insight into motivation and feeling, his own and that of his parents.

Psychoanalytically-oriented psychotherapy, as we shall see, accepts the basic principles and techniques derived from psychoanalysis but the experience is less intense and less protracted and the aims are more circumscribed.

2. Donald Winnicott's contribution

Donald Winnicott, a psychoanalyst and paediatrician, developed his own quite original and imaginatively effective method for helping children with neurotic conflicts and their parents in the setting of a busy out-patient practice. He would ask parents to tell him about the problem, its development, and background. He would have a single lengthy interview with the child himself, using his own famous squiggle game as the main mode of communication. Taking turns, he and the child would draw a squiggle on a sheet of paper, get the other one to complete the picture and comment on what it represents. Because of his exceptional combination of gifts: acute empathic understanding of children, serious concern, and the capacity to allow his own childhood self to participate playfully in the encounter, he often achieved more in one session than other therapists might during prolonged treatment. Follow-up was often done with parents by telephone. Whether other less intuitive therapists can use his methods as effectively remains in doubt. While giving us ample illustrations of this approach, Winnicott (1971), himself a Kleinian, did not establish a 'school' or training programme of his own.

3. Non-directive play therapy: Virginia Axline

Virginia Axline's two volumes (1967, 1971) give eloquent accounts of Carl Rogers's non-directive psychotherapy applied to children. The books are written for teachers and other non-medical professionals as well as for psychiatrists. Axline's play therapy can be practised by teachers in schools, by care staff, and others in children's homes as well as in psychiatric clinics. Children are treated individually or in groups and, an ususual feature, they can bring their friends!

Her basic belief is that each individual has a potential for self-realization, and her aim in play therapy is to release the curative forces present in every child. Even without treating parents she holds that play therapy helps children through insight and self-understanding to become stronger and capable of withstanding even very adverse conditions.

While the exposition of her theories of personality, of its development, and of childhood psychopathology are frankly anti-Freudian and also unclear, she conveys most graphically a way of interacting with children and their parents that is a model for all professionals who wish to help emotionally and behaviourally-disturbed children. Her two books are full of practical examples of how to deal with common problems, e.g. the reluctant child in the waiting room; the child who wants to take toys home; physical attacks by one child on another; and how to react to handicapped children.

She sets out eight simple principles for non-directive therapists:

(1) the rapid creation of a warm and friendly relationship with the child;

(2) total acceptance of the child exactly as he is;

(3) establishing permissiveness so that the child is free to express his feelings openly in the relationship with the therapist;

(4) alertness to the feelings the child expresses and reflecting these back to him so that he gains insight into his behaviour;

(5) a deep respect for the child's capacity to solve his own problems if given the opportunity, and leaving him with the responsibility for choices and the initiation of changes;

(6) no attempt to direct the child's behaviour or conversation: where the child leads the therapist follows;

(7) no attempt to hurry the treatment along; and

(8) the setting of limits only to the extent of anchoring the treat- ment in reality and making the child aware of his responsibility in the relationship.

She does not believe that a transference relationship is an essential component of treatment and she is opposed to the therapist fostering dependence on himself by supportive activities for and lifting of responsibilities from the child. Her play-room contains not only small representational toys and material for artistic creativity, but also large toys such as rockers and punchball, puppets, and dressing-up clothes.

Her approach is of immense value for beginners and for relatively untrained workers with disturbed children. Her principles, if followed, will ensure that vulnerable and damaged children, for example disturbed children in care, are not harmed by intrusive and excessive therapeutic zeal. Child psychiatric clinic staff need to add to her basic recipe more focused and more energetic interventions, if neurotically ill children are to be helped within a reasonable time. Although entirely unself-critical and at times quixotic, Axline's writings have sturdily withstood the passage of time.

Practical aspects of therapy

Every point made by Jerome Frank in his introductory chapter to this book applies also to children.

1. Qualities of the therapist: personal characteristics

Although Kolvin and his colleagues found extraversion, therapeutic assertiveness and openness, rather than empathy and warmth, in therapists to be related to good outcome, we must remember that this was a study of *group* psychotherapy for children (Kolvin, Garside, Nicol, Macmillan, Wolstenholme, and Leitch 1981). There has been no other challenge to the three qualities deemed to be essential in psychotherapists (Truax and Carkhuff 1967): respect, empathy, and non-possessive warmth (to which John Reisman 1973 has added the wish to be of help). These qualities are integral to all civilized relationships between adults but are less universally cultivated by grown-ups in their approach to children. Inevitably adult therapists bring to their encounter with children memories of how they themselves were treated in their youth. Unless they are among the fortunate few with clear early memories, and unguarded about their own childhood selves, special efforts are needed not to be patronizing and educative but seriously attentive to child patients and, just as in psychotherapy with adults, scrupulously to avoid value judgements. When a child shares one of his school successes, a morale-boosting 'You must have been pleased with yourself' is preferable to 'That's very good'. If the following term ends less happily, it will help the child to see his therapist as invested not in his actual success but rather in his capacity to cope, even with setbacks.

2. Qualities of the therapist: the special knowledge base for work with children

Because children are less able to describe their thoughts and feelings, accurate empathy is possible only if one can make informed guesses about how the child at his particular stage is likely to have experienced certain life events or circumstances. This requires a working knowledge of cognitive and emotional child development, both rapidly growing fields of knowledge (see Wolff 1983 for an overview). The under-sevens, for example, tend to personalize their life experiences excessively so that when a father leaves home after repeated violent quarrels with his wife, the child believes the quarrels were about him and that, if his father had loved him more, he would have stayed. If a 4-year-old is admitted to hospital after an accident, she is likely to interpret this event as a punishment for some misdeed. Logical relationships are hard to grasp in these years and children do not reason on the basis of their observations. For example, an intelligent adopted half—Chinese boy of seven, disliked his face and being called 'chinky' by other children. He knew his adoptive parents were not his real parents. He longed for the people he had heard so much about who had looked after him for part of his first year of life, and he clung to his belief that *they* were his real parents although photographs showed that they were clearly not Chinese.

We need to be aware also that the timing of events and circumstances affects not only how children are likely to think and reason about these experiences but what their emotional impact will be. Exposure to prolonged group care, for example, can expand the horizons of a 12-year-old, but it can seriously impair the capacities for emotional responsiveness if it happens during the first three years of life. The accidental loss of a finger tip, while stressful at any stage, may have quite disproportionate emotional effects if it occurs between the ages of three and six when, symbolically, the injury represents a retaliatory punishment for excessive sexual curiosity or assertiveness.

Moreover, young children cannot give clear accounts of their life histories. It is essential to get these from parents in order to understand the meaning and significance of what children tell one. The sudden tears of a 10-year-old recounting how his mother took his rather too destructive kitten to the vet to be put down, convey their full meaning only when one knows he is the one child his unmarried, borderline psychotic mother kept; long before his birth she abandoned three other children; and recently she had a further baby she gave up for adoption.

3. The first interview

Children are brought to treatment, usually by their parents, and sometimes at the request of teachers or the courts. It is adults who identify the problem, in part because young children (especially under seven or eight), cognitively still immature, are poor observers of themselves. One of the therapist's first tasks is to clarify with the child why he has come, what the problem is, and what the therapist can do to help. In this initial stage of treatment there are many opportunities to demonstrate a therapeutic attitude. The therapist conveys interest in the child's own views of the encounter and indicates his own readiness to be frank.

When children are referred for stealing or soiling, for example, symptoms usually evoking angry concern in parents and teachers and associated with shame and often guilt in the child, it is helpful, after an initial discussion of more neutral topics, for the therapist to declare frankly this knowledge: 'Your mother is very worried about your stealing. That must be a big worry for you too.' In a non-judgemental way he conveys that he appreciates (and quite deliberately 'reads') the aberrant behaviour as a symptom the child himself would wish he did not have; that it is associated with anxiety, and that it has a meaning the child himself may not know. Because he is careful not to put direct questions, the child is likely to respond not with defensive denial but a more open revelation of his feelings. If this is not possible in the first encounter, the therapist can helpfully acknowledge that it may be 'too difficult' to talk about that just now.

Many children externalize their problems, aware of their conflict with parents or teachers but not of the need for change within themselves. For such children, especially delinquents, the therapist must try to foster a positive bond and provide real satisfactions. Although Anna Freud in her later years (Sandler *et al.* 1980) did not like to call this process in child analysis one of seduction, in fact it is often necessary to exert oneself to give children positive experiences in order to help them tolerate the more demanding and stressful aspects of treatment.

4 The role of the therapist

The most distinctive features of child psychotherapy are the relationship between therapist and child and the modes of communication between them. These features spring from the child's immaturity and his actual dependence on adults. Anna Freud (Sandler *et al.* 1980) thought children were more difficult to psychoanalyse because of their intolerance of anxiety and frustration, their preference for action over words, their inability to engage in free association, and 'the unavoidable intrusion of parents'!

(i) *Transference*

Although Melanie Klein (1963, 1961) held that the transference in child psychoanalysis, was equivalent to that of adult patients, Anna Freud (1946*b*) was clear that there were two distinct differences (see Sandler *et al.* 1980). These are important also for psychotherapy. First, when children interact with their therapist as they would with their parents, projecting similar feelings onto him and expecting similar responses from him, the parents are in the present and not the past. The patient is not interacting with others 'as if' he were still under the control of powerful parents: he is actually still a child. While he certainly experiences in treatment that other adults can be different from parents, he cannot, as do adult patients, put his parents behind him. Second, the therapist, however neutral, is always a real adult in the life of the child and to that extent has both nurturing and educative influences. He becomes both an auxiliary ego, helping the child to cope and to mature, as well as an alternative role model.

(ii) *Setting limits*

It is an error to think that children benefit from releasing aggression, as if there were a certain amount which had to be let out. In fact when this happens children often become very anxious indeed, terrified of their own power and its possible dangers. As in adult therapy, the child is encouraged to reveal his feelings in words (and in play) with no limits on the content and form of his communications. The therapeutic intervention is to help the child to understand, tolerate, and master his feelings, not to enact them in reality. But, when occasionally children do become wild and possibly destructive, the therapist scrupulously avoids the common adult to child prohibition: 'Don't do that', a response most likely to result in non-compliance and loss of face for child and therapist. Instead, while welcoming the child's expression of his feelings and wishes, he assumes full responsibility for the maintenance of safety without conveying that he expects more self-control from the child than he can manage. The therapeutic message is 'I won't let you hurt yourself or me; or damage the room. . . . If you feel so angry that you can't control yourself I will help you make sure no harm is done.' Often verbal comments on how the child is feeling, acknowledging his emotions and their validity, is enough to prevent their enactment. Sometimes the therapist has to step in physically, even holding a child on his lap, until control has been regained. This approach is anxiety-reducing: it relieves the child of responsibility and guilt without shaming him. It also presents a model to the child of non-hostile control.

(iii) *The therapist's relationship with the parents*

The therapist is responsible for his interventions not only to the child but also to the parents. Moreover the child's attendance depends on his parents' motivation as much as (sometimes more than) on his own. The therapist relies on parents for important information. Finally, if the child is to change, the parents must be able to tolerate this. If we enable an inhibited, phobic child to become more openly assertive, negativistic, and questioning, we must be sure that his parents can put up with such behaviour. It can help, in the child's presence, to ask the parents whether their child can ever get cross with them; to indicate, if this never occurs, that the symptom may be an expression of 'bottled up' feelings and that an important stage in treatment is for the child to become more awkward and oppositional with his mother and father. Many parents declare themselves willing to accept this, while a few are adamant they could never tolerate 'cheek'. Whatever the response, the parents' real attitudes can then be acknowledged by child and therapist in treatment. Most parents require support and many quite active treatment while their child is in therapy. Often, especially when the presenting problem indicates open conflict and mutual hostility between parents and child, a period of psychotherapy for child and parents separately and with different therapists can helpfully precede joint family interviews.

The emotional and behavioural difficulties of children often, but not always, arise from family conflict and parental personality disturbance, and they fulfil a function within the network of family transactions. A constipated 3-year-old boy, for example, ate poorly and woke up nightly, crying for his mother. She, grossly overweight, would regularly rise to make for herself and him a midnight feast of 'hot chocolate'. She went to bed early each night in anticipation of her toddler's demands, frustrating her husband's needs for sex and affection. She justified this pattern to herself in terms of not wanting to wake her hard-working husband. But she was also clear that, although she wished it were otherwise, she could not face intercourse since her son's birth. Her unassertive husband, resentful of his son, accepted the situation mindful of the violence he had witnessed as a boy between his parents.

A fine judgement is always needed about the most appropriate method and, in particular, whether the initial approach should involve the family as a whole or whether, if the child's intrapsychic disturbance and his individual needs require this, the parents can tolerate and help to promote a period of individual psychotherapy for the child.

(iv) *Frankness and confidentiality*

In general, as with adults, the therapist approaches children with genuineness and frankness, demonstrating to the child that important matters affecting him can be talked about without fear. But one must always remember the child's cognitive level and what aspects of an event are likely to impinge on him. The aim is not to have the child understand the details of some life event but to declare the topic open and help him express his own thoughts and feelings about it. This is especially important when there is a possible family secret surrounding, for example, a child's adoption, the replacement of his first mother in early childhood, or a father's imprisonment. Children are often aware of these events but dare not voice their knowledge. The therapist must be absolutely clear about what the parents have told the child. He may need to help parents towards greater frankness. Some parents are adamant that secrecy must prevail but this does not close the door to treatment. However, once children reveal their knowledge in the course of therapy this in itself can change the parents' views.

Over the years I have come to regard the requirement of frankness as less than absolute. When a mother reveals in private that she is the only one who knows her 12-year-old boy is not her husband's son, is it necessarily helpful to press her now, and as a prerequisite for treatment, to face her family with this shattering news? When the alcoholic father of a backward 8-year-old in foster care kills his alcoholic wife and is imprisoned for murder, does it help to present the facts to the boy against his foster parents' judgement, except in terms of an 'accident' caused by drink, in which his mother died and for which his father was held responsible, although he tried (as indeed he did too late) to get help?

Apart from such rare and shocking circumstances however, the rule of frankness between therapist and child should stand.

As in the treatment of adults, the individual therapy sessions with the child are private; the products of his play remain in the room which the parents should not as a matter of course enter. Nor are his communications revealed to parents. The evidence of battle scenes in the sandtray or of messy daubs of paint on hands and paper remain part of the evanescent fantasy shared by child and therapist, with no real life consequences, and clearly separated from the world outside.

Termination of treatment

In contrast to the treatment of adults, child therapy ends by returning the child not to his own care alone but to that of his parents. The therapist aims not only to have the patient look at himself more squarely but to promote between child and parents a more courageously open relationship which can better meet the child's emotional needs as he grows up. This means that parents must come to understand their child better. Indeed many bring the child for this very purpose. Often, when the parents' own personalities are essentially healthy, the therapist can, after a period of individual treatment, act as mediator and prop, enabling the child in joint interviews with parents to have his say. Such encounters should occur only with the child's agreement and when the therapist is sure the parents can tolerate and accept the communications.

The tasks of dynamic child psychotherapy

A primer (Adams 1982), Reisman's text (1973), and Axline's works (1967, 1971) all contain good advice for beginners in child psychotherapy.

1. General principles and aims

Basic to child as to adult dynamic psychotherapy is the idea that repetitive maladaptive behaviour and psychogenic symptoms are expressions of thoughts and emotions outside the patient's awareness. Because the experiences are in conflict either with his conscience or aspirations (his super-ego or ego-ideal) or, in the case of the child, with the real demands of his parents, they are repressed and kept out of conscious awareness by a number of psychological defence mechanisms.

A primary aim of treatment is to create a relationship with the child in which he will feel so secure that he can abandon these defensive manoeuvres and face and accept his own inner thoughts and feelings squarely however dangerous or foolish they might seem. It is the therapist's job to help the child like himself and his inner life better. The validation of his thoughts and feeling, the notion that any child of his age, given his experiences would have reacted similarly, brings relief. Self-esteem is raised and anxiety reduced. Many repressed thoughts and feelings stem even in children from the past when the child was cognitively less mature than he is now. To recognize this brings relief.

2. The importance of the child's actual environment

Often it is insufficient for the therapist to provide non-critical acceptance of the child's inner life. When there is real conflict because of the demands put on him by his parents, or their intolerance of normal child-like modes of being, the therapist must endeavour, often with the help of colleagues, to modify the child's actual environment. When constitutionally normal parents are either themselves under excessive external pressure or suffer from minor or moderately severe personality disorder which interfere with the upbringing of their children, practical help or intervention focusing on their own needs can lead to a shift in their reactions to their children. Often, more active intervention using behavioural or family therapy techniques, outside the scope of this chapter, are helpful in addition.

When parents are either absent or not able to make such changes (e.g. when they are psychotic, brain-damaged, schizoid, borderline psychotic, or seriously psychopathic) auxiliary parental care such as in a residential school, may have to be sought.

3. Four basic psychotherapeutic tasks

The child therapist's four main tasks are:

—to create a non-critical and secure relationship with the child;
—to enable the child to express freely his inner thoughts and feelings;
—to understand the underlying meaning of the child's communications; and
—to reflect this back to him.

We need to be clear that the last and most effective task can only be undertaken when children enjoy real security in their lives. An 8-year-old who has lost two parents and whose temporary foster placement is about to break down cannot possibly face his grief and fury, however skilled his therapist, until new parent figures have made a permanent commitment to him. He needs all the defences he can muster even if, to preserve a cheery front, he has to soil or steal.

Once new security has been found, interpretative treatment can start.

(i) *Creating a therapeutic relationship*

The principles of non-critical acceptance and a friendly but non-intrusive approach apply as in adult psychotherapy. But with children one has to explain more and question less, aware all the time of children's disadvantage in relation to adults; they know less, their understanding is different, they are socially less skilled, and, of course, smaller.

Questions demand answers and children may not know or may think they do not know what to say. It is better to turn a question into a statement. The child is then free to take it or leave it (e.g. 'I was wondering if your mother knew how you felt' or 'that must have been quite upsetting for you'). If the child is too anxious to reply, his silence is not a mark of failure or non-compliance.

When a therapist has information about the child he should be frank and say what he knows. Children should not be given the opportunity to lie.

Adams (1982) is very clear about the need for the therapist to explain the purpose, aims, and process of treatment to the child. '. . . a general or permanent stance of non-direction . . . will turn off most children' (p. 107), who interpret it as meanness. The therapist should feel free to share all information he has had from parents with the child, but tell them nothing about the child except with his knowledge and agreement, and preferably in his presence. This has the added advantage of modelling for parents how children can be helped to say what is on their minds.

As a symbolic expression of the therapist's wish to understand the child seriously at *his* level, he always sits on a chair of the same height: even small children if busy at a table or participating in a family meeeting sit on adult chairs, while the therapist sits on a small chair with him when the child (standing or sitting) is at the sand tray.

Although child therapists should be more communicative and more giving, even, for example, by sending postcards during holidays or when treatment has ended, they should (at least until treatment has been completed and just as in psychotherapy with adults) guard against revelations about their personal lives. Of course, if asked one can explain that one does not actually sleep in the clinic. But it does not help to reveal facts about the therapist's own family. All too readily this becomes a standard for hurtful comparisons with the child's own family. The child should be free to imagine the other family in any way he likes; and the therapist should treat such communications as transference phenomena.

(ii) *Helping the child to express his thoughts and feelings*

This requires materials and opportunities for the child to communicate indirectly through play with small representational toys and creative activities (drawing, painting, modelling). Questions about his earliest memories, what his three magic wishes would be if anything he wanted could happen, what he will become when he grows up, and what his dreams are about, all encourage children to convey their fantasy life. Children are helped also when the therapist has enough courage to reveal his guesses as to what might be on the child's mind.

A 7-year-old, John, was brought to the clinic because of aggressive attacks on his mother. She had a mild schizophrenic defect state and he recalled vividly her delusions (involving him) when he was three years old. He was repeatedly asking her for money to buy icecream and sweets: his hard-working and worried father was always angry with him at night.

In the first session John drew a 'fight' between a large and confident looking 'woodpecker' and a small, misshapen dog. When asked who would win, he paused and said 'the woodpecker, because it's bigger'. When asked who he thought *should* win, John said 'the dog'. His therapist then commented that she knew he really wanted his mother to win over him and that he probably felt quite bad when she did not. John explained at length how he always asked his mother for money and she always gave it to him. When asked what she *should* do, he replied 'Not give it to me'. 'My ma's going to buy me a piano', he went on to say, and this idea seemed to make him uneasy.

Different techniques are needed for children of different ages. Toddlers often feel most at home, at least initially, with a sandtray equipped with animals and people of different kinds, and with water. Latency-stage children express themselves well with paper and crayons or paint, with plasticine, and through more structured make-believe play, e.g. in a doll's house. Even at this stage children often need the opportunity to regress to more infantile play in order to express less differentiated thoughts and feelings. Play and paperwork are helpful mediators in the process of therapeutic conversations. Older children may prefer to talk merely using clay, plasticine, or drawing as accompanying activities. Going for a walk can also be of help for the therapeutic process for older, inhibited children.

Jigsaws and board or card games are less helpful, except for extremely inhibited youngsters, because they allow for little expression of fantasy; since they are interesting in themselves, they often divert both patient and therapist from their therapeutic tasks.

(iii) *Understanding the underlying meaning of the child's communications*

Comments on the underlying meaning of the child's communications encourage further communications so that these two processes are intimately linked. When John, for instance, spoke of the piano his therapist thought this meant the mother would give him anything he asked for, however big, rather than that a real piano was about to be purchased.

Guesses about certain universal connections in childhood are often appropriate, for example, that fear of the destructive effect of one's own impulses leads one to be more rather than less aggressive in an attempt to reassure onself that nothing really bad can happen. The phobic anxiety when parents go out—in case an accident should befall them—often stands for feelings of anger towards those very parents, which the child (usually for good reason) is too fearful to face.

(iv) *Interpretations*

The reflections to John of the underlying meaning of his communication went beyond a mere commentary on how he felt. It was already a form of interpretation.

In contrast to psychoanalysis where children are seen daily, it is important in once-weekly, brief psychotherapy that interpretations should be framed in such a way that they enhance the child's positive feelings about himself (his self-esteem) and are ego building but, at the same time, just as in psychoanalysis, they foster insight and the giving up of inhibiting defences. When an 11-year-old with anorexia nervosa reports that she dreamt it was kinder to eat vegetables rather than people, it will not do to point out her cannibalistic impulses. It is more helpful to focus on her defence of reaction formation: to stress her wish to be kind; her discomfort when she is angry; and her preference to eat nothing at all rather than risk hurting anyone. When in time she reveals her frustration at her mother's restrictiveness, a comment indicating that such feelings are universal in children of her age, is likely both to give relief and to encourage further expressions of previously suppressed or repressed emotions. In contrast to the impression gained by the naive reader of much of the psychoanalytic literature, interpretations should, as Adam (1982) tells us, be a comforting 'corrective experience' and not an 'unmasking' device.

The two major affects involved in the unconscious conflicts of adults and children with neurotic disorders are anger and sexual longing. In child psychotherapy (as contrasted with psychoanalysis) Adams (1982) again helpfully counsels us to focus on the child's anger first. Our adult sexual preoccupations may confuse and seduce children, and can foster excessive dependency which, in brief treatments, is misplaced. This does not mean that a child's unsatisfied sexual curiosity should not be acknowledged. Therapists can often be helpful mediators, enabling parents to enlighten their child. This increases intimacy between child and parents and often the child's esteem among his peers.

Interpretations regarding transference play an important part in child psychotherapy. Right at the start comments to a silent child that it is, of course, difficult to talk to someone he hardly knows, open up the relationship between child and therapist as a topic for discussion. Once familiar with the treatment setting, aggressive pre-school and early schoolage children often become extremely hostile towards their therapists. They may project onto the therapist their feelings for an impulsive and physically punitive parent and their fears of their own destructiveness. Repeatedly the therapist provides a corrective experience by taking full responsibility for kindly and non-threatening control, by relating the child's present behaviour to his past experiences, and by focusing on feelings of affection as well as anger and disappointment. Even a father violent in drink usually loves his children and does not intend to cause harm. Much aggression in childhood is a means for testing the strength of parental affection: how bad can one be without being rejected?

At the close of treatment too an awareness of the meaning to the child of the severing of contact, in the light of his past experiences of the loss of important people, will help the therapist to end the relationship in a positive way. Disguised disappointment and anger will need to be acknowledged. A consolation is that there will be mutual remembrance; people do not disappear from one's mind. Follow-up postcards are allowed.

Perhaps the most important goal of interpretations for children is to reduce anxiety by fostering a cognitively more mature view of the world. Neurotic symptoms, even in adults tend to have their origins in those stages of childhood when thinking is still pre-causal and animistic (Piaget and Inhelder 1969) and the distinction between thoughts and wishes on the one hand and actions on the other is blurred. Child therapists need to stress repeatedly that murder and bloodshed in the sandpit have no real consequences, and that thoughts and words, however bad, carry no risk.

4. Matching the therapeutic resources to the child's needs: the duration of treatment

Most treatment in the National Health Service is once-weekly except when children are so ill or disturbed that they need to go into hospital. Short-term treatment can be sustained more easily by parents, is more economical of staff resources, has on the whole proved effective (see Kolvin *et al.* 1981), and can be carried out without change of therapist by short-term trainees (in psychiatry, child psychology, and social work) under supervision. This is the commonest form of child psychotherapy, despite the fact that more frequent and more long-term treatment may be more effective (see below).

(i) *Brief, dynamic psychotherapy is focused*

As in the case of all brief psychological treatments, short-term child psychotherapy must have a focus. This necessitates a full initial assessment of the child's condition, its aetiology and underlying psychopathology, and of the psychiatric status of his parents. Of course the therapists's formulation of the child's basic conflicts must be open to revision in the light of subsequent knowledge, but it helps to keep in mind throughout the treatment its primary aims. These may be to reduce the anxiety of a sleepless toddler about the destructive effects of his angry impulses on the parents; or to counteract the self-doubts of an over-compliant six-year-old, who steals from her step-mother for fear of being openly assertive, in case she is once more rejected; or to help a 12-year-old school phobic to see that her angry, oppositional impulses could not possibly have caused her widowed mother's depression.

(ii) *The place of long-term supportive psychotherapy*

When children have minor physical or educational handicaps and are likely to be under chronic stress, a more long-term if less frequent contact with the psychotherapist (who then needs to be in a senior position and thus unlikely to move away) can be very helpful for child and parents. Older children, handicapped by deficiencies within their own families—for example a psychotic mother or the absence of siblings *and* one of the two parents—may be greatly helped in their personal development by knowing that their therapist is identified with their future needs and plans, and is available on a long-term basis. This is still the case if they are seen only a few times a year following a short, intensive phase of treatment.

Children with constitutional 'ego-deficits' that is with handicaps affecting their capacities for interpersonal relationships, can also be helped to function better by a long-term but non-interpretative therapeutic contact.

5. Indications for child pychotherapy

Amid the wealth of treatment methods now available in child psychiatry, and in the absence of research-based knowledge of what kind of treatments work best for which conditions under what circumstances, the choice of treatment for the individual child and his family may seem arbitrary.

There is general agreement, however, that children considered suitable for psychotherapy are mainly those with reactive (not constitutionally-based) disorders. If the child's emotional or behavioural symptoms are likely to respond to environmental change alone, e.g. change in family interactions or in his teachers' approaches, then family therapy, parental therapy, or consultation with teachers may be the treatment of choice.

If the disorder is more deep-seated, the result of past traumatic life experiences, and it has led to the excessive use of defence mechanisms and the arrest of personality development, especially when the clinical picture is that of a neurosis, individual psychotherapy for the child is indicated, quite apart from other treatments (family therapy, parental or teacher counselling, behaviour modification, medication with anti-depressants) that may also be necessary.

6. Contra-indications to exploratory psychotherapy: the treatment of children with constitutional impairment ('ego-deficit')

Psychoanalysts regularly treat children with 'borderline states' whose defensive structure is abnormal. Such children have also been described as having Asperger's syndrome or as being schizoid in personality (Wolff and Barlow 1979). Special techniques for long-term psychoanalysis have been described (see for example, Rosenfeld and Sprince 1965).

7. Psychotherapy for severely deprived children

Psychoanalysts have until recently been very clear that children without a permanent home, that is children lacking basic security, should not be exposed to interpretative therapy (p. 236). Yet foster and houseparents as well as social workers often ask for treatment for seriously emotionally deprived children because they are so worried about these children's level of aggression, their withdrawn isolation, or their abnormal sexual activities.

Attempts to help greatly traumatized children in care to cope better in whatever homes they have or to prepare them for a permanent new home by means of intensive and long-term analytic psychotherapy have recently been described (Boston and Szur 1982). Sadly, while this book does help the reader to grasp the extreme difficulties faced both by the children and their therapists, there is no attempt to evaluate the outcome nor even to present the clinical data systematically. What is clear is that only experienced therapists, able to stay with the child for several years should attempt such interventions.

Although such children may be helped by very long-term treatment with frequent sessions, the psychotherapist should be absolutely clear about their diagnosis before embarking on short-term dynamic psychotherapy. While the latter helps most children with neurotic, emotional, or conduct disorders, who are constitutionally healthy and have normal psychological defences, it is totally inappropriate for autistic children and can be harmful for 'borderline' and for some brain-damaged children. Interpretations can further impair the already limited capacity for distinguishing fantasy from reality in 'borderline' children, can increase their tendency for paranoid projection, and can lead to frightening and explosive losses of impulse control. For autistic children the dynamic approach is ineffective. Moreover, such treatment sets up unwarranted expectations for improvement in child and parents which inevitably lead to disappointment. Constitutionally-impaired children respond better to a supportive, non-intrusive approach which respects the chronicity of their condition. Environmental changes, at school 'and at home, can help such children obtain a better social and educational adjustment. Parents of these children need to be regarded as therapeutic allies. The therapist must make it absolutely clear to them that they are in no way responsible for their child's difficulties so that the burden on them of having a handicapped child is not compounded by misplaced guilt.

The outcome of child psychotherapy: research findings

Excellent reviews of outcome studies of child psychotherapy are provided by Heincke and Strassmann (1975), Barrett, Hampe, and Miller (1978), and Kolvin *et al.* (1981). We need to be clear that while there is as yet no scientific proof that the various procedures outlined in this chapter are effective, there are no grounds for therapeutic gloom. Detailed prescriptions for practice currently rest on the accumulated clinical experience of child psychotherapists, especially on their points of agreement. There is evidence from controlled studies that, overall, child psychotherapy works, especially in the long term, and when treatment is intensive or protracted. However, the salient question concerning the conditions under which specific therapeutic interventions are effective for particular psychiatric disorders has not yet been answered (see Schaffer 1984).

Helen Witmer and her colleagues (quoted by Barrett *et al.* 1978) found that 25 per cent of child guidance clinic attenders were 'successfully adjusted' at the end of treatment and 51 per cent 'partially adjusted'. This early optimism was wrecked by Levitt's (1963) apparent finding that studies of treated and untreated child psychiatric clinic attenders showed the improvement rates of treated children at discharge and follow-up (67 per cent and 78 per cent) to be no higher than those of the untreated (72 per cent). In both groups roughly one-third improved, one-third partially improved, and one-third were unchanged. Barrett *et al.* (1978) point out that many of the apparently treated children received psychiatric care but not psychotherapy, and Kolvin *et al.* (1981) have once and for all discredited Levitt's baseline of success. Many children in the studies he summarized had developmental disorders, among whom the spontaneous 'much improved' rate was 54 per cent as compared with the following improvement rates for other conditions: neurosis 15 per cent, mixed disorders 20 per cent and antisocial disorders 31 per cent. It is, therefore, unwarranted to aggregate the results of different outcome studies when the baselines for improvement differ so greatly according to the proportions in the samples of different diagnostic groups of children.

Individual psychotherapy was not a treatment method studied in the major evaluation of school-based treatments for disturbed children in Newcastle (Kolvin *et al*. 1981). But child psychotherapists can nevertheless take heart from the very positive outcome results of direct therapeutic work with children demonstrated in this study. Short-term, non-directive group psychotherapy increased the good outcome of antisocial and emotionally disturbed children from 29 per cent and 19 per cent for the non-treated groups of disturbed primary and secondary school children respectively, to 35 per cent and 37 per cent after an 18-month follow-up period, and to 56 and 53 after three years. Its efficacy was similar to that of nurture work (by classroom aides assigned to help primary school children) and to behaviour therapy (for secondary school children). Group therapy was greatly superior to a combined programme of parent counselling and teacher consultation in which there was no direct contact with the children themselves.

The Newcastle study stands as a model for future evaluative research into the efficacy of treatment methods including individual child psychotherapy.

Heincke and Strassman (1975), in a comparison of once-weekly and four-times-weekly psychoanalytic psychotherapy for diagnostically-matched groups of 9-year-old children, found more frequent sessions to be more effective at one- and two-year follow-up in terms of reading ability, ego-integration, flexibility, and peer relationships. As with other studies emanating from the Hampstead Clinic, one cannot be sure that the meticulously collected and clinically highly relevant data (in this instance subjected to numerical analysis) about the children and their treatment were in fact gathered and recorded in a uniform and replicable manner, and that the outcome evaluations were 'blind', that is, made by independent observers and not by the children's own therapists. Nevertheless, this is one of the few studies of a defined aspect of child therapy: frequency of sessions.

Wright, Moelis, and Pollack (1976) in line with Heincke and Strassman's study (1975) and with the Newcastle findings (Kolvin *et al.* 1981) stress that the comparative benefits of child psychotherapy become apparent only one or two years after the end of treatment and cite evidence that more prolonged treatment (30 or more sessions) are more effective than briefer intervention.

The field is wide open for scientific exploration. Dynamic child psychotherapists should take heart from the fact that the literature on ostensibly more 'scientific' behavioural treatments for children also contains many single case reports, studies of small groups of treated children (often without controls), and rather few well-controlled investigations of large groups.

Training

As for other forms of psychotherapy, training in child psychotherapy has three components: (1) acquiring the knowledge base—and about this no more will be said here; (2) supervised practice; and (3) a personal psychotherapeutic experience.

Supervised practice

In the United Kingdom, only London offers opportunities for training to become a professional child analyst or analytical child psychotherapist. The training institutes providing these long and intensive courses normally require the trainee to undergo a personal analysis also.

Yet there are ample opportunities for training in practical child psychotherapy outside the metropolis. In fact, many trainees in general psychiatry welcome their attachment to child psychiatry departments because of the training in psychotherapeutic methods for children, parents, and families, offered.

There is one danger at the present time that needs to be faced. Some child and adolescent psychiatry departments are so keen on family therapy approaches that children are rarely seen on their own even for initial interviews. This robs the novice of the experience of therapeutic communications with children and, without this, his efficacy, even as a family therapist is likely to be impaired. Every child psychiatry department must ensure that trainees from all disciplines (psychiatrists, social workers, and psychologists) do get adequate experience in the assessment and ongoing psychotherapy of individual children, whatever the particular treatment orientation of the clinic or department as a whole.

Supervision of psychotherapy usually takes place in three possible settings:

(i) in individual, regular meetings of trainee and supervisor (often the consultant);

(ii) in weekly or twice weekly multidisciplinary team meetings; and

(iii) in special child psychotherapy groups or workshops, which may also be multidisciplinary.

(i) *Individual supervision*

This occurs weekly or fortnightly and enables the consultant to get to know the trainee personally, to orient him to the work, and to plan his clinical experience in the light of training needs.

Individual supervision provides opportunities for the regular and detailed discussion of the trainee's psychotherapy with a limited number of patients only. But this will be a help in his treatment of other children too, whose progress and management is referred to more briefly.

The great merit of individual encounters between consultant and trainee is that, without in anyway encroaching on the trainee's privacy and autonomy, revelations can be made, which are salient for the treatment of children and rarely possible in a team or workshop. One trainee, for example, a single mother, was able to discuss her initial hesitancy when confronted by an illegitimate boy, the only child of an unmarried mother. Another, who had himself been deprived of mothering in middle childhood, was able to see this not as a disadvantage (for example, in relation to his professional colleagues), but as enabling him to understand similarly deprived children better.

(ii) *Multidisciplinary team meetings*

Here psychiatrists, psychologists, and social workers discuss their ongoing work. How much the focus can be on individual psychotherapy with children will depend on the team itself. For example, whether the team's composition is currently stable or in a state of change, whether there are concerns perhaps relating to inter-professional collaboration, and on the team's workload. Management decisions inevitably take priority and some cases, also inevitably, take up inordinate amounts of discussion time. It is enjoyable and makes for team cohesion if individual psychotherapy with children can regularly feature on the agenda. Most important, it is much more illuminating to discuss a child's psychotherapy in a setting where both the child's and the parents' therapists are together, and a complete picture of the family dynamics and the treatment processes can be built up.

(iii) *Child psychotherapy group meetings or workshops*

These can be a forum for discussions between members from different disciplines, just like the team meetings, with the advantage that there is less pressure on the group in the form of urgent discussions of management, personal, or team concerns. The workshop can focus on the psychotherapeutic process with more leisure and calm. If the group is cohesive and stable, personal revelations relevant to the treatments can greatly add to the interest, enjoyment, and mutual understanding of the workshop members.

Workshops also offer opportunities for reading, for discussions of the literature, and for more formal case or topic presentations on special study days.

The use of video- and audio-recording

It is enormously helpful to see other therapists at work, and salutary to view oneself. The benefits for the therapist of being able to improve his techniques by objectifying his own performance must be set against the time taken and the consequent encroachment on time for free-floating discussion in team or workshop.

Conclusion

The general principles of psychotherapy for children are the same as for adults. However, the framework of practice differs because of the processes of personality development in childhood, and because children are dependent on their parents and on a network of other adults with responsibilities for their education and care. The rewards of child psychotherapy are of an exceptional kind. The notion that early treatment will prevent later psychiatric ill-health is quite unsubstantiated; the treatment of children is not likely to prevent the major mental illnesses of adult life. Nevertheless, the chances of reducing the degree and duration of childhood distress are considerable and the opportunity to exert a benign influence on the lives of children and their families is great.

References

Adams, P. L. (1982). *A primer of child psychotherapy* (2nd ed). Little, Brown, Boston.

Axline, V. M. (1969). *Play therapy*, Chapter 7, pp. 73-7. Ballantine, New York.

—— (1971). *Dibs: in search of self*. Penguin, London.

Barrett, C. L., Hampe, L. E., and Miller, L. (1978). Research on psychotherapy with children, Chapter 11, pp. 411-35. In *Handbook of psychotherapy and behavior change: an empirical analysis* (eds S. L. Garfield and A. E. Bergin) (2nd ed). John Wiley and Sons, New York and Chichester.

Boston, M. and Szur R. (ed) (1983). *Psychotherapy with severely deprived children*. Routledge and Kegan Paul, London.

Erikson, E. H. (1968). *Identity and the life cycle*. Faber, London.

Foulkes, S. H. and Anthony, E. J. (1957). *Group psychotherapy: the psychoanalytic approach*, pp. 169-88. Penguin Books, London.

Frank, J. D. (1974). Therapeutic components of psychotherapy: a 25-year progress report on research, *J. nerv. ment. Dis.* **159**, 325-42.

Freud, A. (1946*a*). *The ego and the mechanisms of defence*. Hogarth Press, London.

—— (1946*b*). *The psycho-analytical treatment of children*. Imago Publishing Company, London.

—— (1965). *Normality and pathology in childhood: assessments of develoment*. Hogarth Press, London; International Universities Press, New York.

Freud, S. (1959). Analysis of a phobia in a five-year-old boy (1909). In *Collected Papers*, Vol. 3. Hogarth Press, London.

Group for the advancement of psychiatry (1982). *The process of child therapy*. Brunner-Mazel, New York.

Heincke, C. M. and Strassmann, L. M. (1975). Toward more effective research on child psychotherapy, *Am. Acad. Child Psychiat.* **14**, 561-88.

Holmes, D. S. and Urie, R. S. (1975). Effects of preparing children for psychotherapy, *J. consult. clin. Psychol.* **43**, 311-18.

Klein, M. (1961). *Narrative of a child analysis*. Hogarth Press for the Institute of Psychoanalysis, London.

—— (1963). *The psychoanalysis of children*. Hogarth Press for the Institute of Psychoanalysis, London.

Kolvin, I., Garside, R. F., Nicol, A. R., Macmillan, A., Wolstenholme, F., and Leitch I. (1981). *Help starts here: the maladjusted child in the ordinary school*. Tavistock Publications, London.

Levitt, E. E. (1963). *Psychotherapy with children; a further evaluation.*

Behav. Res. Therapy **1**, 45–51.

McAuley, R. and McAuley, P. (1977). *Child behaviour problems: an empirical approach to management*. Macmillan, London.

Patterson, G. R. (1974). Interventions for boys with conduct problems: multiple settings, treatment and criteria, *J. consult. clin. Psychol.* **4**, 471–81.

Piaget, J. and Inhelder, B. (1969). *The psychology of the child*. Routledge and Kegan Paul, London.

Reisman, J. M. (1973). *Principles of psychotherapy with children*. Wiley-Interscience, New York.

Rosenfeld, S. and Sprince, M. P. (1965). Some thoughts on the technical handling of borderline children, *The Psychoanal. Study of the Child* **20**, 495–517.

Sandler, J., Kennedy, H., and Tyson, R. L. (1980). *The technique of child psychoanalysis: discussions with Anna Freud*. Hogarth, London.

Schaffer, D. (1984). Notes on psychotherapy research among children and adolescents, *J. Am. Acad. Child Psychiat.* **23**, 552–61.

Truax, C. B. and Carkhuff, R. R. (1967). *Toward effective counselling and psychotherapy: training and practice*. Aldine, Chicago.

Winnicott, D. W. (1971). *Therapeutic consultations in child psychiatry*. Basic, New York.

Wolff, S. (1981). *Children under stress* (2nd ed), Penguin, London.

—— (1983). Personality development. In *Companion to psychiatric studies*, pp. 61–78 (eds R. E. Kendell and A. K. Zealley) (3rd ed). Churchill Livingstone, Edinburgh.

—— and Barlow, A. (1979). Schizoid personality in childhood: a comparative study of schizoid, autistic and normal children, *J. Child Psychol. Psychiat.* **20**, 29–46.

Wright, D. M., Moelis, I., and Pollack, L. J. (1976). The outcome of individual psychotherapy: increments at follow-up, *J. Child Psychol. Psychiat.* **17**, 175–85.

Recommended reading

General

Adams, P. L. (1982). *A primer of child psychotherapy* (2nd ed). Little Brown and Company, Boston.

Reisman, J. M. (1973). *Principles of psychotherapy with children*. Wiley Interscience, New York.

Models of child psychotherapy and psychoanalysis

Axline, V. M. (1969). *Play therapy*. Ballantine Books, New York.

Freud, A. (1946). *The psychoanalytical treatment of children*. Imago Publishing Company, London.

Haworth, M. R. (1964). *Child psychotherapy.* Basic Books, New York.

Klein, M. (1961). *Narrative of a child analysis.* Hogarth Press for the Institute of Psychoanalysis, London.

—— (1963). *Psychoanalysis of children.* Hogarth Press for the Institute of Psychoanalysis, London.

Winnicott, D. W. (1964). *The child, the family and the outside world.* Penguin, London.

Child development

Bowlby, J. (1979) *The making and breaking of affectional bonds.* Tavistock Publications, London.

Donaldson, M. (1978). *Children's minds.* Fontana, London.

Erikson, E. H. (1971). *Identity, youth and crisis.* Faber, London.

Piaget, J. (1929). The child's conception of the world. Kegan Paul, London.

—— (1982). *The moral judgement of the child.* Routledge and Kegan Paul, London.

11

Supportive psychotherapy
Sidney Bloch

Supportive psychotherapy has several connotations but in this chapter refers to a form of treatment used for the chronically handicapped psychiatric patient. After attempting to define the term, Bloch considers the aims of treatment and its indications. There then follows a section on the nature of the therapist–patient relationship in, and the components of, supportive therapy. With basic practical issues in treatment discussed in general, a particular model whose central concept is that of an 'institutional alliance' is recommended. The critical problem of dependency is then examined and the chapter ends with brief accounts of research and training aspects.

The term supportive psychotherapy has many different meanings. In this chapter it will be used to refer to a form of psychological treatment given to patients with chronic and disabling psychiatric conditions for whom basic change is not seen as a realistic goal. Applying the term in this way it is likely that supportive therapy is one of the most commonly practised forms of psychotherapy. Apart from its widespread use in psychiatry, the therapy is also extensively applied by, amongst others, general practitioners, social workers, psychiatric nurses, and, less formally, by other professionals like the clergy and teachers. Yet relatively scanty systematic attention has been paid to it in textbooks on mental health and it has been rather neglected by psychotherapy research workers. This state of affairs is not altogether surprising: supportive psychotherapy is perhaps the most ill-defined and nebulous of all psychotherapies and tends to be recommended when no other more specific form of treatment is available. Commonly it is also regarded as an inferior form of psychotherapy only to be used in patients for whose problems we currently lack curative or even moderately effective techniques.

Thus we often offer supportive therapy when we have nothing else in our treatment cupboard. When we do, it is on the premise that we know what we are doing and that what we are doing is of some value. The premise however is fragile: supportive psychotherapy cannot be regarded merely as the provision of support to a patient. On the contrary, it is a therapy which calls for an intricate blend of art and technique and which can be carried out either effectively or harmfully.

This chapter attempts to define supportive psychotherapy and considers its aims, indications, therapeutic strategies, and the problems that may arise in the course of treatment. I shall also discuss one particular model whereby therapists can provide the treatment.

Definition

Supportive psychotherapy has always been difficult to define satisfactorily. At first we must emphasize that we are dealing here with a particular form of psychotherapy in which the therapist's provision of support is the chief component of treatment. All psychotherapies obviously entail some element of support and the therapist–patient relationship can be regarded as a helping one (Rogers 1961) but this support is only one of several therapeutic factors used and not the main mechanism underlying the treatment.

Noting the derivation of the word 'support' helps to understand the type of therapy under consideration: Supportare: Sup = Sub + portare—to carry (*Webster's new world twentieth century dictionary* (2nd end.), World Publishing, Cleveland, Ohio 1971). The therapist 'carries' the patient; he helps to prop him up, to sustain him, to keep him from falling or sinking. The obvious implication is that some patients are so handicapped by their psychiatric condition that they require from the therapist a form of psychological aid which enables them to 'survive'.

With the above in mind and for the purposes of this chapter, supportive psychotherapy can be defined as that form of psychological treatment given to a patient over an extended period, often many years, in order to sustain him, because he is unable to manage his life satisfactorily without such long-term help.

An inability to cope may be temporary or enduring. If temporary, the individual experiences a stressful situation such as bereavement, divorce, or change of job which leads to a degree of emotional upheaval not met by his own resources. Additional help from elsewhere is required. The person is said to be in crisis and the treatment necessary is usually referred to as crisis intervention. This is dealt with fully in Chapter 5 and will not be discussed further here. Enduring inability to manage independently is seen in some patients who are disabled by their chronic psychotic or neurotic state, or by the nature of their personality. They may require supportive therapy for an indefinite period. The rest of this chapter is concerned with this type of chronic patient and with his need for long-term help. We will limit ourselves to supportive psychotherapy as practised in the community although some of the points to be made also pertain to patients living in hospitals, hostels, or half-way houses.

Background

Supportive therapy has a long tradition. For centuries society has allocated to some of its members the role of helping those who become chronically disabled, either psychologically or physically. Religious orders particularly have played, and continue to play, an active part as 'therapist'. In addition, in relatively stable and cohesive societies, family and friends have commonly served as the providers of long-term support to those who were in need of it. With the advent of 'professional' psychotherapy in the 1890s, some psychiatrists turned their interest to the application of psychological measures for their patients, but confined themselves to the neuroses, and later to certain personality disorders. Chronic incurable psychiatric patients however continued to be relegated to the backwards of mental hospitals, there to receive custodial care.

The discovery of the major tranquillizers in the 1950s and the widespread adoption of the concept of community-based mental health care soon after has paved the way for large numbers of patients with chronic psychiatric states to be managed in the community. One result of this change has been the increasingly important role of supportive psychotherapy. The changes have also brought many problems and a salient question today is how the mental-health professional can care effectively for people with chronic problems who live outside of protective institutions, often isolated and with minimal or no natural support.

In addition to the increasing relevance of supportive therapy in the context of community mental health, it has also been highlighted in the clinical practice of the family doctor. Balint and his colleagues (Balint, Hunt, Joyce, Marinker, and Woodcock 1970) in their research on general practice, studied the role played by the doctor in treating the typical chronic neurotic patient—the patient who attended regularly with physical complaints not attributable to organic cause and who seemed to need continuing support in order to sustain himself adequately.

We shall return to both these contexts later in the chapter.

Aims of treatment

What are the aims of supportive psychotherapy? These will be influenced to an extent by the characteristics of the patient—his age, diagnosis, prognosis—but common objectives of treatment are:

(a) To promote the patient's best possible psychological and social functioning by restoring and reinforcing his abilities to manage his life.

(b) To bolster his self-esteem and self-confidence as much as possible.

(c) To make him aware of reality, i.e. of his own limitations and those of treatment—of what can and cannot be achieved.

(d) To forestall a relapse of his condition and thus try to prevent deterioration or rehospitalization.

(e) To enable the patient to require only that degree of professional support which will result in his best possible adjustment, and so prevent undue dependency.

(f) To transfer the source of support (not necessarily all of it) from professional to family or friends, provided of course that the latter are available and able to handle the role of support-giver.

Indications

Supportive psychotherapy is indicated in psychiatric patients who are severely handicapped both emotionally and in their interpersonal relationships and in whom there is no prospect of basic improvement. Because of their disability they simply cannot carry on their lives without some external help. They are intolerant of life's stresses and sometimes of even the most trivial demands. Relatives and friends who might be a source of support are often absent, or cannot cope with the needs of the patient. The severity of their conditions and the associated vulnerable quality of their personalities preclude the use of other forms of psychotherapy which involve the acquisition of insight as a central therapeutic factor.

In terms of traditional diagnosis the patients are chronic schizophrenics, recurrent or chronic depressives, chronic neurotics, particularly those with continuing anxiety and/or hypochondriacal features, and severe personality disorders. The last category includes patients who show typically paranoid, hysterical, passive-dependent, inadequate, or schizoid traits, but who also show, in common, disturbed interpersonal functioning and poor coping. Some persons with a low IQ or other permanent handicap like a chronic physical illness or disability may require supportive therapy in order to cope reasonably. The census of one 'supportive clinic' gives an idea of the type of patient treated: 56 per cent were psychotic, 24 per cent neurotic, and 16 per cent personality disorders (MacLeod and Middleman 1962).

As the concept of chronic neurosis is used in a variety of ways, and as many patients receiving supportive therapy have this diagnosis applied to them, it warrants closer attention. More often a woman and usually middle-aged, the chronic neurotic suffers continuous anxiety and/or depression, both mild to moderate in intensity; responds poorly and ineffectively to even trivial life events and generally is intolerant of stress; is in need of constant attention from spouse, children, relatives, and professionals, especially general practitioners; is unable to ask for help in an adaptive way or to use what help is available; is relatively unable to express dissatisfaction or distress in emotional terms but rather tends to use body language, i.e. 'offers' non-specific physical symptoms like headache, weakness, and tiredness, which lack an organic basis; is commonly preoccupied with health and bodily function; has had little experience of pleasure and joy in life and is basically unfulfilled with limited or no interests.

This type of patient may be able to cope—albeit in a far from satisfactory fashion—but any psychological or social change may upset the equilibrium and lead to symptom formation and professional consultation. For example, a woman with a stable, tolerant, and supportive husband may function more or less adequately until he becomes ill or dies or makes some major change in his life. The neurotic pattern may then become overt and visits to the doctor or other therapists may ensue.

Deciding whether a patient is suitable or not for supportive therapy does not usually pose a problem. The treatment has no place in patients in whom there is good evidence of personal resources and strengths, sufficient for independent coping with life's ordinary demands and pressures. As noted in Chapter 5, it can be used as part of 'intensive care', i.e. in crisis intervention where a person with normal coping ability is temporarily overwhelmed by some major stress, but then only for a circumscribed period during which the therapist temporarily assumes responsibility. This responsibility is transferred to the patient as soon as possible.

The therapist-patient relationship

The patient for whom supportive psychotherapy is indicated experiences difficulty in maintaining intimate relationships with others. An intense personal relationship which may involve issues of closeness, trust, and possible separation, constitutes a major threat to him. This must be borne in mind in considering the nature of the relationship between patient and therapist in supportive psychotherapy (Balint *et al.* 1970; Rada, Daniels, and Draper 1969; MacLeod and Middleman 1962). Balint and his colleagues (1970) have shown, for example, that patients who request repeat prescriptions (mainly of psychotropic drugs) from their general practitioners, make frequent contact with them but always indirectly. These patients are lonely and isolated people with chronic neurotic traits who 'tolerate badly any proximity or intimacy with their partners'. They maintain a safe distance from their doctors as well by 'offering him bodily complaints' and receiving repeat prescriptions from them—the drug represents the 'something' they need badly. These patients are quite unable to make use of the trusting, intimate relationship which is the basis of almost all psychotherapy.

Thus the relationship between patient and therapist in supportive therapy is of a particular kind: the therapist assumes a helping role, attends to the patient's needs through the use of a variety of strategies (to be discussed below), and maintains only a modest level of closeness.

Another reason for this type of relationship is more pragmatic: patients receiving supportive therapy suffer from chronic conditions and will require help for extended periods, sometimes for life. The same therapist will generally not be available for such a long term commitment as he moves from one part of an institution to another or to a new position elsewhere. Fostering an intimate relationship only paves the way for a greater sense of loss in a patient and the danger of deterioration when a therapist has to leave. An obvious alternative is the patient's relationship with the 'institution' and we will return to this later in the chapter when considering a model of providing supportive therapy.

Apart from the issue of intimacy, the other main feature that characterizes the therapist–patient relationship is the more directive role which the therapist plays. He assumes a measure of responsibility—not seen in most other forms of psychotherapy—on the premise that his patient is chronically handicapped and therefore unable to care for himself independently. To an extent the relationship resembles the bond between parent and child, i.e. the therapist creates and maintains an association whereby he offers security and caring on which the patient depends (Strupp 1973). The therapist also uses the relationship as a vehicle for a number of specific therapeutic strategies.

Components of therapy

What are the components of therapy? In this section we briefly discuss each of them separately, though it will be obvious that they are not discrete. I hope, however, that by teasing them out their specific application will be made more obvious. We should also note that they are not considered in any particular order. Any of them may be applied at any time.

(1) Reassurance

The therapist can reassure his patient in at least two ways: by removing doubts and misconceptions and by indicating that the patient has certain assets. Patients commonly harbour thoughts about themselves which are ill-founded and lead to considerable anxiety and distress. For example, a middle-aged married man who believed he was going mad was relieved at the therapist's reassurance that he was definitely not destined for such a fate but that his jealousy was an exaggeration of a normal emotion and perfectly understandable in the light of his obviously deprived and insecure upbringing. Reassurance can be used to good effect to relieve fears in the patient that he is insane or becoming so, that he will be permanently locked up in a mental hospital, that he has cancer or other serious physical illness, or that his symptoms are unique to him alone etc. The chronic psychiatric patient has often also lost his self-confidence and when he assesses his life, can see nothing but failure and missed opportunities. Although this may be true in part, he tends to omit from his evaluation that he also has assets and abilities. The therapist can help bolster his patient's confidence by pointing these out to him. A word of caution is necessary—reassurance must, to be effective, be realistic. To promote a patient's hopes unreasonably by giving him reassurance that is groundless may be effective in the short term, but is bound later to backfire. The therapist should therefore aim to create a climate of hope and positive expectation, but without deceiving the patient in any way.

(2) Explanation

This strategy is used quite differently in supportive therapy compared to psychotherapy in which a chief aim is to promote insight in the patient (see Chapter 2). We should emphasize that, in the former, explanation (or to use a more customary term, interpretation) of such phenomena as transference, resistance, characteristic defences, and unconscious determinants of behaviour, is entirely inappropriate and to be expressly avoided. Instead, explanation is focused on day to day practical questions, on the current and external reality with which the patient must contend. The goal is not to deepen self-understanding but to enhance his ability to cope by making clearer the nature of the problems the patient faces and how he can best attempt to resolve them.

Reality testing of this kind is of central importance to the chronic patient. He has to become aware of the nature of his condition and of any unrealistic fantasies he may be nurturing. He must also acknowledge the limits of the therapist and of his techniques, i.e. 'I cannot expect any magic cure from my therapist'. The patient, following appropriate explanation, should be better equipped to accept that he must live in spite of his chronic handicap in the best way he possibly can. He should acknowledge 'I have to live with this for the rest of my life; what can I do to try to control my problems and master them?'.

The therapist may clarify a wide variety of issues among which are: the nature of the symptoms (e.g. 'Your headaches are due to your scalp muscles tightening up when you get tense and not to a brain tumour'); the reason for taking medication (e.g. 'These tranquillizing tablets will keep you more relaxed and this will help to prevent your breaking down again'); the reason for relapse (e.g. 'It's not surprising you're feeling bad considering the pressure you have been under since your husband became ill'); and so forth. Note that all the examples given are in straightforward, everyday language. Explanations in highly technical terms may impress the patient but have no impact because they are often quite beyond his comprehension.

(3) Guidance

Supportive therapy not uncommonly entails the therapist's guidance of the patient in a wide range of situations, mainly by means of direct advice. As with explanation the focus is on practical issues, including the most fundamental like budgeting, personal hygiene, nutrition, and sleep. Advice may be necessary in respect of work, e.g. how to apply for a particular position, whether to change jobs, how to approach the boss to make a reasonable request; or about family, e.g. how best to relate to an aged parent, what to do about a rebellious adolescent son; or about leisure time, e.g. how to join a social club, how to pursue a particular hobby.

The therapist's goal is not merely to assist the patient to deal with a particular problem but also to teach him the requisite skills for coping with that and other similar problems. Ideally the patient is shown how to recognize and assess common life pressures and how to identify measures that can be taken to deal with those pressures; in this way he should be able to handle stresses and decisions on his own. Particularly important in this regard is teaching the patient how and when to ask for help appropriately. Many patients have been unable to do this throughout their lives. Instead they have expressed their emotional and social difficulties exclusively in terms of bodily symptoms, or made impulsive suicide attempts, or delayed consultation until they were either excessively distressed or functioning very poorly. In summary, the therapist tries both to enhance the patient's coping skills and to teach him how to seek help when this is necessary.

Occasionally advice is ineffective or inadequate and *persuasion* is then required. The therapist moves from a gently directive stance to a more controlling one as he tries to convince his patient to think or act in a particular way. This may be related, for example, to an obvious decision the patient is obliged to make or to a specific programme of action the therapist believes the patient should pursue. The therapist must obviously feel confident of his ground before resorting to this strategy and preferably try to use other means like advice and explanation beforehand. The danger always lurks that the therapist's persuasion will reflect his own personal attitudes and beliefs rather than be more objectively determined.

(4) Suggestion

This strategy is similar to guidance but the patient is offered less choice in deciding whether to co-operate or not. The therapist attempts to induce some change in the patient by influencing him implicitly or explicitly. An example of implicit influence is for the therapist to show approval of desirable behaviour: 'The way you stood up for yourself last week was excellent', with the obvious implication that the patient ought to repeat this type of behaviour. As was the case with persuasion, guidance and explanation in which the patient plays a more collaborative role are preferable to suggestion and should be attempted first.

(5) Encouragement

To encourage a patient is so commonsensical that we are apt to take it for granted. The most effective use of encouragement is made however when the therapist is aware of what he is trying to achieve with it. Most chronic patients need to be given 'courage' or confidence regularly, but this is best done in relation to a particular situation in their lives or their therapy. Thus, rather than give encouragement in vague general terms, the therapist should use this therapeutic strategy within a specific context. Contexts vary considerably from patient to patient. What remains constant are the basic objectives behind the use of encouragement: to combat feelings of inferiority, to promote self-esteem, and to urge the patient to adopt courses of action or behaviour of which he is hesitant and frightened (Lamb 1981).

The therapist encourages in various ways according to need and circumstance. He can use the full force of his authoritative benevolent role by commenting, for example: 'From my long experience of dealing with the sort of problem you are describing, I am confident you will be able to master it'. He may also demonstrate his sense of confidence non-verbally through a display of eagerness and optimism. As was the case with reassurance, the therapist can exploit any past or current progress in the patient by positive reinforcement, either explicit or tacit. He may comment: 'Last year you proved how effectively you could discuss your work schedule with your boss—I'm certain you have the courage to do it this time too'.

A word of caution is necessary regarding encouragement: its use may be not only futile but also counter-therapeutic if given inappropriately. To encourage a patient unrealistically and towards a goal which is hopelessly out of his reach may well have the opposite result to that intended: he becomes dispirited as he battles to attain what the therapist hopes for but which he finds too demanding. The limitations imposed by the patient's condition must be recognized and respected. In any event, he should be encouraged to take small steps so that the chance of successfully negotiating them is increased. Each success experience then promotes self-confidence and serves as a source of encouragement for subsequent steps (see Chapter 1).

(6) Effecting changes in the patient's environment

Patients, particularly those with a chronic psychiatric condition, are markedly influenced by the social forces, both human and institutional, that impinge on them. The deleterious effects on the schizophrenic of a family atmosphere typified by high emotional expressiveness is a good illustration (Brown, Birley, and Wing 1972). In supportive psychotherapy one considers the patient in the context of his social environment with the goal of removing or altering elements in it which are detrimental, and conversely, of maximizing other elements which benefit the patient. The therapist therefore asks himself the question: 'How can I help to modify my patient's social environment to his best advantage?'.

Stressful environmental factors need to be carefully assessed so that they can be suitably modified. The range of factors is infinite, but the following are common to a large proportion of patients: the patient's job has become too demanding and outstretched his resources; the family atmosphere is tense and hostile; the patient's housing situation is poor; he is socially isolated; he is under financial pressure etc. Environmental changes of a more positive kind, i.e. adding something to the patient's world, are as important as the removal of stressful factors. Thus encouraging the patient to participate in appropriate social activities like those found in Elderly

Citizens' Clubs, the church, and community centres, or helping him to start up or resume hobbies and pastimes, can be of considerable value. Social contacts are enhanced but in a protective type of setting and the patient can derive pleasure from pursuits that are intrinsically enjoyable and worthwhile.

There are two dimensions to this therapeutic strategy (1) working directly with the patient by helping him, for example, to obtain a suitable job or to approach the appropriate authorities for sickness or other benefits, or putting him in touch with suitable social clubs and the like (social workers are most helpful with these aspects of supportive psychotherapy) and (2) working with people who are important to the patient, particularly relatives. Here straightforward counselling will often be helpful both to the relatives, and indirectly to the patient. If we remind ourselves that one aim of supportive psychotherapy is the transfer of some of the source of support from professionals to a patient's family or friends (assuming of course that they exist) it follows that the more skilled they are for the task, the more likely they are to succeed. This task is often no easy matter. Caring for a chronically ill patient calls for perseverance and discretion. The therapist in assisting the relatives or friends can use many of the strategies we have already discussed including guidance, encouragement, and reassurance.

It is important to recognize that failure in the care of the chronically ill patient is sometimes due to the therapist's neglect of the family's needs. He may have overlooked the marked positive effects on the patient's welfare that can result when using the family as an ally in treatment. For the family to be successfully incorporated into supportive therapy however, requires that they be properly informed and counselled. They need to be instructed as to what to do and how to do it. In addition the family needs help in their own right in caring for their ill relative as the process can be extremely burdensome at times.

The work of Leff and his colleagues (Leff, Kuipers, Berkowitz, Eberlein, and Sturgeon 1982) illustrates how crucial a role the patient's family can play in reducing his vulnerability to relapse. In a splendidly executed study, schizophrenic patients with a high risk of relapse because of their exposure to relatives who are overly critical and/or over-involved with them, were followed up for nine months after the families were given either routine out-patient care or the opportunity to participate in a relatives' group and in family sessions. The goal of these social interventions was to reduce the level of expressed emotion and/or social contact in the family. The relatives' group was designed to enable its members to discover new coping strategies to deal with problems they encountered at home; the family sessions were intended to complement the group. Using well-validated outcome measures the experimental and control groups were compared over a nine month follow-up period. The results are striking: the relapse rate was 50 per cent in the control group and only 9 per cent in the experimental group. Although this social treatment was designed for schizophrenics alone, and then for a specific subgroup of them, the research suggests that there is scope for intervention at the family level in other chronic conditions. Further clinical investigations will no doubt clarify what constitute the most appropriate forms of intervention.

In long-term care the occasion will arise when there is a need to alter the patient's environment radically because his condition has deteriorated or he has become exposed to a particularly stressful situation. Options will include in-patient admission to a psychiatric ward, attendance at a day hospital, or participation in a sheltered workshop or other occupational-therapy programme. Such a development need not necessarily be construed by either therapist or patient as a failure if they both understand that the patient's resources will from time to time be outstretched by circumstances.

(7) Permission for catharsis

The relative safety of the therapist–patient relationship permits the patient to share—with a sense of relief—pent-up feelings like fear, sorrow, concern, frustration, and envy. The therapist's office is usually the only place where the patient can feel sufficiently trusting to do this. The therapist, by showing that he is a sympathetic, active listener who accepts the patient unconditionally, grants the latter permission to share his 'secrets' whatever they are and however painful or embarrassing they may be. Although the sharing of emotionally charged material is not necessarily effective in itself (Yalom, Bond, Bloch, and Zimmerman 1977), the process can lead to a sense of marked relief and serve as a vehicle for other therapeutic strategies.

Associated components of therapy

Apart from the specific type of relationship and the therapeutic strategies discussed above, various other methods can be added to a programme of supportive psychotherapy when appropriate. Drug treatment may have a place, e.g. a maintenance major tranquillizer in the case of the chronic schizophrenic (Davis 1975), a minor tranquillizer in a patient with high levels of anxiety especially when he is exposed to stress, the possible use of lithium in a recurrent depressive. The chronic neurotic, treated in general practice, is often prescribed a minor tranquillizer such as diazepam. The pharmacological value of such a drug in these patients is dubious and any positive effects are probably placebo in nature. There is also growing evidence that physical or psychological dependence may develop thus complicating psychotherapeutic management (Petursson and Lader 1984). The 'tablet' however does have a symbolic value and tends to serve as a concrete bridge between therapist and patient and as a tangible reflection of the former's interest and caring. Such grounds for prescribing drugs are obviously quite unsound; the therapist should clarify the precise role for psychotropic medication in a particular chronic neurotic patient, and only use drugs when adequate clinical criteria are satisfied.

Other treatment methods which may be used as part of supportive therapy include relaxation training, social skills training (Trower, Bryant, and Argyle 1978), social clubs (Bierer 1964), industrial workshop or other occupational therapy. In some cases treating the patient together with his spouse or family may be indicated but the approach adopted is primarily supportive with no attempt made to examine in depth the nature of intra-familial relationships. The therapist uses the therapeutic strategies discussed above and attempts to help the family as a group to cope more effectively.

Supportive psychotherapy in practice

More often than not, trainees (rather than the trained) in the mental health professions, especially psychiatrists, are asked to take on patients for long-term supportive psychotherapy. (There is a growing trend, however, for this type of work to be done by community psychiatric nurses.) Typically the registrar (I shall refer to the registrar only although other professionals may also be involved) 'slides' into this work rather than mapping out objectives or a comprehensive treatment plan. Therapy tends as a result to be unfocused, even haphazard at times. Supervision of his work is invariably limited as if this form of psychotherapy were regarded as reasonably straightforward and uncomplicated. This is an unfortunate state of affairs and an effective model of therapy to remedy it is discussed in the next section. Before turning to this model, some general practical issues warrant our attention.

The therapist in starting treatment with a chronically disabled patient must ask a series of questions—How often will I see this patient? How long will each session be? How long will therapy continue for? Is it likely that I will be able to refer this patient back to his general practitioner in the foreseeable future or will he probably require long term care from a psychiatrist? At what point will I review the effectiveness of therapy? Should anyone else be involved in treatment, e.g. spouse, other relative? Should I draw upon specific resources in the community such as a social club? Is medication necessary? If yes, under what circumstances?

These are but some of the questions the therapist needs to ask. Accompanying his inquiry is the preparation of a problem list—an attempt to clarify in what specific areas help is necessary. The use of a problem-orientated approach guides the therapist in his setting of appropriate therapeutic goals and enables him to assess at later points the value of his intervention. Much of the product of his preparation should be shared with the patient and a form of contract negotiated.

Anticipation of problems which may hamper the course of therapy is useful from the outset. In particular, what is the danger of this patient becoming overly dependent on me? How likely is he to comply with my recommendations? Will it be necessary to set limits? What arrangements should I make with regard to sessions requested between set appointments, the patient's use of emergency services, and my availability on the telephone? Do I need to set any conditions to prevent the development of certain problems? (e.g. 'It is essential that you continue in your job if treatment is to be worthwhile'). Periodic review by the therapist is an essential feature of a long-term treatment like supportive therapy. As mentioned earlier the problem list will be valuable for this purpose. In addition, certain questions need to be asked: Is my original plan working? Am I making the patient worse? Is he becoming unduly dependent on me? Have any new problems arisen? Should I modify the goals I set previously? Am I still the most appropriate person to be providing help? If not, who is best suited—the general practitioner, the family?

Careful consideration of these practical points will facilitate the provision of more efficient and more effective treatment. Yet the question does arise: is there an optimum model for the practice of supportive therapy?

A model for the provision of supportive therapy

In this section we consider one model which appears to be effective and suitable. In 1962 MacLeod and Middleman reported a preliminary evaluation of their 'Wednesday Afternoon Clinic' (WAC), a novel pattern of supportive care for chronically-ill psychiatric patients. Since then other similar clinics have sprung up, particularly in the United States (see for example, Sassano and Stone 1975; Masnik, Bucci, Isenberg, and Normand 1971; Masnik, Olarte, and Rosen 1980; Rada, Daniels, and Draper 1969; Brandwin, van Houten, and Neal 1976). The structure and function of a clinic of this kind are worth examining in some detail. It is held regularly, without fail, on the same day of the week at the same hour. Patients having been assessed as suitable for this type of out-patient care are seen at intervals ranging from weekly to bi-monthly. Although patients are seen by appointment they have free access to the clinic. If they wish to attend earlier than scheduled they make an effort to notify the clinic accordingly.

The staffing arrangements call for two constant figures: a receptionist and a co-ordinator. The receptionist, rarely given enough credit in mental health clinics, is a particularly important person in that she provides a sense of continuity for the patients. The co-ordinator is most conveniently a psychiatrist, for example a senior registrar (advanced resident) since there is a need for drug prescribing in many cases. The remainder of the staff, among them psychiatrists, clinical psychologists, social workers, and psychiatric nurses, work in the clinic for a period of several months, usually as part of their training programme.

Let us now follow the 'career' of a typical patient (who has already been previously assessed and deemed suitable for treatment in the clinic). On arrival he is welcomed by the receptionist and then shown to the waiting room where he can avail himself of light refreshments. There he meets other patients whom he gets to know over the course of several months. This informal prelude to the actual session with the therapist has considerable therapeutic value in itself in that the clinic is perceived as hospitable and welcoming. The receptionist plays a useful role in this respect as she fosters the sort of climate necessary to reduce the patient's anxiety. The 'coffee atmosphere' also allows the patient to recognize through his contact with other patients that his problems are not unique to himself. He is seen by a different therapist on each occasion with the session lasting about 15–20 minutes. During that time the therapeutic strategies discussed earlier in this chapter come into play.

At the end of the clinic all staff meet to review the progress of the patients seen that day and to discuss any problems in treatment that have been encountered. This session enables the staff to become familiar with the problems and management of all the patients which facilitates a consistent approach to treatment and promotes continuity of care despite the change of therapist. The results of the discussion are recorded in the file of each patient including suggestions for future treatment. In addition the staff use the period to learn about the principles and practice of supportive psychotherapy and to support one another for what is often experienced as extremely demanding work! We will return to these latter issues below.

The rationale behind the pattern of treatment is that it allows an 'institutional alliance' to develop, i.e. the patient forms a relationship with the 'clinic' rather than with one particular psychotherapist (Daniels, Draper, and Rada 1968). The sort of patient we are considering is threatened by too intimate a therapeutic relationship. The fact that he is treated by different therapists but in the secure framework of the clinic is more suited to his needs. As discussed earlier in the chapter a pragmatic issue is also involved—the patient is likely to require continuing care for an indefinite period. Because of their own training requirements and job movements, the staff will not be available for such a long-term commitment. The problems of separation and loss would then arise for the patient. By contrast the clinic meets regularly without exception and is always dependable—there is no threat to the patient of losing it.

In summary, the WAC model involves the institution as the ever-present, constant, and accessible source of help. The waiting room, the refreshments, the receptionist, and the rotating staff together constitute the agency of support. Personal attention is given in this clinic but at a level which can be tolerated by the patient and at the same time without the threat to him of losing his therapist.

A model for supportive therapy in general practice

To set up a clinic as described above is not always feasible. In any event many patients, particularly the chronic neurotic, do not require referral to a psychiatric service and can be given long-term supportive therapy by their general practitioner. Indeed this is common practice. One possible approach for the physician in his own practice is to negotiate a contract with the patient as follows: he will be seen on a regular basis, once a month on average, for a specified period, usually about 15 minutes. Under this agreement, the time allocated 'belongs' to the patient and the appointments are in a sense guaranteed to him. When the programme of help is so predictable and constant the patient feels secure while the therapist is relieved that in all likelihood he will be spared anguished telephone calls or repeated requests for additional appointments. Clinical experience shows that the patient adheres to the programme as scheduled, probably because he is confident that his 'lifeline' remains intact. I have often been intrigued that chronic psychiatric patients can be satisfied with appointments which are brief in duration and infrequently spaced. The important factor seems to revolve around the patient's fantasy that the person on whom he relies will not abandon him and will in fact always be available in an emergency.

During the 'quarter-hour' the therapist is an active listener and displays interest in what the patient has to say. As in the WAC he applies, when appropriate, the various therapeutic strategies we have discussed previously. Particularly relevant in the general-practice setting is the therapist's approach to somatization. Since the patient commonly expresses his psychic distress in somatic terms and seeks relief from physical symptoms, the therapist should gently encourage him to 'express his feelings with his mouth rather than with his body' (Wahl 1963) by enquiring about various aspects of his current life-situation, like his job or his family. At the same time it should be made clear to the patient that the doctor does not regard his physical symptoms as imaginary. On the contrary explanation should be provided as to how emotional states, especially tension, can produce pain and other symptoms.

The model allows for continuing contact perhaps indefinitely. As a consequence there is no pressure to accomplish a set amount in any one 15 minute session. After all there will be opportunity to talk further the following month, and thereafter.

Problems in the course of treatment

Undoubtedly one of the most common dangers in the practice of suppportive therapy, no matter the model used, is the fostering of excessive patient dependency to an extent that he relinquishes all responsibility for himself and becomes entirely reliant on his therapist. As Kolb (1973) warns: 'In employing supportive therapy, the physician should bear in mind the dangers that he may thereby encourage dependence and a regressive passivity in the patient'. Whatever the nature of the chronic patient's disability the 'prospect exists that dependency (which is intrinsic to the treatment) will both escalate and persist in a way that is not necessarily in the patient's long term interests' (Bloch 1977). Dependency in some measure is inevitable in every therapist—patient relationship (Balint 1964), but even more so in supportive psychotherapy where the patient is actually permitted to 'lean on' the therapist. The thorny question arises as to how much leaning is desirable? The condition and needs of the patient will often dictate the answer but in general the therapist's goal is to promote self-sufficiency to the maximum degree possible and to transfer some of the source of support to the family and other intimates.

One could argue that continuing dependence on the therapist in the chronically disabled population is of no major consequence. A parallel is the use of narcotics in the terminally ill—concern about drug addiction is not relevant since the relief of severe pain is the top priority. The problems with the patient in supportive therapy, however, are that he will be deprived in his passive role of any opportunity to practise coping behaviour that he may well be capable of, and that, should the therapist move elsewhere, the patient will rapidly crumble unless he finds a substitute source of support.

Neki (1976), in an excellent overall review of the topic of dependency in psychotherapy, highlights the resistance that Western practitioners display to the patient's yearning for dependency on them; they work assiduously to promote the patient's active self-reliance and his full autonomy. Such efforts are perfectly applicable to those psychotherapies which aim towards personality change but is quite unsuitable in the case of supportive therapy. Therapists, in giving supportive therapy, have to overcome their bias, accept their role as a support figure, but at the same time take care not to foster undue passivity and dependency. This is a taxing job. Not uncommonly the therapist fulfills the supportive role initially but later encounters considerable difficulty as he grapples with the patient's entrenched dependent stance and his own discomfort in trying to alter his clinical role, that is to lessen the amount of support he will provide. He may resort to setting limits or 'withdrawing' from the patient. The relationship usually becomes strained and the therapeutic process is thrown into disarray. The patient tries to cling all the harder while the therapist, feeling progressively more angry and frustrated, endeavours to keep him at bay.

A therapist may nurture undue dependency unwittingly because of his own personal needs: to prove to himself and others that, first, he actually has a significant role in helping patients, and second, even in 'incurable' cases he can be useful. In many of the conditions he deals with there is only equivocal evidence that his efforts result in improvement. I suspect that the therapist unconsciously deflects the uncertainty of whether he is effective or not by relying on the concept of support. Since supportive therapy by definition denotes an active role for the therapist in the therapeutic relationship, he can obtain comfort from the notion that for the patient he *is* a significant figure as a benevolent authoritative provider of support even if the precise effectiveness of his intervention remains unclear.

In the case of the incurable patient, in whom the therapist is by and large unable to produce any change, he may offer excessive support to satisfy himself that he is doing something. This effort is comparable to that of some physicians and surgeons in their management of the terminally ill: their resort to 'heroic' measures, which only prolong the patient's agony, when they find it difficult to concede that they no longer have an active health-restoring function (Bloch 1976).

As the scope of this chapter does not permit more detailed discussion of this important question of dependency, the reader is referred to Neki's contribution (1976).

Supportive therapy is generally not regarded by therapists as satisfying as intensive psychotherapy where one is in a sense participating in a journey of discovery or as the therapies discussed in this book in which specific goals are laid down and often accomplished. For the chronic patient there is no chance of 'cure' and the work involved tends to be less interesting, to some even dull. Not only this, therapists often find the practice of supportive therapy arduous, demanding, and frustrating. They are repeatedly reminded of their ineffectiveness in the face of a broad range of psychiatric conditions—fertile ground for the growth of demoralization.

Moreover, as we saw earlier, the patient typically cannot tolerate the close relationship that ideally (and gratifyingly to the therapist) obtains in the therapeutic relationship of the intensive psychotherapies and this can be a potential source of therapist frustration (Kahn 1984).

The WAC model becomes all the more important because of these pressures on the therapist. There the clinic shoulders the major task and no one therapist is over-burdened. Furthermore, the staff in their own meeting following the clinic provide mutual support to one another (Sassano and Stone 1975). The general practitioner does not obviously have this opportunity although he may, if in a group practice, use his colleagues as a source of support. The development in recent years of Balint-groups for doctors in general practice—groups which meet regularly to discuss the psychotherapeutic aspects of their work—has proved helpful (Balint, Balint, Gosling, and Hildebrand 1966). The doctor can, of course, always refer his more complicated patients to a psychiatric clinic.

Supportive therapy practised in an appropriate setting can, despite what we have noted above, bring satisfaction and present challenges. A patient's success at achieving a goal, notwithstanding how limited and unambitious, can be a rewarding experience for him and the therapists who have assisted in the process (Daniels *et al.* 1968). The positive experience for the latter is more likely to occur if they remember to '. . . content themselves with settling for what is possible' (Lamb 1981).

Effectiveness of supportive therapy and training

The effectiveness of supportive psychotherapy is extremely difficult to assess. What criteria of outcome can be used in the case of patients for whom a cure is not the goal of treatment? Although chronicity is a common feature of the group of patients we are discussing in this chapter, we are still dealing with a heterogeneous group of patients with varied diagnoses. Obviously we would have to separate out these diagnostic groups if we were to try to test effectiveness adequately. We would also need to note carefully what other treatments were being given, e.g. medication, non-professional support like social clubs, and so on. The formation of a control group against which to test the effectiveness of supportive psychotherapy would be possible although difficult. The likely approach would be to vary one parameter of treatment at a time.

With regard to the first methodological problem of outcome assessment, suitable criteria might include: the pattern of clinic attendance (e.g. failure to keep appointments, dropping out of treatment, excessive use of the clinic between appointments), incidence of psychiatric hospitalization, use of psychiatric emergency facilities, number of crisis telephone calls at irregular hours, the overall pattern of help seeking, the quality of relationships with intimates and others, performance at work, and ability to cope with everyday demands and tasks.

With the methodological hurdles involved in assessment measurement as well as in the other areas cited, it is no suprise to find that outcome studies are few and far between. The WAC model has however been studied for its effectiveness although only impressionistically. MacLeod and Middleman (1962) compared the outcome of patients in treatment at their WAC clinic with similar types of patients attending a regular psychiatric out-patient clinic and found that there were 'considerably more indications of improvement' in the former group. However, the criteria which their assessment was based on were not mentioned. Brandwin *et al.* (1976) in assessing the value of their 'continuing-care clinic' used the rate of hospitalization as a criterion and compared the rate for a period before the patients began their attendance at the clinic and for a period thereafter. The number of patients hospitalized, the frequency of admissions, and the total number of in-patient days were all substantially reduced while attending the continuing care clinic.

Another study reveals similar findings. Masnik and her colleagues (1980) followed up 71 patients who had attended a supportive, regular 'coffee' group for an average of five years. The therapists' ratings, conceded to be subjective, showed that patients were minimally improved in terms of their symptoms and ability to cope. Rehospitalization rates were also reduced. Improvement correlated only with attendance suggesting that the group acted as a support system with peer identification and encouragement as salient therapeutic elements. The work of Leff *et al.* (1982), including its efficacy, has already been noted on p. 263.

Supportive therapy as practised in a clinic especially designed for the chronically ill appears to achieve better results than more conventional out-patient approaches but we cannot say much more about this question until further systematic research is done.

As with effectiveness, we are in relatively uncharted territory and have little idea of what constitutes an effective *training* for therapists in supportive therapy. Training programmes usually emphasize the hospital care of the chronically ill patient. Following the patient's discharge into the community, trainees are often left to their own devices as to how to continue treatment. In a sense their training has lagged behind the dramatic development of the community mental health movement over the past couple of decades.

What are the important ingredients of training? Instruction on theory is less pertinent than in other psychotherapies simply because theoretical models for supportive psychotherapy are still lacking. Interestingly, no school of psychotherapy has attempted to adopt the chronic patient under its wing although certain behaviour therapy techniques such as token economy have been applied in hospital settings (Atthowe and Krasner 1968). The treatment remains by and large empirical and consists of a number of related procedures that clinical experience has shown to be useful and appropriate. As important as theoretical knowledge is the trainee's familiarity with the nature of those chronic illnesses—clinical course, aetiology, prognosis—for which supportive therapy is indicated. He will then be better aware of the needs and problems that these patients present.

Practising supportive therapy under supervision is undoubtedly the main aspect of training. By working with a range of chronic patients over a period of at least several months the trainee ideally accomplishes several tasks. His attitudes to the care of these patients becomes more balanced and realistic, as well as positive. Instead of regarding them nihilistically as 'crocks' or 'incurables' the trainee comes to recognize that a particular approach is necessary, one in which treatment goals are limited (Daniels *et al.* 1968). To the therapist these goals initially are frustratingly minuscule, but later he can understand that *for the patient* their achievement may be of the greatest significance. In this way the therapist learns that he can be helpful to the patient. Another attitude to modify is the commonly held one that supportive therapy is merely 'brief, commonsensical chats . . . which consist of little more than sympathetic listening and more-or-less considered advice' (Smail 1978). The trainee realizes that treatment involves much more than this and requires skill and expertise to be done satisfactorily.

Teaching should preferably be closely-related to patient care. The WAC model is most appropriate. As mentioned earlier a group of trainees assembles together at the end of the clinic to discuss the cases seen. Each therapist compares his clinical encounters with those of his peers as well as receiving guidance and suggestions from an experienced clinician who serves as supervisor. Since the patients have a different therapist at each visit the trainee sees a wide range of cases. A useful spin-off is that trainees from different professions—psychiatry, clinical psychology, social work, nursing, and occupational therapy—can participate in the same programme with the clear advantage of inter-disciplinary exchange and the sharing of different perspectives to the care of the chronic patient. Even if a WAC-type clinic is unavailable for training, clinical experience under supervision remains the core of any training programme.

Summary

Supportive psychotherapy with the chronically handicapped patient has as a main aim the promotion of his best possible adjustment. To achieve this the therapist enters into a particular type of relationship with the patient and uses a number of specific therapeutic strategies such as explanation, reassurance, and guidance. Undue patient dependency is without doubt the most important problem facing the therapist and its prevention requires careful skill on his part. A useful practical model of treatment, which centres around the concept of an 'institutional alliance' can help to minimize the problem of dependence as well as provide suitable clinical care. The effectiveness of this model, however, and of supportive therapy in general, still remains to be tested. Indeed there are many questions waiting to be explored through systematic research.

References

Atthowe, J. W. and Krasner, L. (1968). A preliminary report of the application of contingent reinforcement procedures (token economy) on a 'chronic psychiatric ward', *J. Abnorm. Psychol.* **73**, 37–43.

Balint, M. (1964). *The doctor, his patient and the illness.* Pitman Medical, London.

——, Balint, E., Gosling, R., and Hildebrand, P. (1966). *A study of doctors*, Tavistock, London.

——, Hunt, J., Joyce, D., Marinker, M., and Woodcock, J. (1970). *Treatment or diagnosis. A study of repeat prescriptions in general practice.* Tavistock, London.

Bierer, J. (1964). The Marlborough experiment. In *Handbook of community psychiatry* (ed L. Bellak). Grune and Stratton, New York.

Bloch, S. (1976). Instruction on death and dying for the medical student, *Med. Educ.* 10, 269–73.

—— (1977). Supportive psychotherapy, *Br. J. hosp. Med.* 18, 63–7. Reprinted in *Contemporary Psychiatry* (1984) (ed S. Crown). Butterworths, London.

Brandwin, M. A., van Houten, W. H., and Neal, D. L. (1976). The continuing care clinic: outpatient treatment of the chronically ill, *Psychiatry* 39, 103–17.

Brown, G. W., Birley, J. L., and Wing, J. K. (1972). Influence of family life on the course of schizophrenic disorders: a replication, *Br. J. Psychiat.* 121, 241–58.

Daniels, R., Draper, E., and Rada, R. (1968). Training in the adaptive psychotherapies, *Compreh. Psychiat.* 9, 383–91.

Davis, J. (1975). Overview: maintenance therapy in psychiatry: 1. Schizophrenia, *Am. J. Psychiat.* 132, 1237–45.

Kahn, E. M. (1984). Psychotherapy with chronic schizophrenics, *J. Psychosocial. Nursing* 22, 20–5.

Kolb, L. C. (1973). *Modern clinical psychiatry*. Saunders, Philadelphia.

Lamb, H. R. (1981). Individual psychotherapy. In *The chronically mentally ill* (ed J. A. Talbott). Human Sciences Press, New York.

Leff, J., Kuipers, L., Berkowitz, R., Eberlein, R., and Sturgeon, D. (1982). A controlled trial of social intervention in the families of schizophrenic patients, *Br. J. Psychiat.* 141, 121–34.

MacLeod, J. and Middleman, F. (1962). Wednesday afternoon clinic: a supportive care program, *Archs gen. Psychiat.* 6, 56–65.

Masnik, R., Bucci, L., Isenberg, D., and Normand, W. (1971). 'Coffee and . . .': a way to treat the untreatable, *Am. J. Psychiat.* 128, 164–7.

——, Olarte, S., and Rosen, A. (1980). 'Coffee groups': a nine-year follow-up study, *Am. J. Psychiat.* 137, 91–3.

Neki, J. S. (1976). An examination of the cultural relativism of dependence as a dynamic of social and therapeutic relationships, *Br. J. med. Psychol.* 49, 11–22.

Petursson, H. and Lader, M. (1984). *Dependence on tranquillers*. Maudsley Monograph No. 28. Oxford University Press, Oxford.

Rada, R. T., Daniels, R. S., and Draper, E. (1969). An out-patient setting for treating chronically ill psychiatric patients, *Am. J. Psychiat.* 126, 789–95.

Rogers, C. (1961). *On becoming a person*, Chapter 3. Houghton Mifflin, Boston, Mass.

Sassano, M. P. and Stone, C. L. (1975). Supportive psychotherapy: Thursday afternoon clinic. In *Psychiatric treatment: crisis, clinic, consultation* (eds C. P. Rosenbaum and J. E. Beebe). McGraw-Hill, New York.

Smail, D. J. (1978). *Psychotherapy: a personal approach*. Dent. London.

Strupp, H. H. (1973). On the basic ingredients of psychotherapy, *J. consult. clin. Psychol.* 41, 1–8.

Trower, P., Bryant, B., and Argyle, M. (1978). *Social skills and mental health*. Methuen, London.

Wahl. C. W. (1963). Unconscious factors in the psychodynamics of the hypochondriacal patient, *Psychosomatics* **4**, 9-14.

Yalom, I. D., Bond, G., Bloch, S., and Zimmerman, E. (1977). The impact of a weekend group experience on individual therapy, *Archs gen. Psychiat.* **34**, 399-415.

Recommended reading

Lamb, H. R. (1981). Individual psychotherapy. In *The chronically mentally ill* (ed J. A. Talbott). Human Sciences Press, New York.

MacLeod, J. and Middleman, F. (1962). Wednesday afternoon clinic: a supportive care program, *Archs gen. Psychiat.* **6**, 56-65. (Description of a clinic designed to provide supportive therapy.)

Neki, J. S. (1976). An examination of the cultural relativism of dependence as a dynamic of social and therapeutic relationships, *Br. J. med. Psychol.* **49**, 11-22. (An excellent review of the problem of dependency in psychotherapy.)

Wolberg, L. R. (1977). *The technique of psychotherapy*, 3rd edn. Grune and Stratton, New York. (Includes a clear practical account of supportive psychotherapy.)

Index